The Manager's Troubleshooter

THE MANAGER'S TROUBLESHOOTER

Pinpointing the Causes and Cures of
125 Tough Supervisory Problems

Clay Carr
Mary Fletcher

PRENTICE HALL
Englewood Cliffs, New Jersey 07632

Prentice-Hall International (UK) Limited, *London*
Prentice-Hall of Australia Pty. Limited, *Sydney*
Prentice-Hall Canada, Inc., *Toronto*
Prentice-Hall Hispanoamericana, S.A., *Mexico*
Prentice-Hall of India Private Limited, *New Delhi*
Prentice-Hall of Japan, Inc., *Tokyo*
Simon & Schuster Asia Pte. Ltd., *Singapore*
Editora Prentice-Hall do Brasil, Ltda., *Rio de Janeiro*

© 1990 *by*

PRENTICE-HALL, Inc.

Englewood Cliffs, NJ

10   9   8

Library of Congress Cataloging-in-Publication Data

Library of Congress Cataloging-in-Publication Data
Carr, Clay, 1934-
   The manager's troubleshooter: pinpointing the causes and cures
of 125 tough supervisory problems / by Clay Carr and Mary Fletcher.
      p.   cm.
   ISBN 0-13-552647-7
   1. Supervision of employees.   I. Fletcher, Mary,   II. Title.
HF5549.12.C36   1990   90-35141
658.3'02--dc20   CIP

ISBN 0-13-552647-7

PRENTICE HALL
BUSINESS & PROFESSIONAL DIVISION
A division of Simon & Schuster
Englewood Cliffs, New Jersey 07632

Printed in the United States of America

About the Authors

Clay Carr and Mary Fletcher currently manage an internal consulting and training group with centers in five major cities. Prior to this assignment, they held a variety of positions as operating managers. In all, they have more than 25 years of management experience between them (and have the scars to prove it).

We affectionately dedicate this book to:

Bryan Carr
Heather Arsham
Lisa Conant
Chris Erdman
Lynn Marker
Michael Fletcher
and
Matthew Fletcher

How This Book Can Help You Overcome Your Toughest Supervisory Problems

Picture this situation. You're driving through an unfamiliar part of the city, late at night. Suddenly, your car coughs and dies. There's no service station nearby, not even a public telephone. You have no idea what direction to walk for help. Then suddenly, you remember the troubleshooting manual in your trunk. It takes a few minutes, but you find the problem, fix it, and get under way again. Whew!

Being a manager can seem like that sometimes. Problems come up that don't have quick and easy answers. The standard solutions you've been taught or read about don't seem to work. You feel stuck, like someone whose car has stalled in a strange part of town.

Well, here's the troubleshooting manual you need. Between us, we have been managing people for more than 25 years. We don't have all the answers—no one does—but we've learned some useful things. We've written this book to share them with you. *The Manager's Troubleshooter* will help you identify and solve some of the thorniest people problems you'll encounter as a manager.

Let us warn you at the beginning that this isn't the typical book that deals with the easy problems. You won't find advice on how to counsel a worker who comes in late one morning, or how to conduct a performance appraisal. Instead, we've tried to identify harder problems, ones that they didn't tell you how to solve in your basic supervisory training—ones that make or break you as a people manager.

How to Use This Book

How many times have you had to read pages and pages—perhaps even chapters and chapters—to find how to deal with a problem you faced? You won't have to do that with *The Manager's Troubleshooter*. Like all good troubleshooting manuals, it will help you find the cause and cure of your specific problem quickly and easily.

Here's how you use it:

- The manual describes 125 difficult people problems, grouped into 14 different chapters. Each chapter deals with a specific theme (such as "Problems with Your Workgroup" or "Ethical Problems"). This helps you zero in on the right topic and the right problem in a hurry.

- Look in the Table of Contents and find the chapter that deals with the type of problem you have to handle. Then look down the list of problems in that chapter. Find the problem that sounds closest to yours and turn to it.

- Each problem begins with a brief description or vignette, The Scene. Read the description carefully. If the The Scene describes a problem similar to yours, keep going.

- But what if it isn't similar? Look at other problems in that chapter, or even in other chapters. Find the problem that's most like yours. If it isn't quite the same, don't worry—we'll tell you why in a minute.

- Once you've found the right problem and read the description of it, read about its Possible Causes. We spell out for you the most common causes of each problem. It's important to read this carefully. Why? Because problems that look the same can have very different causes and cures. You have to find just what caused them before you can successfully cure them.

- Once you understand the cause of the problem you need to know The Cure. That's the next part of each section. It's also the longest, because we talk you through all the steps you need to take. If you've identified the cause of your problem and follow these steps, you're on your way to curing it.

- In most cases, there are two or three different sets of steps to take, depending on the cause of the problem. Read and think about each set carefully before you decide which one to use. Then use it.

- What if a problem in the manual sounds like yours, but turns out to be not quite the same? You're not stuck. Each section ends with a part called "And If This Doesn't Quite Fit Your Situation ...." This part includes two helps for you:
  - It identifies other, closely related problems in the book that may be more like yours. You can turn to them and see if those

descriptions are more helpful. Often you can combine the steps from two problems that are something like yours and come up with the way to cure your problem.

- It also identifies one of the checklists in the back of the book that you can use instead of, or in addition to, the steps in a specific problem. You might look on these checklists as general problem-solving processes. There are eight checklists: a General Checklist which can be used with any problem and seven specific checklists for problems such as poor performance and substance abuse.

We've even added a feature to help you prioritize your problems. Not all people management problems are equally important. When you have more than one problem to work—and you usually do—it's crucial to work the most serious one(s) first. (Just in case you haven't found it out yet, a manager can get into trouble just as quickly by setting the wrong priorities as by doing the wrong thing.)

We've provided specific guides to help you choose which problem(s) to deal with first. These guides aren't hard and fast; they're our best guess about how critical the problem will be in *your* unit. This is the way we identify how serious a problem is:

If a problem is a *Shark*, it requires your total attention right now! Postpone it, work something else first—and you're history.

If it's an *Elephant*, it will trample you to death if you let it—but you have a little time to deal with it. Elephants are what you concentrate on as long as you don't have any sharks.

If it's a *Wolf*, it lurks around, just waiting to jump you. If you're lucky, wolves are the most serious problems you have day in and day out. If you have sharks and elephants, work them first. If you don't, work on your wolves. Don't ignore the wolves, though, or they'll eat you alive.

Finally, if it's a *Mouse*, it's one of the irritations and annoyances that every manager has and works when the situation permits. There aren't a lot of mouse-type problems in this book, because it's written to help you with serious problems. We've included a few, though, because even mice will eventually nibble you to death if you ignore them.

A Final Suggestion

This is *your* book, and it will help you solve your people management problems efficiently and effectively. It's written around problems, and its goal is to help you solve these problems—but we'd like to give you this hint: When you solve a people problem, don't settle for just getting things back to what they were. Use the problem to develop a *better* situation. What does that mean?

- It might mean solving the problem in a way that increases the trust between you and the worker. The more you trust each other, the easier it is to solve problems.

- Or solving it in a way that helps the worker manage himself more effectively. The better your workers are at managing themselves, the fewer the problems that will come to you.

- Or in a way that increases the worker's sense of responsibility for and commitment to the job. A strong commitment to the job prevents many problems from occurring.

You can think of more ways to improve things as you solve problems. The important thing is to keep looking for ways to make the situation better and the worker more effective. The more you do this, the fewer problems there'll be for you to solve in the future.

Contents

Chapter 3 □ Troubleshooting Problems Caused by the Personal Life of an Employee   61

1

Troubleshooting Problems with Your Employees

— 1-1 —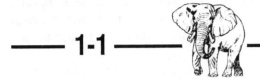

The Problem: Your employees frequently produce unacceptable work.

The Scene

Sunday morning finds you seated at the breakfast table with a cup of tea and Paul Strauss's latest work report. You eagerly begin to read, then note to your dismay that most of it doesn't make any sense. You can't follow his logic, sentences aren't clear, and you have no idea where his conclusions came from. You're especially disgusted because this is the third major product you'll have to return to one of your employees this month. Can't just *one* of them do something right?

Possible Causes

Your employees may not know what's expected of them. This is most likely if you're new to your work unit or if requirements have recently changed in some way.

Your employees may not see any advantage to themselves in doing a better job. Is there any reward to them for doing better work? What happens when the work is unacceptable? Do you rework the product for them, or are they required to fix the problem themselves?

The work environment may discourage good work. Do your employees have access to all the materials they need to do their jobs well? How hard is it to get new tools or resources? Does your organizational structure facilitate the right people doing the right parts of a project?

Hint: Poor performance by an entire organization requires treatment different from that for poor performance by an individual. You may have a situation where the poor performance is the result of a number of different individual performance problems. It's more likely, though, that your problem is systemic; something in the way your work is organized, or communicated, or reviewed, *as a whole,* is causing large numbers of your people to produce substandard work.

If most of your people are producing poor quality work, don't be misled by the one or two who do well. They don't necessarily prove that you don't have a systemic problem. Some people will perform well in spite of almost any adversity.

Cures

If your employees don't know what's expected of them:

Review the unit's work products again to see if there are aspects that are consistently being done poorly. Identify two or three changes in work procedures or processes that would correct the most common problems.

Determine the training method that would best teach your employees how to do those two or three things better. Maybe a local training source for formal training? Or an employee who does one of those aspects well and could do some on-the-job training?

Tell your employees what you plan to do to help them learn the job better and that you intend to concentrate on specific items. Then provide regular feedback to them on how well they're doing and what *specific* areas they still need to work on.

If your employees don't see any advantage in doing a better job:

Set up an informal system of recognition for each job that's done well. This can be a public "pat on the back" or a more tangible form of recognition such as a certificate, a bonus, a gift certificate, or some other item that says "Good job!"

Discuss with your employees what motivates them. If they trust you, they'll probably tell you what turns them on. As much as possible, try to devise rewards intrinsic to the job (better assignments) rather than extrinsic rewards like time off work.

While you may have limited authority to set up your own recognition and reward systems for your employees, you can see to it that they, not you, are the ones who suffer the consequences of their unacceptable work. Give your employees regular feedback on what they're doing well and not so well. When it's not done well, make sure they do the work over again until it's right. Devise other "natural consequences" for their poor quality, even if that means denying them a vacation day so they'll have time to rework an important assignment.

If the work environment is discouraging good work:

Review your work situation to see just what's getting in the way of doing a good job. Talk to your staff; they know better than you do what's getting in their way.

Examine the work flow and your organizational structure. Restructure the work if necessary to see that tasks are done in a logical sequence and that segments once completed don't require rework by another person or function. Make sure that someone is ultimately responsible for the quality of every product and that that person sees the final result before it goes to you or to the next section for review.

If materials or equipment are getting in the way of quality work, make a friend of your local supply department. Visit them to see what bureaucratic roadblocks stand in the way of their serving you. Offer to help, and follow through, in whatever way your position allows, to make their job easier.

Something to Think About

Most employees don't like to work in an organization that does poor work. If your employees do know what's expected of them and how to perform to those expectations, they'll probably be the best source of information on barriers to improved quality. But before they tell you what those barriers are, they need to trust you and believe that you have their best interests in mind. That trust takes some time to develop, but it's worth the effort.

And If This Doesn't Quite Fit Your Situation . . .

Look at Problems 1-6 and 1-7 to see some other examples of organizational poor performance. Problems 2-3, 4-3, 5-1, and 5-5 also deal with poor performance, but from an individual perspective.
Use Checklist 1 to develop a cure of your own.

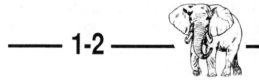

— **1-2** —

The Problem: Your employees are competing with one another when they need to cooperate.

The Scene

You lean back in your chair and sigh. The talk with Jack Webster and Ellen Highland went just as you expected—with each of them blaming the other. You know that your employees would be much more effective if they could just work together, but you just can't get any of them to work with anyone else. They're all a bunch of individualists.

Possible Causes

No payoff for teamwork; big payoff for individual performance. Whatever else may be wrong, you can be sure that this is a major part of the problem. And the problem won't go away until you solve this.

Weak cooperative skills. We talk about people having "interpersonal" skills. Actually, there are a wide variety of interpersonal skills. Some people are very good at giving and taking orders. Others are good at the give-and-take of cooperative relationships. Your people may be short on cooperative skills.

"Personality conflict." This may be the cause—but not very often. It's amazing how "personality conflicts" vanish if cooperation is strongly rewarded.

Hint: When people aren't performing the way you want them to, the first place to look is for the real rewards they're getting by acting as they do. Most of the time, that's all you need to know to understand their actions.

Cures

If all of the rewards are for individual performance:

Take a cold, honest look at what the rewards really are for your people. Are the individual "stars" the ones who're selected for promotions? Do pay increases depend solely on what the individual has done with his own work?

Do you really *need* cooperation? That's not a silly question. In many circumstances, it's best to put up with the friction and let people handle projects independently. If that's the way it should be, though, don't expect them to work together well. Don't make joint assignments unless you're forced to.

If you need cooperation, reward cooperation. Revise your reward structure so it pays for cooperation. Make cooperativeness one of the factors that pay increases depend on. Give bonuses to people who help others get their jobs done. Borrow an idea from college football teams and let your employees give stars to other employees that have been particularly helpful to them. Each month or quarter, give the employee(s) with the largest number of stars a day off, or a steak dinner.

Expect flak, listen to it, and keep on track. If individual performance is what's been paying off, your people have been "trained" to compete. It will take time for them to change, and they'll be uncomfortable. Many of them will try to get you to go back to the old ways. Don't. If cooperation is what you need, hang in there until cooperation is what you get.

If your employees have weak cooperative skills:

Go through the steps in the paragraphs above; make sure that you need cooperation and will reward it. It doesn't matter how skillful your employees get at cooperation—they won't use the skills if individual performance is what pays off for them.

Get your employees together and tell them how the way they work is going to change. Make it clear that cooperation will be important, that it will be rewarded, and how it will be rewarded.

Arrange with your training department to provide training support for the change. Just sending your people to one training course probably won't be enough. To make the change effectively, you'll probably need several courses or workshops spread over several months. You may also need someone to serve as an observer or consultant at times.

Identify some assignments which require your people to work in two's or three's—so they can start practicing cooperation. Tie this in as closely as you can with the training they get. Give them a chance to practice what they're learning as soon as possible after they learn it.

Expect your employees to be uptight. They're not only changing the way they work, but they're having to learn and practice a whole new set of skills. Encourage them, help them as you can—but make sure that they keep moving in the direction you want.

If there is a "personality conflict" between employees:

Most "personality conflicts" result from different ways of thinking and acting. These may be cultural or ethnic, or they may be individual differences. This is really a different problem from general lack of cooperation, and you might find some suggestions for resolving it in such problems as 2-4, 3-6, 3-9, 3-10, and 3-11.

Something to Think About

People—including people as employees—will do what they have the opportunity to do and know how to do, if it pays off for them to do it. As a manager, it's up to you to provide the opportunity, the training (if necessary) and the rewards.

And If This Doesn't Quite Fit Your Situation . . .

Look at Problem 4-5 if you have a new employee who won't accept help, possibly because of the competitive environment. If the competitive environment is causing an individual to do sloppy work, look at Problem 5-3. It could also be causing an individual to produce a high volume of low-quality work; if so, see Problem 6-5. If the competitive environment is leading workers to try to discredit one another, see Problem 7-5.

Use Checklist 1 to develop a cure of your own.

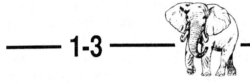

— 1-3 —

The Problem: A group of employees tells you they've just heard a rumor that the company is going to lay off employees.

The Scene

"Hey, boss," remarked Bob at yesterday's staff meeting, "I was over in the personnel office yesterday, and there was a lot of talk about 'downsizing' here. We want to know if we're going to lose our jobs."

"That's right," added Michelle, "two of the technicians in production are leaving for new jobs the end of the week. Do they know something we don't?"

With 11 anxious faces turned toward you, what could you say? "I'll see what I can find out," you replied lamely.

Possible Causes

The rumors of impending layoffs may be true. You may already be aware of the company's plans, or word may not have filtered down through official channels.

The rumors may be untrue, but instead reflect employees' anxieties over other matters. Any potential change, whether in the immediate organization or even in the surrounding community, can cause employees to feel insecure. And when they're feeling insecure and vulnerable, they tend to worry about their paychecks—whether there's good reason to or not.

Hint: The best way to combat rumor is with truth. But you can't explain the truth to your employees unless you know what it is. As you're probably painfully aware, being in the management chain does not guarantee you inside knowledge. So you may need to do some digging to find out what's really going on—whether there's any truth to the rumors of downsizing and layoffs and what the whole truth is.

This is one place where a well-developed network with your peers can be invaluable; you may well be able to find out more through informal channels than through the formal chain of command. But check your sources! If you feed bad information into the rumor mill, it can do a lot of harm—especially since what you say as a manager has the ring of authority.

Cures

If the rumors of impending layoffs are true:

Let your employees have all the information they need to make plans for their own futures. This may be trickier than it sounds. At any stage in the planning process, some decisions will have been made firmly, but other issues will still be under consideration. And some things that sound like firm decisions may still be subject to change. Tell your employees everything that you know is firm, but use a little judgment about the rest. Let them know matter-of-factly what options are under consideration, but don't speculate. This is a very troubling time for your employees; panic won't help anyone.

Find out what your company's policy is on informing employees about drawdowns and layoffs. Be sure you understand the rules completely so you won't reveal information that's supposed to be limited.

Within the limits of your company's policies, tell your employees as much as you're allowed to about how the company will decide who stays and who goes. Reassure the employees whose jobs are secure, then concentrate on the ones most at risk. Identify available outplacement services (including the company's own personnel office) and direct employees to them.

Keep in touch with your boss and your own informal network so you'll know what's going on as planning for the layoffs progresses. Then pass that information on to your employees, with the cautions we've discussed.

If the rumors are untrue, but instead reflect employees' anxieties over other matters:

Put your employees' immediate fears to rest by reassuring them that the rumors are false. But, again, check before you speak! Employees expect management to reassure them, and then issue pink slips next week. If you're to have any credibility with your employees, you need to be absolutely sure that they won't be affected before you attempt to allay their fears. If there will be layoffs that affect some other section of the company, tell your employees who will be affected and why that section is downsizing. Then explain what conditions in your unit are insulating it from the damage.

Try to identify the real source of their anxiety. If other companies in the area are laying off employees, find out what's different between their situation and yours, and let your employees know. If your company is discussing major changes that are causing your employees' insecurity, explain to your employees what the real impact will be on them at the same time that you reassure them of their continued employment.

Something to Think About

Difficult as the situation may be, it's important to keep up production even when employees are more concerned about finding new employment than about the job they know (or suspect) they will be leaving soon. Yet a drop in market share is a major reason for downsizing companies. If productivity or quality decrease, you may create a problem where none existed before. So make sure that your employees understand that the best job protection may be their own high performance.

And If This Doesn't Quite Fit Your Situation . . .

Look at Problems 2-1 and 2-2 to see some other examples of the rumor mill in action, this time against you or an individual employee.

Use the Basic Checklist to develop a cure of your own.

— 1-4 —

The Problem: Your employees are openly resentful of a newer employee you've just promoted to a senior position.

The Scene

You've just listened to the third employee so far this week complain about the performance of Nancy Wallace. You just promoted Nancy to a senior job in the work unit, even though she has been with the organization for less than a year. The employees who've been there longer—and that's most of them—are openly resentful of her promotion. The resentment is so strong that it's beginning to affect productivity.

Possible Causes

You've violated the group's expectations for who should get promoted. All groups have "norms" for who should be promoted. If there are few opportunities to get ahead in the unit, these norms may be even more important.

Your employees resent a woman in a senior position. This isn't as common as it was a decade ago, but it's still there. Your employees may believe that Nancy got the promotion for EEO reasons instead of her own abilities. If promotions are rare, any sign of EEO favoritism will be resented even more.

Your employees may believe she doesn't know the job well enough. In other employees' eyes, it often takes a long time for an individual to "prove" himself or herself on the job. Your workgroup may think she hasn't been there long enough.

You may have promoted her for the wrong reasons. These include personal relationship (whether or not sex is involved); liking Nancy, without regard for how well she performs; or promoting her purely to meet EEO goals.

Hint: Whenever you decide to take an action that isn't what your employees expect, be prepared for an adverse response.

Cures

If the basic reason is your employees' expectations:

This is a common situation in all organizations. If promotions are few and far between, most employees expect them to go to the experienced, proven employees.

If you made your choice carefully (and there's no excuse if you didn't), stick by it. Some of the resentment is meant as pressure, to get you to change your decision. Make it clear that you won't, that you fully support her.

Help Nancy be successful quickly. If the position she's been promoted to is just an extension of what she was doing, this may be easy. If there's a longer learning curve, you'll have more of a problem. Even in this situation, you can assign her projects that she can handle most effectively. Make sure she's a success, and that the other employees know it.

If there are specific reasons why Nancy was the best qualified, see that the other employees know what they are. In fact, it would have been a good idea to do this at the same time that you announced her promotion.

Don't expect it to be easy; it won't be.

If they're resentful because she's female:

It may take a good deal of sensitivity to tell if this is really the case. Don't jump to it as an explanation without good reason.

There are other problems in this book which deal with discrimination (especially Problems 2-8, 2-9, and 9-4). You should read them for additional information on this problem.

If you're reasonably certain that discrimination is involved, you need to deal with it—head on and quickly. Call a group meeting, or have a talk with one or two key employees. But make it clear that you won't tolerate discrimination and that you expect the situation to change NOW.

If they believe she doesn't know the job well enough:

As in the first situation, the key here is helping her be successful as quickly as possible.

This doesn't mean doing her work for her, or giving her simpler jobs so she'll look good. You promoted her because she was good; now give her the support she needs and challenge her to perform.

If you did promote her because of favoritism or other non-performance reasons:

It's probably too late to change the action, so you'd better do whatever you have to to make her successful.

It would be a really good idea if you learned from the situation and never let it happen again.

Things to Think About

All work units develop their own "norms" about who should get promoted and why. If you're going to change them, lay the groundwork for your action in advance.

In this situation, it would have been helpful for you to have identified the qualities you wanted in the senior position loud and clear to everyone well before you filled the job. That way, anyone who wanted a shot at the job would know what was expected of them. If Nancy was the one best suited, you'd have a clear rationale for her promotion.

And If This Doesn't Quite Fit Your Situation . . .

If the resentment is leading other employees to perform poorly, you may find some suggestions in the problems in Chapter 5 or in Problems 7-4, 7-5, and 7-7.

Use Checklists 1 or 2 to develop a cure of your own.

——— 1-5 ———

The Problem: There's serious ingroup fighting among your employees.

The Scene

"I should have known I'd pay for this later," you remarked wryly to no one in particular as Bill left your office. "*One* afternoon off to do some shopping and now half the staff's mad at me."

Unfortunately, most of the rest of the staff had been gone too—including the senior employees you usually left in charge during your absences. So you told Pete to take over the office while you were gone, and now you've spent most of the morning hearing about "favoritism" and that it's not fair that you're "grooming Pete for the next promotion." With three hours of supervisory experience!

"But if it weren't this, it would just be something else," you muse, "Such a talented group of people, but they're always fighting about something!"

Possible Causes

Some occasional dissatisfaction among your employees is probably inevitable. If what you're faced with is this sort of "annoyance bickering," the best thing you can do is nothing. Any attempts on your part to make things better will probably just make them worse—by giving the behavior a prominence it doesn't deserve.

However, there are two cases where you can't afford to ignore infighting:

- When it's caused by real or perceived inequity in the way employees are treated, or

- When it's the result of serious dissatisfaction and employees' perception that they're trapped in meaningless work with no potential for advancement.

In those cases, you *must* analyze the situation and take action. Otherwise, things will only get worse.

Cures

If the infighting is caused by real or perceived inequity in the way employees are treated:

First determine the source of the apparent inequity. Is it the system itself (e.g., the way work is assigned, raises and promotions given)? Is it something you're doing? Or something someone higher up the chain is doing?

The next step is education. Often, employees don't even know that there is a system or a set of rules for making certain decisions. Let your employees know what the rules are and how you've applied them in the past. (In this case, you put Pete in charge because he had the next highest level of seniority with the company—though some of the others had more seniority in their position. If you explain how the decision was made and show that you'll be consistent in applying that rule, things will improve noticeably.)

If there are no rules, consider drawing up a set of guidelines for your own unit that covers the situations that most often cause contention. You can't make a rule for everything! And you shouldn't try. But you can identify for employees the criteria you use in making some decisions. Once the staff know what criteria you use and are convinced that you're following them, much of their dissatisfaction will cool.

And, of course, if rules are not being followed, the solution is obvious: Follow them. If it's someone further up the chain of command who's the source of the inequity, you can point out to them the impact on morale and productivity. But if you can't change your boss's behavior, you may need to make some adjustments at your level to mitigate the damage.

If the infighting is the result of your employees' dissatisfaction with their jobs, the solution is not nearly so straightforward (and you may have less satisfactory results):

If you can change the way work is structured to make it more meaningful or increase advancement potential for even *some* of your employees, as long as you're not hurting the others—do it!

Manufacture opportunities for your employees to increase their direct contact with their customers. All work products should be of benefit to someone—either within the company or outside. (If they're not, you'll want to consider whether that work ought to be done at all.) As your employees have greater contact with the recipients of their efforts, the work will become more meaningful—and the group can unite around the common purpose of serving the customer.

Let your employees know you're on their side. If the work truly is boring and dead end, let your staff know you're aware of their dissatisfactions, that you'll do what you can to make things better, and that if they do a good job for you you'll help them to move on to better jobs. If your staff knows you as an empathetic boss, it will be harder for them to imagine you treating them unfairly.

Something to Think About

Don't confuse infighting with honest disagreement. In any group made up of strong, talented individuals, there is bound to be disagreement and conflict. In this situation, the proper cure is to manage the conflict creatively, not try to suppress it. (If you're not sure how to do this, there are a number of good books which will help you.)

And If This Doesn't Quite Fit Your Situation . . .

Look at Problem 1-4 and Problem 2-4 for discussions of group infighting when the resentment is directed against one co-worker. Problems 3-9, 3-10, and 3-11 deal with individual employees who don't get along with the group. And Problem 12-1 discusses another case of group dissatisfaction.

Use Checklist 1 to develop a cure of your own.

—— **1-6** ——

The Problem: Your employees are demoralized and only produce so-so work.

The Scene

Your new boss was right; the performance of this group of employees is mediocre. Their work always meets the minimum standard—just barely—but never gets much better. If you try to get them to improve, they ask you to tell them what to do in detail, or come up with a dozen reasons for why it can't be improved. Worst of all, they just don't seem to care.

Possible Causes

Their last manager was no better than marginal. If a manager is barely competent, it doesn't take long for him to pass his shortcomings on to his employees.

Their last manager refused to support them. This is another effective way to wreck a group of employees. If the manager never stands up for his employees, always sides with the people who criticize them—it doesn't take long for them to get the word and hunker down.

Hint: Once in a rare while, you may find employees that even an effective supervisor can't get good performance from. Most of the time, though, an ineffective work unit is the result of ineffective supervision.

Cures

If their last manager was marginal:

Your number one task is to prove your competence at the same time that you build up their self-confidence and willingness to produce.

Make it clear from the beginning that you know your job. This doesn't mean that you have to have all the answers; you don't. But you do need a clear sense of how to do the job, and you need to act on this sense.

Make it clear to the group what level of performance you expect from them. Do this at a group meeting, and explain it carefully. Invite them to ask questions (though they probably won't at this stage). If it's necessary, put your expectations in writing. The important point is for them to know what you want and that you're serious about it.

Insist on getting the performance you want. If a job isn't acceptable, explain what's wrong and have it redone until it's right. Depending on the group, this may be a long struggle. For both your sake and theirs, you need to win it.

Keep your eyes peeled for one telltale sign. Managers sometimes get into the habit of accepting substandard work and (bad) having someone else redo it or (worse!) redoing it themselves. If you see signs that this was how the last manager did things, make it clear that you don't work this way, that you expect jobs to be done right the first time. Then work the situation until they are done right.

There's another bad habit work units fall into: not getting things done on time. There is virtually no excuse for this, period. If your employees have too much work to do, it's your responsibility as their manager to get the work load adjusted. Except for that, your employees should expect to meet every deadline—or to renegotiate the deadline *in advance* with you.

Are you doing all of this to be hard on your employees? Not at all. You're doing it because it's the only way they'll ever be able to take pride in what they do again.

If their last manager refused to support them:

Normally, this is the only situation other than marginal management which can really demoralize employees. Some otherwise competent managers always side with the people who complain about their employees.

The group is probably hoping that you'll be different, but afraid you won't be. In other words, they'll be cautious and wait for you to prove yourself.

Your basic tactics here are easy. When someone comes to you with a complaint about your employees, listen carefully to him, get all of the facts as he sees them, and tell him you'll look into the situation and get back to him. If he's in a hurry, or very upset, promise to get back to him quickly—but don't make any commitments until you've talked with the employee(s) he's complaining about.

Talk to the employee or employees. Get their side of the situation. If you can back them, do it (always, not just in the beginning). If possible, let them take care of the problem with the individual who complained. If you have to come up with a different solution in order to satisfy a reasonable complaint, do it—but let them present the solution to the individual if you can.

In other words, see that the situation is resolved, but don't make your employees the bad guys. If they were careless or unresponsive or otherwise did a poor job, let them know it and let them know what you expect. But do it in private. And never correct them because someone complained; correct them because what they did was inadequate—whether anyone complained about it or not.

Things to Think About

If you want your employees to trust you and really produce for you, you need to protect them from outside harassment. This doesn't mean overlook it when they screw up; it does mean dealing with their screw-ups in private and helping them be good guys to the rest of the organization.

There's one last, very important point. To succeed as a manager, you have to delegate effectively. When you delegate, you let the person act for you. Whatever he does, as long as he does it conscientiously—he does for you. Support it and support him (even if you have to undo his decision). This is the only way that your delegations can be successful.

And If This Doesn't Quite Fit Your Situation . . .

Chapter 4 and Chapter 6 look at performance problems which could be caused by an individual employee who is demoralized or frustrated.

Use Checklist 1 to develop a cure of your own.

—— **1-7** ————

The Problem: Your employees have a very low (self-imposed) production bogey.

The Scene

As you strolled unobtrusively through the Claims section yesterday afternoon, you noticed the same lack of industry that you'd observed before. No one was really "goofing off," but no one seemed to be working very hard either. The whole atmosphere was relaxed and laid back.

Back in your office, you reviewed the last two months' production figures. As you suspected, the other sections doing claims processing all had higher output than yours. Of course, employees in those sections complained more too. "But maybe," you mused, "it was worth it. My people do what they have to, but not one claim more."

Possible Causes

If employees are producing acceptable work at an acceptable rate, but nothing more, it's probably because they see no advantage in working harder. If it's important that they begin to produce at a higher rate, there are two areas that you should examine as potential sources of improvement:

Employees may not see any benefit from increased production. Some things in your operation may even discourage higher production. Are there rewards for doing more work?

There may not be any penalty for producing at the low level, and there may be positive reasons for not doing more. Employees may feel they'd be exploited if they did more work for what they're getting paid.

Hint: Before you rush full tilt into a production improvement program, there's one other statistic you should check—acceptance rate. If other sections are producing at higher rates, but there are more appeals of settlements on claims their sections processed, then the company as a whole hasn't really gained. First make sure your quality level is where you want it to be, then you can work on improving production (and show your boss how higher quality, even with slightly lower production, helps the company in the long run).

Cures

If employees see no benefit from enhanced production:

Look at your compensation system to see if there's any way employees can share in the gains from increased production. Establish specific production goals at several levels and link some form of recognition to each level. This recognition, particularly for small production improvements, need not be monetary. An essential ingredient, though, is that the recognition must be public; it should serve as a stimulant both to the recipient and to other employees who see how they can benefit from production improvements.

Discuss with your employees what you might do to increase production. Ask them what benefits are worth striving for, and then implement as many suggestions as you can.

As you implement these recognition systems, be sure that they're administered fairly and impartially. Let your employees know what the criteria are for recognition, and don't change the rules without letting them know and telling them why you're making the changes.

If the employees see some positive reason to continue their low level of production:

Identify what it is that's encouraging employees to produce at a low level and what's discouraging higher production. Review employee complaints over the past couple of years. Is there a common theme (or underlying message) in many of the grievances you've received?

Do what you can to remove the barriers to higher production and let your employees know what you can do and what you can't. If the disincentive is something as basic as the pay scales for their jobs, over which you have no control, talk with them about what you might be able to substitute for a change in pay rates.

As when your employees see no incentive to higher production, look at your compensation and recognition system to find ways to let employees share in the company's gains. If employees feel that the company's fortune is their own, they'll be much more interested in increasing its profitability.

Something to Think About

Employees have many different reasons for setting production bogeys lower than the level management believes is a "fair day's work"—but they all boil down to one: this is what pays off best for them. To change the bogey, you have to change the payoff.

And If This Doesn't Quite Fit Your Situation . . .

Look at Problems 1-1 and 1-6 in this chapter for other cases of organizational performance improvement. Problem 12-1 deals with the situation where employees are rebelling against a production increase.

Use Checklist 1 to develop a cure of your own.

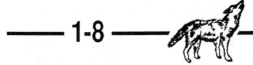

—— 1-8 ——

The Problem: Your employees respond to suggested changes with "we've always done it this way."

The Scene

You bite your tongue to keep from yelling at Floyd and stalk back to your office. He's the third employee this week who's answered "we've always done it this way" when you suggested doing things a different way. You thought you were taking over a conservative group of employees, and, boy, were you right!

Possible Causes

The employees really don't know any other way to do things. The group may have been so stable and done things the same way for so long that no one has ever thought that there might be another way to do them.

The employees like the way they do things and are resisting change. Employees often see a new manager as someone who's going to force a lot of new ideas on them and "dig in" to resist the changes.

The employees are actively fighting specific changes that you want to make. They may be fighting the changes not because they don't want to change, but because they don't like the changes you want to make.

Hint: These situations sound similar, but are actually quite different. You need to listen carefully and ask effective questions to find out what your problem really is before you can to solve it.

Cures

No matter what the cause is:

It's not true that people don't want to change. Most of us choose to change many times. But we only do so when we can answer "yes" to these three questions: (1) Will it pay off for me? (2) Can I do it successfully? and (3) Is it worth the effort it will take?

When someone else wants us to change, we must have a "yes" answer to a fourth question: Do I trust the person who wants me to change?

These four criteria are what we each use to decide whether or not to change. When anyone, including you, us and your work unit, can't answer "yes" to all four questions, we'll resist the change. On the other hand, when a proposed change meets all four criteria, we will change.

Your basic job, then, is to establish trust with your employees, and show them "yes" answers to the first three questions.

If they really don't know any other way:

Find a change that you're sure meets the first three criteria and then explain to your employees what you're going to do and why. Give them a chance to ask questions. Be patient. No matter how good you think your idea is, and how good they may later decide it is, making the change is going to make them uncomfortable.

If you can, wait to make more changes until the first change has "taken" and the group is comfortable with it. If it was an effective change, they'll be happy that you did it. This will make the next change easier. If you string together a succession of successful changes, change will probably become natural to them. Then they'll begin suggesting changes, and you'll know that you've succeeded.

If the employees are actively resisting change:

Don't get angry at their stubbornness. If you let the situation disintegrate into you versus them, you'll both lose.

Select a change that meets the three criteria. In this circumstance, it helps if the change is in response to a clear problem ("We've got to do something to reduce the number of errors or we're going to be in big trouble.")

Here's a technique that often works. Start with a compelling reason to change. (Perhaps you've been directed to cut copier expenses by 10% by the end of the month or else.) Call the group together; tell them that it has to be done and how you propose to do it. Then tell them that if anyone has a better idea you'll be glad to consider it. If you don't get any ideas from them, go ahead and do what you said you'd do. If you do get ideas—and sooner or later you will—do your best to implement them (at least in part).

Remember, pick changes that clearly have to be made and make sure they're effective. This will start to build employee trust in you. Then you can start persuading employees to make changes that aren't required and may not be so obvious.

If the employees are actively fighting specific changes you want to make:

First, examine the changes you're trying to make. Are they really going to help? Are they what the work unit needs now? Will they make the group more effective or efficient, or are you just changing to make the situation more comfortable for you? In other words, do the changes meet the first three criteria?

If they do, try to persuade your employees that they do. If you can't, but try to force the change through, you'll create a situation where it's you vs. your employees. Don't do this unless the change is absolutely essential (or absolutely required).

If you can't convince them the change will help them, at least convince them you're going to do it—no matter what.

If their opposition is really strong, you might try this: agree to stop pushing the change if they'll come up with a better way to do it. That gives them an out and puts the ball in their court, without your backing down from the change.

Do whatever is necessary to make sure the change succeeds. Forcing through a change which doesn't work is disastrous!

Things to Think About

You may be forced to make a change that doesn't meet all three tests, or before you can build trust with your employees. If you must do this, do it as gracefully as possible. But don't ever initiate a change on your own when this isn't true.

The more experienced your employees get at changing successfully, the easier it will be. Getting those first few successes is the hard—but very necessary—part.

And If This Doesn't Quite Fit Your Situation . . .

It might be related to the problem just before this one (1-7), which deals with self-imposed group production bogeys. If you have individuals who refuse to change, see Problems 5-4 and 6-9.

Use Checklist 1 or the General Checklist to develop a cure of your own.

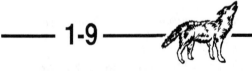

1-9

The Problem: Your employees have a poor reputation in the organization.

The Scene

Angered and hurt, you slammed down the phone. "That's totally unfair," you fumed. "What kind of a statement is that, 'I knew this proposal would be garbage as soon as I saw your unit's name on the cover'? I've worked hard with my group to make sure we only put out products that we can all be proud of. It doesn't make any difference how good a job we do, Analysis and Design has had some bad press, and now nobody will give us a chance!''

Possible Causes

Your unit may have produced substandard work in the past. It may be that your poor reputation is at least partially deserved. Customers (including internal customers) will not be likely to take a risk with you again if they've been burned in the past—unless you can convince them that they won't be disappointed again.

Your unit may have produced technically adequate work that failed to satisfy your customer's expectations. Customers don't necessarily know what's accurate or correct, but they do know what they want. Your job is to provide them with what they want *or* convince them that what you're offering them meets their needs even better.

Your unit may truly have gotten "bad press" for something that wasn't their fault. No one wants to admit error, and we're all falsely blamed at one time or another. An organization that really was at fault for poor products may have passed the blame on to you, or competitors may have made misleading comparisons between their offerings and yours.

Hint: As your mother probably warned you, reputation is a fragile thing. That's true corporately as well as personally. And much of the business we get is on the basis of our reputation—for solid, accurate, reliable, responsive work. The best way to safeguard your reputation is never to allow it to be sullied in the first place. Corporate image is not just the concern of the Public Relations department; it must be a concern in every customer contact.

Cures

If your unit has produced substandard work in the past:

Be honest with potential customers and clients who are worried about your previous performance. Tell them what you've done to improve, and show them examples of good work you've produced since the problems have been remedied. While you're in the process of reestablishing yourself, consider offering services on a contingency basis: you'll only get paid if the client accepts your work.

Try to expand your customer base. Approach people you haven't dealt with before, who may not have preconceived notions about the quality of your work.

Bite off only as much as you can chew. Start small. Be willing to spend a little extra effort at first producing a "perfect" product. You can use those first samples to show new customers (or to convince previous customers to give you another chance), and your "ultrasatisfied" customers can give good testimonials to your later prospects.

If your unit has previously produced technically adequate work that failed to satisfy your customers' expectations:

Work out in advance with your customers exactly what you intend to do for them. Listen closely to their needs and wants and articulate back to them what you think you hear them saying. Tell them (in a formal contract, if it's appropriate) exactly what you're offering them and which of their concerns your offering will satisfy. Make sure you both agree on the product or service you'll supply and what it will do for them, before you provide the product or service itself.

If you're offering a product that will take some time to produce, set up a series of checkpoints along the way. These can be meetings with the customer or they can be sets of formal specifications. But whatever form they take, you'll need periodic points where you and the customer examine progress to be sure that he or she is satisfied. That way you can clear up any misunderstandings early—before they become major disconnects.

If your unit received some "bad press" for something that wasn't their fault:

As closely as possible, identify the source of the erroneous information. It's tough to tackle an opponent you can't see.

If the bad press appears to be the result of innocent misinformation or misunderstanding, confront the source directly. Explain the true situation and try to enlist his or her aid in repairing the damage.

Consider an information campaign aimed at your most crucial customers. Through any of a variety of media and methods, public and individual, you can provide information to counter the "disinformation."

Contact some of your most loyal customers to explain the poor publicity you've received and to ask them for references or testimonials that you can use with prospective new customers. Develop, through special attention and high quality of delivery, a cadre of customers that you can count on for support even if times get tough.

Something to Think About

When a work unit is accused of poor work, it attacks the reputation and self-esteem of each employee in it. If the accusation turns into a poor reputation, the employees' self-esteem may drop sharply. One of your priorities should be to help them increase their self-esteem, by demonstrating your confidence in them and identifying and praising (on the spot) every improvement they make.

And If This Doesn't Quite Fit Your Situation . . .

If your poor reputation is the result of continuing poor quality work, you need to fix your quality problem before you can improve your reputation (See Problem 1-1). Problem 4-11 discusses a problem with a supplier caused by an individual employee. And Problem 11-2 deals with a manager's attempts to ruin your personal reputation.

Use Checklist 1 to develop a cure of your own.

—— **1-10** —— 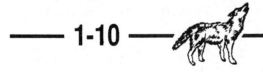 ————

The Problem: You've just taken over a group of employees that takes long lunch periods and breaks.

The Scene

Your desktop luncheon is punctuated by the incessant ringing of the telephone in the offices around you. "Where has everyone gone?" you wonder. Stepping from your office, you see two employees scrambling frantically to answer six phones and service three customers—all at the same time.

"Where are Lynda and Kyle?" you ask the employees.

"Oh, they're still at lunch."

"What about Jesse?"

"He's out on a break; he'll be back soon."

After just a couple of weeks, it's obvious to you that, between lunches and breaks, not a lot of work is getting done around here.

Possible Causes

Your unit's former manager may never have told them their long absences weren't acceptable. He or she may not have been as concerned about getting the work out or may just have been more laid back about absences.

Your unit may feel too pressured or stressed out. They may be resorting to long breaks in the workday as a way to relieve that pressure. Other symptoms of unhealthy stress include excessive absences or illnesses and irritability or petty arguments among your employees.

Hint: If this is not a production environment, your regulation of your employees' lunch periods and breaks is appropriate only to the extent that their over-long absences affect the quality of their work. If they're gone slightly more than you'd like, but they still do as much work as you can reasonably expect, you'll need to be very careful about stricter enforcement. The more liberal hours may be one of the benefits that keeps them in your employ. (Regulation of production workers' breaks is, of course, a different issue.)

Cures

If your unit was never told their long lunches and breaks weren't acceptable:

Make a rough estimate of the amount of time your unit is losing on their overlong absences; then translate that estimate into production, or profits, or whatever other measure is most meaningful to your employees.

Establish specific rules regarding breaks and lunch periods that will apply to all employees. Decide in advance how you'll treat requests for exceptions to those rules. Then communicate to your employees both the rules you've established and why it's necessary for you to control absences (by referring to the estimates you've computed).

Observe your employees fairly closely for the first couple of weeks, reminding them of the new rules whenever you see them slipping back into old patterns. When the new behavior is well established, make a point of recognizing their cooperation in a staff meeting or other gathering.

If your unit is using the long breaks and lunch periods to relieve the stress of the job:

Identify the source of the stress. Are your employees being pushed to produce too much? Are the pressures the result of management decisions or customer demands? Are there things that you can do to eliminate the source of the stress directly? Or must you live with the demands while trying to mitigate their adverse effects on your employees?

If the stressors are items that you can control directly, then make the adjustments necessary to control the work demands before you make any efforts to set or enforce time limits for lunches or breaks.

If the stressors are items that you cannot control directly, decide whether there are other, perhaps more effective, measures you could take to reduce the stress. You may want to consult with a professional to identify means of reorganizing the work to make it more efficient, and thus less stressful, or to confer with a stress-reduction consultant. While you're working out the underlying problem, make as few changes in work rules as possible—that means that you may have to live with the long lunches and breaks a little while longer.

Something to Think About

When your unit appears to take advantage of the work situation (such as the one in this problem), look carefully for the reason. The two reasons discussed here are very different, and the treatment needs to be different. In particular, look to see if they're compensating in another way; for instance, they may take long lunch breaks but keep working after the normal quitting time. As with so many other situations in this book, it's critical to know the cause before you can find the right cure.

And If This Doesn't Quite Fit Your Situation . . .

Look at Problem 7-6 for the case of an individual employee who is consistently late to work. The long lunches and breaks could also be related to work unit demoralization or low production bogeys (discussed in Problems 1-6 and 1-7). They could also be part of the cause of the unit's poor reputation discussed in the problem just before this one (1-9).

Use Checklist 2 to develop a cure of your own.

2

Troubleshooting Problems Caused by Today's Social Environment

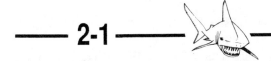

—— 2-1 ——

The Problem: An employee brags to others (falsely) that she's your lover.

The Scene

You sit dumbfounded as Sheila Smith, another manager and a friend of yours, walks out of your office. She's just told you that Alice McKenzie, one of your employees, is hinting to others that she's having an affair with you. Alice is young and relatively attractive; she's also a relatively poor employee that you've had to counsel repeatedly. You're sure you haven't done anything that she could have interpreted as an advance.

Possible Causes

Alice may be more immature than you had realized and is looking for attention. She may have found that claiming to be her manager's lover gets her attention she needs but can't get otherwise.

She may be setting the stage for a sexual harassment charge if you try to deal with her poor performance. She may be a poor employee, but nothing says she has to be dumb, too. She may believe that if she can get enough people believing the story, she can prevent you from doing anything about her performance. If you don't act quickly and well, she may be right.

She may also be setting the stage to try to trade sexual favors for advancement. She may have decided that since her performance won't make points with you, setting you up for an affair might.

Hint: Even though you're innocent, this is an extremely serious situation, and a very sticky one to deal with.

Cures

No matter what the cause is:

Go to your boss immediately and tell him the situation. Ask him to help you with rumor control.

Talk to someone in your firm's EEO office. Take your boss with you if he's willing to go.

Schedule an appointment with Alice. *Do not* meet with her alone; have another woman with you. (If you need to keep counseling her about performance, by the way, make sure you do it where someone else can see the two of you at all times.)

If possible, have Sheila or someone else with firsthand knowledge with you. (You may want to have someone from the EEO office there also.) Confront Alice with what you've been told.

Don't let yourself become emotional. Confront her with the situation, and let her know how very serious it is. Give her a chance to explain herself.

If she's apparently doing it from immaturity:

Evaluate very carefully whether she's salvageable as a employee. How honest is her response? Is she willing to correct the damage immediately?

If she seems worth saving, make the terms of it clear. She must agree to tell the truth immediately and to work on her performance. She must also understand that if anything like it happens again, she'll be dismissed—period.

If there's any question at all about her salvageability or honesty, give her the opportunity to resign and terminate her if she doesn't.

If she's apparently doing it to set you up:

Be prepared for a rough session—perhaps even a rough few days or weeks. If she was willing to lie originally to get what she wanted, she'll be willing to keep on lying.

Before things are over, the whole issue may depend on your demonstrated integrity. If you've been straight with female employees in the past, it will pay off now. If you've had serious complaints before—even if they've not been proven—you're in deep trouble now.

The organization may believe your story but still want to settle with Alice to prevent notoriety. Try to prevent any settlement which would make it sound like you had done something improper.

She may also be setting the stage to try to trade sexual favors for advancement.

This may be very difficult to spot. After all, if you're sitting there with someone else, she'll hardly make overtures to you there.

Think about her actions over the past few weeks and observe her carefully for a few days. Is she doing anything that might be interpreted as coming on to you? Have you perhaps been overlooking it, or been flattered even though you've not responded?

If she is dropping subtle hints, you need to respond to them—clearly and cleanly. You don't have to be harsh or angry; just make sure she gets the message.

Now's a good time to think about your relationships with your women employees in general. Have you been doing anything that might encourage Alice or any others to think you might be interested in a physical relationship? If you have, this would be a dandy time to stop.

If you did make any advances to Alice that others saw or know about:

Salvage as much as you can from the situation. If you keep a supervisory job, you'll probably be lucky.

Things to Think About

It's often tempting to "kid around" with attractive, willing employees. Sometimes it's tempting to go further than that, particularly if the other party seems agreeable. Just remember that there are "Alice McKenzies" out there, and if your reputation is a little tarnished before she shows up, it will be midnight black when she leaves.

This is written as though you're male and "Alice McKenzie" is female. That's not at all necessary. Nor, in some circumstances, is it necessary that you be of the opposite sex. The pattern and the dangers are the same no matter the sex of the participants.

And If This Doesn't Quite Fit Your Situation . . .

The other side of this is the employee who accuses you of sexual harassment or discrimination; if that's the case, see Problems 10-2 and 10-5. If the employee accuses another employee of sexual harassment or discrimination, that's covered in Problems 2-5 and 2-8 in this chapter.

Use Checklist 2 to develop a cure of your own.

—— 2-2 ——

The Problem: A group of employees tells you that they've heard another employee has AIDS and they won't work with him.

The Scene

Tom, Al, and Carol strode somberly into your office and quietly closed the door. "We're concerned about Carl," began Al. "Have you seen how thin and haggard he looks? He's out so much of the time—and can't seem to concentrate even when he's here."

"Frankly," interjected Carol, "we think he has AIDS, and it's not fair to the rest of us that you haven't done anything about it!

So we are. You know that team project you put the four of us on? Well, three of us just dropped out. We're not going to work that closely with Carl."

Possible Causes

Your employees may be concerned about the health risks to them. They may be concerned that they could get AIDS as a result of their contact with Carl—or that they could carry the disease home to their families or friends.

Your employees may be making a moral statement about the life-style patterns that are most common among the victims of the disease. The fact is that the highest risk groups for contracting AIDS are homosexuals and users of illegal drugs. Some of your employees may feel that, by working with an AIDS patient, they are showing approval of a life-style they consider immoral.

Hints: Regardless of the cause of your employees' concern, this is a very delicate and emotion-laden subject. Above all, you must treat your employees with tact and sensitivity for their feelings—whatever specific actions you choose to take.

Also, keep in mind that not all AIDS patients choose to tell their supervisors or coworkers what their real ailment is and that not all people who "look like" they have AIDS really do. A number of diseases exhibit similar symptoms and, for example, not everyone who loses a lot of weight has AIDS. If an employee you strongly suspect has AIDS won't tell you, respect his or her privacy—while also protecting your employees from possible infection.

Cures

If your employees are concerned about the health risks to them:

Find out for yourself what the real risks of infection are—from reading or from discussions with informed professionals. Find out what your company's policy is (if there is one) for dealing with AIDS patients and reducing the risks of infection. If there are work situations that could result in infection, fix them. If that means you can't allow the AIDS patient to perform certain tasks or if it means you have to modify the patient's assignments, then explain to him or her what you're doing and why.

Show your employees both what the *real* risks are to them and what you've done to minimize the risks. It's even better if you can get a health professional to come in and talk to your employees either as a group or individually.

Reassure your employees that you will continue to do everything you can to prevent infection.

At the same time, explain to them compassionately, but firmly, exactly what you expect from them—including continuing to work with the AIDS patient when you've decided that's appropriate.

Demonstrate by your own example the level of interaction you expect your employees to have with their sick co-worker. If you withdraw from the patient, you can't really blame your employees for withdrawing too.

If your employees are making a moral statement:

Again, learn as much as you can about risk behaviors and AIDS infection. Do what you can to minimize the risk of contagion in your work unit, and tell your employees what you've done. Be aware that your employees' moral statement may mask a deeper fear, conscious or unconscious, that they'll contract the disease themselves.

Explain to your employees that not all people who get AIDS are homosexuals or users of illegal drugs and that it's not fair to make judgments without knowing the facts. If it's already known that the AIDS patient engaged in behaviors your employees don't approve of, remind them that the behaviors predated the disease. Association with the sick person now, from a moral standpoint, is no different from association before he or she got sick.

As above, explain firmly exactly what you expect from your employees and demonstrate by your own actions how you want them to act.

Things to Think About

One of the big reasons AIDS is such a sensitive issue is that it's been identified only recently and many people don't know much about it. And nothing breeds panic, and prejudice, like ignorance.

Chances are that you *don't* have anyone in your unit now with AIDS, so this is a good time, in a staff meeting or other appropriate setting, to talk to your employees about AIDS. You can explain in general terms about the risks of infection in the kind of work you do and what your, and the company's, policies are for dealing with AIDS patients. Pre-armed with information, your employees will be much less likely to react irrationally when there really is an AIDS patient in their midst.

And If This Doesn't Quite Fit Your Situation . . .

See Problem 2-6 if an employee tells you that another employee is using drugs on the job or Problem 7-5 if an employee is trying to discredit another employee.

Use Checklists 2 or 3 to develop your own cure.

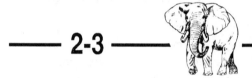

— 2-3 —

The Problem: You've just hired a minority group member with very high ratings who turns out to be a poor performer.

The Scene

You slam down the phone, your suspicion confirmed. Your newest employee, a minority group member who got excellent ratings from his last two supervisors, is a nonperformer. Here you are, in the middle of a production crunch—and now you have to deal with this!

Possible Causes

He may really want to do well and have ability. But he may be lacking in self-confidence or never have gotten the proper training. (Individuals in minority groups usually get formal training but may be missing informal, "this is how you really do it" training from other employees.)

He may really want to do well but lacks the ability. He may lack one or more key abilities for this kind of work. Or he may jut not be temperamentally suited to it.

He may be a poor performer because that's what he wants to be. He may be content to "get by" with as little work as possible. (Remember, though—this could be a symptom of lack of self-confidence, lack of training, or lack of a key ability.)

Hints: Listen carefully and ask probing questions. He will probably have a set of surface "answers" very different from his real thoughts and feelings.

If you settle for the surface answers, you won't find the real cause—and that means you won't be able to cure the problem.

Cures

If he really wants to do well and seems to have ability:

Give him routine but meaningful work to do. You might want to assign another employee to help him, particularly if you have a skilled employee who is also a member of a minority group.

See that help is available to him, but also make sure that no one else will do his work for him. If necessary, provide formal or on-the-job training.

Follow up regularly and frequently—anywhere from every day to once or twice a week. Praise his progress and use his mistakes to help him learn.

Gradually increase the variety and difficulty of what he's assigned until he's performing the full scope of his job. This may take weeks or months. It will be easier and faster if the rest of your employees are willing to work with him.

If he really wants to do well but doesn't seem to have the ability:

Make sure that this really is the case. It's painful to admit it if you have lingering stereotypes, but it's a fact of life. If he really wants to do well, don't decide he can't until he's had a real chance.

Give him routine tasks with plenty of help (as in the cure above), until you have a clear idea of just what he can do. This may take several weeks or months, if you have the time.

When you're sure he can't do the job, discuss the situation realistically with him. Try to arrange a change to a less demanding job in your unit or elsewhere. As long as he's conscientious, support him in every way you can.

Don't "carry" him or overrate him in hopes you can pass the problem on. It may solve this particular problem in the short run, but you may not want to live with the long-range consequences.

You can find more guidance for this situation in Problem 4-6.

If he's a poor performer because that's what he wants to be:

Again, make sure this is really the case, and not just a cover-up for lack of self-confidence, and so on.. Remember to be careful about the stereotypes you may have about that minority group.

Assign him a regular, routine work load—the kind of work his job grade is expected to perform. Give him assistance when appropriate (but make sure no one else does the work for him).

If he gives in and performs, so much the better. If not, follow your organization's procedures for dealing with non-performers. But deal with him.

If you push him and he threatens to file a discrimination complaint:

Double-check your expectations. Make sure you're *not* treating him differently from nonminority workers.

From a purely practical standpoint, some battles just aren't worth fighting. You may be convinced that what you're doing is right and nondiscriminatory. If you think you're likely to lose in a discrimination complaint or that the fight will tear apart your work unit, you need to think hard about the situation. Will the benefits of success outweigh the negative consequences?

If the benefits outweigh the dangers, confront the EEO issue head-on. Tell him that although he has the right to file a complaint, you're convinced that what you're doing is best for him and for the organization. Then document every action or discussion with him and start building your own case!

And what if you think the outcome isn't worth the effort? You have a serious problem on your hands. You can't let him just "slide by" because of his threat. Our best advice is to keep constant pressure on him to perform at the same level as the others. If that's not practical, see if you can assign him meaningful, useful duties which he can perform. The critical point is to somehow see that he becomes a productive member of your work unit.

Things to Think About

Other people let the situation develop for months or years; you don't have to resolve it overnight. Be careful and cautious—and *sensitive*—in your approach to it. Just remember that *not* dealing with it will probably create the greatest number of problems in the long run.

No matter how you deal with the EEO implications, don't forget that this is first of all a *performance* problem. The situation will never be completely resolved unless and until the performance issue is resolved.

And If This Doesn't Quite Fit Your Situation . . .

If the problem seems to be specifically the employee's motivation, see Problem 4-2. If the employee won't follow work procedures or is poor at organizing his work, see Problem 5-1 or Problem 6-1. If the problem appears to be that he won't change the way he's done his work, see Problem 6-9.

Use Checklist 1 to develop a cure of your own.

— 2-4 —

The Problem: You have three new Vietnamese employees who are your best producers, and the rest of your employees are becoming resentful of them.

The Scene

"Come on in," you call in response to a quiet knock on your office door. "What can I do for you?"

"Well, Mr. Paulsen," replies Nguyen in halting English, "I was told something on the floor today that didn't sound right, and I thought I should check it out. Someone warned me I'd have trouble if I didn't slow down. I thought you wanted us to work through as many parts as we could, but this guy says there'll be trouble for me if I go too fast. What should I do?"

You reassure Nguyen that his production is just fine, reflecting as he leaves that the problem is worse than you thought. You knew there was some resentment of your three newest employees—but you didn't know it was this bad.

Possible Causes

Your employees may fear that the new employees' production will raise the standard for everyone. And they may not see any good reason to raise the standard (or any benefit to them).

They may be worried that, in doing so well, the Vietnamese employees will get the lion's share of promotions and bonuses—promotions and bonuses they themselves expected to be next in line for.

Their resentment may stem from real prejudice. This is probably the toughest situation to deal with because you're fighting ignorance and emotion rather than something based in fact.

Cures

If your employees are concerned their production standard may be raised:

Come up with some positive incentives to encourage increased production as an alternative to forcing higher quotas. Even if you're convinced that most of your employees could be doing more than they are, use the "carrot" rather than the "stick" to get employees *voluntarily* to increase their own production.

Consider grouping your unit into teams, distributing the new Vietnamese employees among them. Establish some incentives on the basis of group performance, rather than individual performance. Your new employees will move quickly from being threats to the other employees to being prized team members.

Look at Problem 1-7 for positive ways to increase production without angering your employees.

If your employees are worried that they'll be bypassed for promotions and bonuses:

If you haven't already done so, decide what criteria you'll be using to make promotions and award bonuses. Especially for promotions to lead or supervisory jobs, production isn't the only consideration.

Make sure your employees know what the criteria are, and their relative importance in your decisions.

Offer training and job enhancement opportunities to all of your good performers equally—not just to those who are the very best. Your new employees' higher productivity may be as much a function of their enthusiasm for a new job as of cultural differences. Let your long-term good workers know that you continue to value them and look out for their interests.

If the resentment stems from real prejudice:

Make sure your employees are aware of your personal policy on equal treatment of employees and your intolerance of discrimination. Repeating your company's policy can be a part of that, but it's essential that your employees get a clear and firm message from you about your own personal position.

Look at Problem 2-10 for more information on integrating women and minorities successfully into your work unit.

Something to Think About

This is a situation in which it's essential to know the real cause of your management problem before starting to solve it. Resentment could be either the result of discrimination (which you can't tolerate) or of fear, and maybe embarrassment, which requires a more sensitive solution. Correcting the problem before you know its cause can result in the wrong message being sent to your staff. You could be seen as lacking sympathy when they're being outdone by a bunch of newcomers or as quietly approving their prejudice against a minority group.

And If This Doesn't Quite Fit Your Situation . . .

Look at Problems 1-4 and 2-10 for discussions of easing employees into the group. Problem 1-7 talks about ways of increasing production in your whole unit.

Use Checklist 3 to develop a cure of your own.

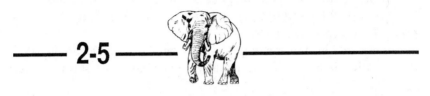

2-5

The Problem: One of your employees tells you another has sexually harassed her, and asks what you're going to do about it.

The Scene

"No, there isn't any question about it!" Velma says emphatically. "Charlie made a serious pass at me when we were in the file room. That's sexual harassment, and I want to know what you're going to do about it!"

Possible Causes

Velma may have misunderstood Charlie. He may genuinely have been kidding, but she took him seriously.

Charlie may have thought Velma was interested in him. His pass was a test to "check it out." Now he knows she isn't interested, he won't try it again.

Charlie may be determined to get something going with Velma. If this is the case, things won't stop but will probably get worse—unless you resolve the situation quickly.

Hints: It doesn't matter which is true; you have a serious situation on your hands. Unless and until you know otherwise, you should assume that Charlie made the pass on purpose and may repeat it.

If it was a verbal pass, the situation is serious. If it was a physical pass, it's very serious.

Cures

No matter what the cause is:

If you have any questions about what your organization's policy is on sexual harassment, find the answers to them immediately. If you aren't sure about your responsibilities, find that out, too.

Tell your boss about the situation, so he's not caught by surprise. Then keep him posted.

Talk to Charlie immediately. Be completely clear about what the situation is and why. Be equally clear about how serious it is.

If it appears that Charlie was only kidding:

The odds are good Charlie will say this no matter what really happened. Don't take it at face value.

If the pass was physical, reject this alternative no matter how loudly Charlie claims he was only kidding. A physical pass is always serious, confirmed sexual harassment.

If the pass was only verbal and Charlie insists he was kidding, you might want to check with a couple of his co-workers you feel you can trust. Do they believe his story? (Don't just go by their words. Their silences, pauses, and nuances may give you the real information.)

If you're completely convinced Charlie was kidding, counsel him on the seriousness of the situation. Then get him and Velma together with you as quickly as possible so he can apologize and promise not to repeat it. See if she will accept his apology and explain her reaction to him.

If she accepts his apology and lets the situation be, breathe a loud sigh of relief. If she doesn't, but you're convinced Charlie's actions were innocent, discuss the situation with her again privately. If you can't convince her, let her do what she must.

If Charlie was apparently testing to see if Velma was interested:

He made a significant miscalculation. Now you have to try and salvage the situation quickly.

See if you can find out from Velma what she wants. She may settle for Charlie's apology and promise not to repeat his actions.

If she will, talk with Charlie immediately. Make sure he understands that if the situation is repeated with any female employee his tenure on his job is in jeopardy. Write up the counseling, using whatever format your organization requires. If the action was blatant enough, take formal disciplinary action.

If Velma demands that you discipline Charlie, the situation is stickier. Discipline of another employee isn't an appropriate resolution for any kind of grievance; the decision to discipline is management's and must be based on the facts of the situation. Try to get Velma to accept your assurance that it won't happen again and let you handle Charlie. If he's willing, it might help to have Charlie apologize to her and promise not to repeat the pass.

What if Velma won't accept this resolution? Tell her that you've dealt with Charlie and it won't happen again. If she won't settle for that, tell her you've done all you can and let the EEO system take over.

If it appears that Charlie intends to "hit on" Velma or if the pass was physical:

Take prompt and appropriate disciplinary action. You can't tolerate an employee who makes unwanted advances at another employee, particularly if physical contact is involved.

It doesn't matter how you feel about Charlie or how good a employee he is. Unless you take firm action quickly you—and the organization—will be subject to a sexual harassment charge. In this case, you're acting to protect both yourself and the organization.

Use your best judgment, but if it appears it might help and he's willing, have Charlie apologize to Velma and promise not to repeat his actions.

Tell Velma that you've taken appropriate action to see that it won't happen again. If this doesn't satisfy her, you have to tell her you've done what you can and she'll have to do what seems best to her.

Things to Think About

The situation is even more serious if Velma is in what has been considered a "man's job"—and this incident is part of an overall strategy of making her feel uncomfortable. If you have any reason to suspect this might be true, deal with it—quickly and firmly. This means disciplining Charlie and making it crystal clear to everyone else that the behavior won't be tolerated.

If this seems harsh, you haven't been reading the newspapers. Sexual harassment is a form of sexual discrimination, and is just as serious as any other form of discrimination. If there was physical contact or Charlie apparently intended to force his attentions on Velma, only prompt action can save you and the firm from a charge of sexual harassment.

And If This Doesn't Quite Fit Your Situation . . .

If the employee complains of racism rather than sexual harassment, look at Problem 2-8 in this chapter. If the claim is that *you've* done the harassing, see 10-2. Problems 2-7 and 2-9 in this chapter may also help, since they deal with situations that could involve sexual harassment.

Use Checklist 3 to develop a cure of your own.

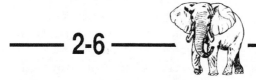

—— 2-6 ——

The Problem: An employee tells you that another employee (one of your best) is using cocaine on the job.

The Scene

You sigh dejectedly. Tom Vasary has just told you that Wilson Edwards is using cocaine on the job. You don't want to believe it, but Wilson has been acting differently lately. Maybe he really is a user.

Possible Causes

Tom is trying to discredit Wilson for some reason. With today's emphasis on drugs, Tom may have decided to use the story to get rid of Wilson or settle an old score with him or . . .

Tom is being honest but is mistaken about what he saw. Again, with the emphasis on drugs people may see abuse in innocent situations. Mistaken or not, their perceptions have to be dealt with.

Wilson is using cocaine or some other illegal drug on the job. Of course, this is the worst situation. It's hard to prove it, but absolutely essential to stop it.

Hint: Your natural tendency may be to delay dealing with the situation. After all, you don't really know. *Don't* put it off. If Tom was mistaken, you need to get the situation cleared up as quickly as possible. If he wasn't mistaken, every day you put it off makes the habit more dangerous to Wilson—and increases the prospect that he will begin to be a performance problem.

Cures

No matter what the cause is:

Question Tom in detail about just what he saw. If there's any doubt, ask why he thinks that Wilson was using cocaine. Be careful; you need to communicate to Tom that you need these facts to act on the situation—and you're not trying to put him on the spot.

If possible, talk to one or two employees whom you believe will level with you. Have they noticed anything unusual where Wilson is concerned? Are they perhaps worried about him? This will be awkward. It will require great tact on your part. Your employees must trust you for this to work, and you must make it clear you're doing this because of your concern for Wilson. But do it. The penalty for not doing it is too great.

If they're sure that Wilson is clean, check to see if anyone knows why Tom might want to discredit him.

If you're not absolutely sure that Tom was distorting the situation, talk with Wilson. You don't have to identify your source, but tell him what you've heard. Be prepared for him to react emotionally, no matter what the situation is. Stick with it, until you find whether or not he has a fully believable explanation.

If Tom is apparently trying to discredit Wilson:

You have a sticky situation on your hands. If you have clear evidence that Tom was lying, take disciplinary action against him for defaming an employee. (You can find some more guidance for this situation in Problem 7-5.)

If you don't have good evidence, follow the guides in the next few paragraphs.

If Tom appears just to have been mistaken about what Wilson was doing:

Call Tom in and tell him what Wilson's explanation was (if an explanation is necessary). Let him react to that.

If Tom reacts with relief (or an other appropriate response), thank him for sharing his concern with you and counsel him gently on being careful about what he says.

If Tom reacts defensively, try to find the reasons for his defensiveness. For instance, he may feel you're attacking him and trying to protect Wilson. Or he may be reacting to your having caught him at trying to discredit Wilson. Counsel him strongly on being careful about what he says about others.

If it appears that Wilson may be using cocaine or a similar illegal drug on the job:

Tell your boss about the situation immediately.

Contact your company's Employee Assistance Program (EAP) manager, or whoever is responsible for assisting with employees who have problems. Ask for his advice and follow it. Also find out from him exactly what your firm's policy is in regard to employees who possess and/or use illegal drugs on the job.

If you don't have enough evidence to confront Wilson, make it a point to have contacts with him throughout the day. Does his mood change significantly? Does he sometimes act secretively? See that your EAP manager knows about anything significant.

If you believe that Wilson is abusing an illegal drug, don't give up until he seeks help or you have to separate him for using or for poor performance.

Things to Think About

In a situation like this, you need to be sensitive, alert and forceful. On the one hand, if Wilson does have a problem the best thing you can do for him, yourself and the company is to get him to seek help. On the other, you can't take formal action unless you get usable evidence that he's breaking the law, or his performance becomes unacceptable.

Be patient but persistent. Cocaine addiction is a powerful, destructive force.

And If This Doesn't Quite Fit Your Situation . . .

If Wilson's problem starts to show up in his performance, look for the specific performance problem in other chapters. If your boss resists your taking action against Wilson, see Problem 14-3.

Use Checklists 2 and 7 to develop a cure of your own.

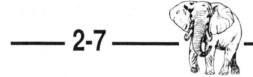

2-7

The Problem: An employee complains that her team leader is sleeping with another employee.

The Scene

Jenny Critchlow left your office looking relieved, while you sat looking at your desk as if a bomb had just dropped there. And in a figurative sense, it had. Carol Kadenski, one of your best leaders, sleeping with another employee! How could she risk everything like that? Her great work record, a good chance at the next promotion—all for some fling.

Well, now you know, and your employees know you know, so the monkey's on your back.

Possible Causes

Why Carol is having an affair with another of your employees isn't particularly important here. It's not even entirely relevant whether she'll admit the affair or not. But there are some questions you need answers to in deciding how to solve this problem:

Is the person Carol is sleeping with one of her employees, or is it someone in another group? Affairs between leads or supervisors and subordinates require significant intervention—both because of the possibility of coercion in the relationship and because of the possible effects on the lead or supervisor's other employees.

Particularly if the person she's sleeping with is on Carol's team, do other employees in the unit feel they've been harmed by the affair? Is Carol giving preferential treatment to her lover? Either tangibly in better ratings, bonuses, promotions? Or less visibly in better assignments, better work space, time off?

Hint: Many companies have specific policies about relatives, including husbands and wives, working together. Fewer have policies about affairs between coworkers. If your company has such a policy, your task is much easier. Explain to Carol what the rules are and give her an alternative: either she fixes the problem—or you will. Then follow through.

Cures

If the person sleeping with Carol is someone who works for her:

Let Carol know immediately that you're aware of the situation. If she denies that she's having an affair with anyone on her team, tell her that her employees are concerned enough that even the *perception* that the relationship exists is causing problems.

Decide whether you need to move Carol or her lover so they're no longer in a superior-subordinate relationship. This isn't always necessary, and it's not always the best solution—but it always needs to be considered. If Carol's people believe they've been harmed by her affair, it's essential.

If Carol's people have been harmed, that is a serious mishandling of her supervisory authority. You'll need to consider whether to take some further action against Carol—including moving her out of supervision/lead duties altogether or firing her.

Make sure you let Jenny Critchlow know that you checked out her concerns and acted on them. It may not be appropriate to tell her specifically what you've done about Carol, but she does need to know that you've responded to her.

If the person Carol is sleeping with is not in her unit:

Consider whether any action is required at all. If the person Carol is sleeping with isn't in her unit, the relationship probably isn't hurting the work or the employees, and they're being discreet (so there's no harm to the organization's reputation), you might not have any reasonable basis for doing anything. (Of course, if there's a company policy on the subject, follow it.)

Any action should start with telling Carol about the report you've received—without revealing the source of the information. Encourage her to reconsider whether the affair is in her best interests—or her lover's, and counsel her to be discreet if she decides to continue the affair.

If Carol denies the affair, tell her that perceptions can be just as damaging as real events and, again, counsel discretion.

Whenever there is any hint that Carol has misused her authority (for instance, using her position or favors she might award or deny to coerce her lover's cooperation), strong measures are in order.

Something to Think About

One of the essential ingredients in a successful superior-subordinate relationship is trust. This situation is a particularly delicate one because it acts specifically to undermine that trust. Your primary aim in solving this problem is to set up an environment where that trust can be rebuilt—either between Carol and her employees or, if that relationship is beyond repair, between the unit and its new leader.

And If This Doesn't Quite Fit Your Situation . . .

Look at Problem 5 for a discussion of sexual harassment when there's coercion involved. Problem 3-6 discusses an office romance between peers.

Use Checklist 3 to develop a cure of your own.

2-8

The Problem: An employee accuses another employee of racism or sexism.

The Scene

"Mr. Jones, I know that you haven't had many women employees here, but that's no excuse. Conrad has been discriminating against me."

"How?" you ask.

"He always gives me the dirtiest assignments," Madeleine replies. "When I ask him for help, he tells me to get it on my own—but I hear him explaining to all of the men just how to do things. He's made two notes in my file this month—for things I couldn't do anything about. If you don't get him to change, I'm going to have to file a complaint!"

Possible Causes

Madeleine is overly sensitive because she is the only woman in the unit right now. When you're a member of a minority group, it's easy to interpret situations as discriminatory, even if no one intends for them to be.

Madeleine is a poor or lazy employee who wants an excuse not to have to perform. It's all too easy to settle for this kind of an explanation for the problem, and in most cases it would be the wrong one. But it does happen.

Conrad isn't used to having women employees and isn't treating Madeleine appropriately. This may be happening even if Conrad has no intention to discriminate at all. He needs educating, quickly.

Conrad really is discriminating against Madeleine because she's a female. Needless to say, this situation has to be resolved immediately (or perhaps sooner).

Hint: The days of obvious discrimination are almost over. Racism and sexism appear in much more subtle ways these days. In fact, displays of racism and sexism are almost never overt or easy to spot. But they're often there, and they're just as dangerous and as illegal as they were before. The moral? No matter how clear-cut things seem on the surface, don't throw discrimination out as an explanation for a problem until you've looked more deeply into the situation.

Cures

No matter what the cause is:

You have a potentially serious situation on your hands. It's important to find out—quickly—all of the facts you can.

Begin by having Madeleine tell you in detail what has happened that she believes is sexual discrimination. Be careful; don't give the appearance of putting her through the third degree. Make it clear that you want the facts so you can investigate what she's telling you. Then get all the facts you can.

If you can, try to observe Conrad for several days to see if he does seem to be treating Madeleine differently from the other (male) employees. Also observe Madeleine herself, to see if she's doing anything that might be causing Conrad's actions.

At some point you'll need to talk with Conrad. How open you are and just how you conduct the conversation will depend on your relationship with him, your confidence in him, and your observation of his behavior.

If Madeleine appears to be a poor or lazy employee who wants an excuse not to have to perform.

Investigate and observe carefully before you reach this conclusion. Ask yourself if it's consistent with Madeleine's performance. If she's new, you may not know. If she's been an employee for long, though, has she always been like this? If not, avoiding work probably isn't the reason for her behavior.

If you're convinced she's trying to find an excuse not to perform as she should, tell her this, make your expectations clear, and then treat her as you would any other employee whose work and/or motivation were questionable. (For instance, see chapters 5 and 7, which deal with these kinds of performance problems.) She may file a complaint against you, but you'll just have to deal with that.

If Madeleine seems to be overly sensitive because she is the only woman in the unit right now:

This is another alternative that you should accept *only* when you've checked out all of the alternatives below and believe that none of them are true.

Talk with Conrad and, if sensible, other men employees. Explain to them how Madeleine is feeling and ask for their help to make life in the unit easier for her.

Talk with Madeleine. Explain to her all you've done to check out what she said and the conclusions she's reached. Explain that you believe Conrad and others genuinely want to treat her as an equal and that you've asked them to be sensitive to her feelings. Ask her to be understanding. Suggest that any time she believe she's being treated unfairly by anyone she come talk to you (and, if she does, be just as thorough as you were this time).

If Conrad is sensitive and willing to do it, you might include him in the conversation in the paragraph above. His assurances to Madeleine might mean more than yours.

If Conrad isn't used to having women employees and isn't treating Madeleine appropriately.

You have a serious situation on your hands, but at least it appears to be unintentional. Act quickly and decisively—but be tolerant and understanding of Conrad (and others, if they're also involved).

Talk clearly and firmly with Conrad. Point out what he's doing. Give him a chance to explain himself, and expect that he may be defensive. But this isn't a discussion; your clear objective is to get him to change his behavior. See that he understands this and follow up to see that he has changed.

Tell Madeleine what you've done to investigate her complaint and the action you've taken. See that she understands you believe Conrad didn't do it on purpose, but that you've directed him to change. Ask her to tell you any time he repeats his "sexist" behavior—and if she does, follow up on it.

If Conrad really is discriminating against Madeleine because she's a female:

Act immediately. If the discrimination is clear and has harmed Madeleine's performance or advancement opportunities, discipline Conrad. If it's just been a correctable irritant—and this is his first offense—counsel him pointedly and tell him exactly what changes you expect. He'll probably be defensive and complain about reverse discrimination. Let him, but make it clear that he's to change, or else.

Follow up, with both Conrad and Madeleine, to see that the situation is corrected. If Conrad hasn't changed, take whatever action is necessary.

Things to Think About

Before you begin, make sure you know what equal opportunity laws and your company's own policies require. Once you understand these, think about how you want your unit to operate within the framework they establish.

The analysis and actions above are equally valid whether the allegation is racism or sexism—or any other illegal discrimination. Check to make sure you have the facts. If possible, observe. Then take the appropriate action—quickly.

Even if you believe Conrad has discriminated, you may be tempted to treat him as though it was unintentional. This may work, but be careful. If you take this course of action, he may not realize the seriousness of the situation. And you may subject yourself to a complaint because you didn't act to resolve the problem effectively.

If there is discrimination, you need to deal with more than this specific occurrence. One solution is to arrange for an experienced facilitator to conduct workshops to help your employees understand the law, company policy and (hopefully) their own prejudices. If there are pockets of resistance to cooperation and inclusion of all employees, schedule the workshops so that these people are separated from each other and intermingled with employees who are already moving in the right direction.

Above all else, fight discrimination through your personal example. If you treat everyone evenhandedly and sensitively and expect each employee to do the same, most discrimination won't ever occur.

And If This Doesn't Quite Fit Your Situation . . .

If the charge is sexual harassment rather than discrimination, see Problem 2-5. The next problem (2-9) deals with a situation where discrimination might be a factor. If the employee has accused you of discrimination, see Problem 10-5.

Use Checklist 3 to develop a cure of your own.

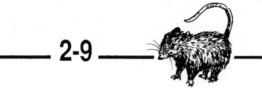

—— **2-9** ——

The Problem: The new (and only) woman in your work unit complains that the men use language which offends her.

The Scene

Georgia strides briskly into your office. Obviously she means business!

"Mark," she begins, "you know I'm not a prude and I can give as good as I get, but the language around here is awful. It sounds more like a sweatshop than an office! I don't think some of these guys know how to construct a sentence that doesn't start with a curse. And the only adjective some of them ever use is 'f___g.' I don't think I should have to put up with that!"

Possible Causes

Your employees may have used that speech style for so long that they don't even realize what they're saying. Language patterns are usually adopted unconsciously. Cursing, swearing, and off-color remarks are common in many single-sex groups. But if your employees associate these speech patterns with the work*place* rather than the work *group*, it may not occur to them to change when a woman joins them and they're no longer a single-sex group.

The offensive language may be a subtle form of harassment. Especially if your new female employee has made it clear to your other employees—verbally or nonverbally—that she dislikes or disapproves of their language, employees who are not openly resentful of a woman in their midst may see this as a way to get back at her, or even to drive her out.

Cures

If your employees aren't consciously aware that the language is offensive:

Make them aware in a straightforward but diplomatic way. Rather than labeling the language as "offensive," you might talk about it as "unprofessional." Then solicit your employees' cooperation in cleaning up their language to improve the company's (or group's) corporate image.

If this is the real cause, then simply making everyone conscious of the language they're using will probably be enough to get them to correct it. Remember though that language patterns are adopted unconsciously, so be moderately patient about expecting significant changes, as you continue to remind employees who fall back into the old, unprofessional ways of speaking.

If the offensive language is a form of harassment:

In this case, your *real* problem isn't the language; it's prejudice—which we've already addressed in several different guises. Look at Problem 2-10 in this chapter for specific steps to take in overcoming bias in the workplace.

Something to Think About

The solutions we've talked about so far assume that your male employees really do use offensive language and that their language is inappropriate in your particular work environment. And that's generally the case in most white-collar environments. In much blue-collar work, however, and in some high-stress white-collar jobs, "risque" language is the norm. If people in most other units or companies in your line of work seem to talk the way your employees do, then changing your employees' language may not be the best idea. Your people may start to sound "wimpy" to their associates and competitors. In that case, you need to take an entirely different approach—reeducate your new female employee. Explain why it's not a good idea to change the way your unit sounds and encourage her to try to get past the language employees use to see what they're really saying. And make sure she knows the language isn't meant to get to her—it's just part of the environment.

And If This Doesn't Quite Fit Your Situation . . .

Look at Problems 2-3, 2-4, 2-10, and 9-5 if the problem is acceptance of a woman in the workplace.

Use Checklists 2 and 3 to develop a cure of your own.

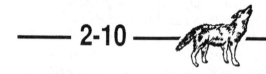

—— 2-10 ——

The Problem: Two of your employees are carrying on an openly homosexual relationship.

The Scene

Your employees have been dropping broad hints for several weeks that two of the newer men employees are "more than just friends." You saw them at lunch today and drew the same conclusion.

Possible Causes

Human nature. People have been trying to figure out for years why individuals fall for one another. It doesn't appear that there's an answer yet. And why does someone fall for someone else of the same sex? Again, no one really knows.

Hint: You have one problem for sure, and perhaps two.

- The "for-sure" problem is that two employees have a personal relationship that may affect their working relationship. This has nothing to do with whether or not they're gay.

- You may also have a problem because they're the same sex. In some parts of the country, that's acceptable—or at least bearable. In other parts, it's still completely unacceptable.

Cures

For the problem that two employees have a "more than friends" relationship:

Whether this is serious, and how serious it is, depends on their work relationship.

If the two of them work in separate units, or completely different jobs, where neither of them deals with the other:

- You may not have a problem. Their work contacts may be so limited that their relationship is unlikely to impact their job performance.

- You might want to alert them that the situation could prevent one or both of them from advancing, since you could never allow one to supervise the other.

- You also need to make sure that the time they spend on their relationship doesn't start cutting into the workday. For instance, they may begin coming back from lunch consistently late. You need to deal with this—remembering that the problem is the lateness, not the relationship.

If they work in the same unit, but don't disrupt work with their relationship, the problem is almost the same.

- In this case, there's probably a greater chance that the relationship could keep either from getting promoted. Make sure that they understand this.

If either of them supervises the other, or makes decisions which affect the performance of the other, the situation is serious.

- You can't allow it to continue. Reassign one of them if you can. If you can't, discuss the situation with them and see if they can come up with an acceptable alternative. If they can, fine. If not, take whatever action is necessary— such as requiring the one who's the supervisor to let you make every decision that directly or indirectly affects the other.

If the fact that they're gay is unacceptable to other employees:

This is a very touchy area. You need to check with your legal office, personnel office, EEO office, or whoever can tell you what the laws are in your state concerning actions based on sexual preference. It may be a form of prohibited discrimination.

If actions based on sexual preference are discriminatory, you may have a serious predicament on your hands. Other employees may ostracize them, perhaps even physically abuse them.

Even if discrimination on the basis of sexual preference isn't illegal, you still have a sticky situation on your hands. If the two employees are good employees, you may jeopardize their chances of getting other jobs if you take any action based on their being gay.

Our last suggestion is threefold:

- First, get the very best counsel you can. This is a very uncertain area in our society and in the law of most states. You need to proceed very, very carefully.

- Second, if you feel you have to take action, give the two individuals as much voice as you can in what will be done. One of them might voluntarily accept a reassignment, or even resign to take another job. Give them the chance to find their own solution.

- Finally, if you have to take an action do it in the way that will least hurt the individuals. Regardless of how you and other employees might feel, the actions of these two individuals are probably as "natural" for them as heterosexual relationships are for others. Respect that, whatever action you have to take.

And If This Doesn't Quite Fit Your Situation . . .

Problem 3-6 deals with two employees who've broken up and the tension between them is disrupting the unit. If the problem involves an individual sleeping with a subordinate, see Problem 2-7.

Use Checklists 2 and 3 to develop a cure of your own.

3

Troubleshooting Problems Caused by the Personal Life of an Employee

 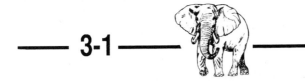

The Problem: An employee has serious health problems.

The Scene

Gloria Singer, one of your most experienced employees, just confided to you that she has a serious illness. She's been absent for days at a time; even when she comes in, she doesn't perform as well as she used to. Sometimes you wonder if there's any point in her being there at all—but she's not so sick you can justify sending her home. Your boss is pressing you for the assignments Gloria usually does, and other employees have begun to complain about having to cover for her.

Possible Causes

She may have a serious illness from which she'll recover. There are many illnesses which are very debilitating but from which individuals do recover.

61

She may have a serious illness which won't get better. This is a real possibility—and a very different problem from a short-term illness.

She may be trying to hide other problems. She may be covering up for serious family troubles, severe depression, or substance abuse. People are often embarrassed by situations like these and find it easier to pretend they're physically sick.

Her doctor may limit what she can do. This will limit what she can contribute, no matter how much she wants to do her job.

Hints: Be careful not to discuss her problem with other employees or to make a point of treating her "special." If she told you about her illness in confidence, respect that confidence.

If you need to talk to someone, talk to a health professional or your organization's Employee Assistance Program counselor.

Cures

If the illness is a legitimate, long term one:

Work out with Gloria how much work she can do and a reasonable reduced-hours schedule that you're both confident she can meet.

Identify the specific job tasks Gloria will keep and which ones she will give up (even if temporarily).

Reassign the tasks she's giving up to other employees or hire a partial replacement (temporary help, part-time employees, etc.) if company policy permits.

Establish a regular schedule (maybe once every month or two) for you and Gloria to discuss her condition again and make any adjustments (upward or downward) in her work schedule.

Help Gloria identify any sources available that might help her make up her lost income (disability benefits, employee assistance program, etc.).

If the illness appears to be a cover-up for another problem:

Insist on talking personally with her doctor; don't accept a written statement.

If there really is another problem, insist that she get help for it. If your organization has an Employee Assistance Program, offer it to her.

Don't let her continue on as she is. If she gets help, assist her in any reasonable way back to full performance. If she doesn't get help, insist that she perform fully or else.

If the illness is short term:

Insist that she not work unless her doctor clearly okays it. She should do whatever is necessary to help herself recover.

Explain the situation to the rest of your employees and ask them to help carry her work load for a short while.

Follow up regularly—every week or so—with Gloria and, if necessary, her doctor. Make sure that she's recovering as expected. If she's not, look at the first alternative above.

Things to Think About

If the employee has been a good, productive worker, you have an obligation to treat her as compassionately as possible.

On the other hand, she has the obligation both to be completely honest with you and to take the responsibility for her recovery.

And If This Doesn't Quite Fit Your Situation . . .

Look at Problem 3-7 if an employee with a health problem can work but his medication is making him drowsy. If the employee's problem is more emotional than physical, see the next problem (3-2). If you think that a health problem is worsened (or even caused) by a stressful work situation, see Chapter 1—especially Problem 1-2, 1-3, 1-5, and 1-6. And Problem 6-4 deals with an employee who goes to pieces under pressure.

Use Checklist 2 to develop a cure of your own.

—— 3-2 ——

The Problem: An employee seems to be becoming unbalanced.

The Scene

You walk back to your office, shaking your head. Martin Kaminsky has always been a little weird, but lately he's been acting truly crazy. You just heard him accuse Sandra Wilson, a new clerk, of hiding the notes from his latest audit. When Sandra left the room in tears, Martin turned to the others and yelled "You think I'm no good, but I'll show you!"

Possible Causes

Martin may be reacting to a temporary stressful situation. Perhaps his home life is bothering him, or changes in the work environment have him "stressed out."

He may have periodic episodes. All of us go through "phases" in our emotions, more "laid back" at times, more "uptight" at others. Martin's swings may be more pronounced than normal.

He may be getting seriously emotionally disturbed. His strange behavior may be a sign that he's becoming irrational, that—in the language of the last generation—he's "having a nervous breakdown."

Hint: The worst reaction you can make is to get angry with Martin. Whatever is happening, getting angry with him will only make it worse.

Cures

No matter what the cause is:

First, remember what we just said. Keep your cool. Observe carefully. Then, if necessary, find someone who's familiar with emotional disturbance and learn all you can from him.

Talk to other employees. Learn everything they know about him. How has he changed? Has this ever happened before? What happened then? How was it handled then? How quickly did he recover?

Talk with Martin. Yes, this is going to be stressful. No, you're not going to play psychiatrist. But you want to get a "feel" for his situation. You want to talk with him about the problem, if possible. If he can talk about it, that increases the chance that it can be resolved with a minimum of stress. If he can't—well, that's important information.

There's another side to the picture. If the situation is deteriorating, you may have to act without knowing all you need to know. It may be a tense time, for Martin, your other employees, and you. But if you act on the best information you have, trying to do the best you can by everyone—you'll bring about the best solution possible under the situation.

If he's reacting to a temporary stressful situation:

How will you know this? You won't, for sure. But if the problem really is a specific situation, he should be able both to tell you about the situation and understand the problem his reactions are causing. In other words, he'll probably be willing to work with you.

(One point to keep in mind. He may really be reacting to something specific, but not be willing to talk about it. Many of us have really serious circumstances in our lives we can't talk about—such as the serious illness of someone we care about deeply. If Martin says he has this kind of problem, listen very, very carefully. You need to discover whether it's a real problem he doesn't want to talk about—or a cover-up for something else.)

You should suggest to Martin, as tactfully as possible, that he get help with his problem. While you want to support him, and his fellow employees probably will want to also, he has to help.

Finally, be as supportive as you can. Simply be a friend to him. Encourage your other employees to do the same.

If this is a periodic episode:

Your best guidance is what he's done before when he's had similar episodes. Remember, though, that the present one may be more or less severe.

It's important to find out whether he understands what's happening. If he does, it may be almost as easy to resolve as the situation above. Many people are able to realize when they're having an episode such as this and respond realistically to it.

You'll probably want to suggest that he get professional help in this case also. In addition, you may want to encourage him to take some time off. That depends, of course, on the severity of his condition. You'll have to walk a careful line between supporting him and insisting that he take whatever actions are necessary to help himself.

If he appears to be getting seriously emotionally disturbed:

He may show this when you talk to him—by denying the situation, responding inappropriately, or becoming very defensive. All of these are signs that he feels caught in something he can't control.

If this is the case and his behavior is deteriorating, you'll have to take swift, effective action. If he's being disruptive, you may have to insist that he take sick time off, use vacation time—whatever is necessary to get him out of the work situation. If company policy permits, you may need to send him for a psychiatric evaluation. Remember, you're not doing this to punish him, but to relieve a condition that's painful both for him and for your other employees.

Things to Think About

Serious emotional disturbance is truly an illness. Regardless of how irrational and irritating Martin may seem, he may not be able to really control his emotions.

If Martin in any way threatens or implies violence to others or himself, respond to that immediately. You must assume that he means it. Get counsel from your company physician or any other professional you can reach, if there's time. If it's serious enough, you may need to involve the police.

And If This Doesn't Quite Fit Your Situation . . .

If the cause of the strange behavior may be alcohol or drugs, see the next problem (3-3). If the individual is going to pieces under pressure, see Problem 6-4. Less serious emotional problems could also show up in the kind of performance problems described in Chapters 5, 6, and 7.

Use Checklist 2 to develop a cure of your own.

3-3

The Problem: An employee appears to be under the influence of alcohol or drugs on the job.

The Scene

Ben Morgan, your lead technician, poked his head in your office door, whispering, "Boss, can you come here a minute? There's something I want you to see."

You followed Ben quietly, pausing at the corner of the open office area.

"Watch, Leo," he said. "See how loud and talkative he's being on the phone? A few minutes ago he said something to Krista and actually *giggled*. *Leo!* He's been acting strange ever since the last break, about an hour ago. Donna said his eyes are kind of glazed, and, look—he's drenched with sweat. I think he's on something, but I thought you'd want to handle this one!"

Possible Causes

There are a number of reasons why employees may appear to be under the influence of alcohol or drugs on the job, but none of them has much to do with the steps you need to take immediately. They *will* affect the way you follow up after this incident is over, but your first concern must be for the impaired employee—for his or her well-being and safety and for the well-being and safety of the rest of your employees.

There's only one piece of information you need immediately: You need to decide if this employee really is physically or mentally impaired—whether by drugs, alcohol, or some other influencing factor. For the short term, it's the *impairment* that's important. You may know positively that it's caused by drugs or alcohol—but it could be caused by a lot of other things too, including dangerously low blood sugar or a circulatory blockage. Your first course of action is to decide whether there is an impairment, not its cause.

If you decide there is an impairment, and there seems to be no immediate danger to the employee, then you can take the time to figure out if drugs or alcohol are the cause. If they are, then it's also a good idea for you to find out, now or later, through discussions with the employee, trusted coworkers, and your own observations, whether the employee has a continuing pattern of substance abuse.

Cures

Whenever you suspect that an employee is impaired by drugs or alcohol on the job, there are two things you need to do immediately:

- First, get him out of any situation where there could be harm to the employee or to others. If the employee is working with a piece of machinery, get him off it! If he refuses, make it a firm order—with physical assistance from you or your company's security personnel if necessary. You already have an impaired employee; you don't need to compound the problem by having somebody hurt.

- Second, observe the employee personally. Describe to him the behavior that makes you think he has a problem. Ask if he knows what's causing it. If it's a medical problem not related to drugs or alcohol, he may recognize the symptoms and be able to offer an explanation or a solution.

IMPORTANT: If the employee is incoherent or displays any of the classic signs of physiological shock, get him to medical help right away! Even if he's drunk or stoned, he may be in physical trauma requiring immediate treatment. This is a situation where it's better to err on the side of caution.

Of course, all of this should be done as quietly and with as little fanfare as possible. Although the employee may become confrontational, your calm, rational approach will help keep everyone from getting more upset. As you observe and talk to the employee, don't make accusations. Even if you're sure he's on drugs or alcohol, telling him, "I think you're drunk," is only likely to start an argument.

If you decide the employee is physically or mentally impaired:

Decide whether treatment is necessary immediately, and, if so, make arrangements for the employee to get treatment. In a large company, you probably have some medical staff, and you can escort the employee to them (or call them to your unit). In a smaller company, an urgent care facility is a good place to go if you can't arrange treatment through the employee's own doctor.

If medical care isn't immediately necessary, see that the employee gets home safely and explain to him why he's being sent home.

After the employee returns to work, follow up with him or her. Explain again what led you to deal with the situation as you did, and, if you suspect repeated drug or alcohol abuse, refer the employee to your company's Employee Assistance Program or to a rehabilitation specialist. Document the referral! If this problem persists and you have to fire the employee, the courts may want to know what you did to help him.

If you decide the employee is not impaired:

You need to decide next whether his behavior is unacceptable or just unusual. If it's within the bounds of acceptability, stop there. No further action is necessary. If it's not acceptable, explain to the employee what he's doing wrong, why it's wrong, and, if it's not obvious, what he should do differently. Then follow up to see that the problem is corrected.

Something to Think About

As we say over and over again, watch carefully for signs of drug abuse in any performance or behavior problems you face. If you suspect that abuse is there, deal with it quickly. The longer you let an employee continue to abuse drugs, the harder it will be for him to stop.

And If This Doesn't Quite Fit Your Situation . . .

Problems 3-1, 3-2, 3-5, and 3-8 deal with other examples of impaired job performance.

Use Checklists 3 and 7 to develop a cure of your own.

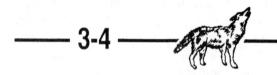

The Problem: An employee takes a lot of time off from work because of serious problems in his personal life.

The Scene

Your heart is breaking for Harley. He and his wife have always been very close, and now she has terminal cancer. You don't have the heart to refuse his requests for time off to be with her.

But you also need him on the job. He's one of your most experienced employees, and the work is falling behind because of his absence. You don't know how much longer you can take not only his absences but his reduced efficiency when he is at work.

Possible Causes

It doesn't require much speculation to see what the cause is. Grief at the thought of losing a loved one is one of the most universal human emotions. It's also one of the most powerful, and frequently disabling to those who experience it.

Cures

For this situation:

It would be wonderful if we could give you an easy answer to the situation. We can't.

We can tell you that becoming angry or impatient with Harley won't work. He knows the problem he's causing you—he probably feels guilty about it. But none of that helps assuage his grief.

Be as supportive as you can. Grief is very draining emotionally. Support from people who care eases the pain and helps an individual cope more effectively with his or her situation.

There are several actions you can take which may help both Harley and the work situation.

- First, very strong emotion—of any kind—is often very disorganizing. (Think, for instance, of how you responded to things the last time you were extremely happy or extremely sad.) It may be useful to insist gently that Harley set a regular schedule, if possible, and follow it. This may help him be more available for work and to concentrate more effectively on work when he's there. It may also help him deal with his grief, by giving him some basic structure he can depend on.

- Another possibility, if the situation and Harley's frame of mind permit, is to let him do some work at home. You have to be careful about this, of course—he may be even less able to concentrate at home than at work. But if he can concentrate and produce an adequate quantity of satisfactory work, it may help both of you to let him work some at home. The two of you should agree in advance on what he's to accomplish and how much time you expect him to take.

- If the illness is a very lingering one, you may have to look at giving Harley an official leave of absence. This permits you to replace him temporarily with someone who can produce the work you need, but the job is there for Harley when he's ready and able to return.

For similar situations:

You have basically the same situation when an employee has to stay home often with a chronically ill child or parent, or otherwise keeps losing time from work because of a demanding personal situation.

- The "work-at-home" solution may be a good one in many of these situations (if your company permits it). A mother who has to take of a sick child, for instance, may still be able to put in almost a full eight hours of work.

- If that won't work, you may be able to divide the work between the employee with the problem and another employee. Another employee could share the work, and they could get together periodically to review their progress. (You can see how this could be combined with the work-at-home alternative.)

- As we suggested, the length of the situation is a critical factor. If it's going to be short, you can afford to make significant accommodations to the individual. If it's going to drag on, your alternatives will be fewer. No matter how long it will be, give the employee every consideration you can.

Something to Think About

When an employee has a serious personal problem, be available to listen to him. Don't begrudge him the time he needs to talk about it. But don't give him "pep talks" or try to talk him out of his emotional responses. He needs companionship and compassion—not advice.

And If This Doesn't Quite Fit Your Situation . . .

If an employee goes to pieces under pressure because of his personal situation, see Problem 6-4.

Use Checklist 2 to develop a cure of your own.

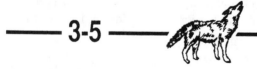

3-5

The Problem: An employee comes to work frequently with alcohol on his breath.

The Scene

"Whew! You don't want to get downwind of Carlo," remarked Jane to Leila, one of her coworkers.

"Is this the first time you've noticed?" replied Leila. "For months, he's been coming back from lunch reeking like a brewery. Somebody ought to say something to him—but it's not going to be me!"

This isn't the first time you've heard this conversation; only the speakers have changed. Everybody seems to have noticed Carlo's luncheon habits. But what can you do? Isn't it Carlo's business what he does on his own time?

Possible Causes

Carlo may just enjoy having a drink at lunch time. It may not affect his performance, and, while his coworkers may discuss his habits among themselves, it may not impair his relationships with them.

Carlo may enjoy having a drink, with no impairment of his performance, but the obvious odor of alcohol may put off some of the people he deals with at work.

Carlo may come back from lunch under the influence of alcohol—to the point where it impairs his ability to concentrate and to handle his work assignments.

Cures

If Carlo is not impaired by his lunchtime drinking, and it seems to have no negative effect on his interactions with customers or coworkers:

It's best to leave it alone. It *is* Carlo's business what he does on his own time, unless his off-the-job activities affect his on-the-job effectiveness. If there is clearly no connection, then you have no basis for intervening.

If Carlo is not impaired, but his interactions with others suffer:

Take him aside quietly and explain that his relations with customers, or others around him, are affected by the alcohol on his breath. Emphasize that he can do what he wants at lunch—except when his activities interfere with his effectiveness later on. And this does. Explain that the odor of alcohol is offensive to some people and that diminished relationships with customers and co-workers diminish his job performance.

Make clear to Carlo the possible consequences of not changing his luncheon behavior—whether that's a change of assignment, or disciplinary action, or firing.

Take this opportunity to make Carlo aware that assistance for his problem is available if he needs it. Refer him to your Employee Assistance Program or, if your company doesn't have one, to an outside source of help for substance abuse problems.

If Carlo's ability to do his work is impaired:

Deal with the problem immediately and firmly. See Problem 3-3 for specific instructions on how to deal with employees who are under the influence of alcohol or drugs on the job.

Something to Think About

Be sure you separate the problem of alcohol on an employee's breath from the completely different problem of an employee whose level of performance is impaired by alcohol or another drug. While the former may be part of an abuse problem, it need not be—and it requires action whether it is or not.

And If This Doesn't Quite Fit Your Situation . . .

Look at Problem 3-3 for a discussion of how to handle impaired employees. Problem 3-10 deals with employees' personal habits that interfere with their effectiveness.

Use Checklists 2 and 7 to develop a cure of your own.

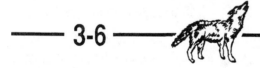

3-6

The Problem: One of your employees was involved with another employee and they've broken up, very messily.

The Scene

Germaine was the last to arrive at staff meeting last Tuesday, and all the places were taken except the one beside Don.

"Well," you said to yourself, "this should be interesting. The hot office romance decays to smoke and ashes. Let's see how uncomfortable it gets in here today."

A pleasant surprise—there were no sharp exchanges and no overt hostilities, but it was obvious that the staff was on edge. Probably because of the blowup the two had had just a few days before. The situation is awkward for everyone. So what happens now?

Possible Causes

As in a several of the other cases we have looked at, it is not necessary here to know what caused the problem, but it is necessary to have some information about the situation:

First, are the employees in any kind of superior-subordinate relationship? If so, look at Problem 2-8 for advice.

Second, does the breakup seem to be affecting the performance of either of the two people involved?

Third, regardless of how well the principals themselves are coping with the situation when they're at work, is it having a negative effect on the rest of your staff? Do you expect the negative effects to be short-lived and to resolve themselves, given a little time, or do they require your intervention?

Hint: We've said this before, but it bears repeating: You're only justified in involving yourself in your employees' personal lives to the extent that what they're doing off the job affects what happens on the job. If these two former lovers hurl epithets at one another, slander each other, or worse, when they're not at work, but are models of decorum on the job, then you have no basis for getting involved. But as soon as what's happening in their personal lives begins to affect their work, or that of others, you should step in firmly and swiftly.

Cures

If the breakup is affecting the performance of either of the two people involved:

Have a talk with the affected employee, explaining in some detail the deterioration you've noticed in his or her work performance. Let the employee know that you're aware of his or her personal situation, and delicately inquire if that situation could be the cause of the performance problems.

Offer to refer the employee to a counselor or to provide other appropriate assistance to help him or her work through the situation. At the same time, make it clear that you expect the performance problems to be corrected. Make it clear that the situation you're concerned about is *not* the breakup, but the deteriorating performance.

If it's appropriate, consider offering the employee a reassignment, permanent or temporary—to allow time for emotions to cool and for the two employees to reach some kind of equilibrium.

If the relationship is having a negative effect on the rest of your staff:

Observe carefully to see whether the actions of the two employees are the cause of the disturbances in your staff, or whether it's the staff's anticipation of trouble that's affecting them badly. If the problem isn't due to anything the two employees themselves are doing (or not doing), then you can't hold them responsible. In that case, time and continued civil relations between the parties will probably solve the problem.

If you can attribute the negative effects on the staff to either of the two employees involved, then talk to the employee(s), explain what behaviors are causing strained relations among the staff, remind them of their responsibility to establish and maintain effective work relationships, and see that they take whatever steps are necessary to mend the relationships.

Something to Think About

Several problems in the book deal with strong emotional attachments between employees (such as Problems 2-10 or 9-6). One problem in any relationship like this is what happens when and if the relationship ends. Keep that in mind whenever you're evaluating the effect of any relationship.

And If This Doesn't Quite Fit Your Situation . . .

Look at Problems 2-7 and 2-10 for other situations involving sexual relationships. If one individual is making unwanted sexual advances to another, see Problem 2-5.

Use Checklist 2 to develop a cure of your own.

—— **3-7** ——

The Problem: An employee is heavily medicated and keeps falling asleep on the job.

The Scene

You've been watching Wally Bozeman through your door for the last 15 minutes. All during the time, he's nodded, caught himself, tried to work, nodded again—over and over.

Wally has told you that he's on strong medication for an illness. But he's been like this for two weeks now, with no sign of improvement. All the other employees are beginning to talk among themselves.

Possible Causes

Wally is on medication for a short-term illness, so the situation will bring itself to an end before long.

He's on medication, but the illness isn't short term. This is clearly more serious, since you can't count on his condition changing by itself.

The drowsiness is being caused by the illness itself. Walt may have been misleading you, or he may not really understand the illness.

Wally is abusing a drug. His story about the medication is just a cover for a habit he's unwilling or unable to change.

Cures

No matter what the cause is:

Call Wally in and go over his situation carefully with him. Don't give him the "third degree," but make your concern clear to him. You need to know just what to expect. If he avoids your questions or gives you vague answers, insist on talking with his doctor—or at least on having his doctor give you a specific statement of his condition and prognosis.

You don't want to offend Wally or give the impression that you're picking on him. But it's very important to know just what his situation is, so that you can be fair to him and to your other employees as well.

If you have a company physician, you'll probably want to send Wally to him for evaluation—especially if you have questions left after you talk with Wally.

No matter what the cause is, you can't let Wally become a safety hazard to himself and others. If he might fall into machinery, or from an elevated platform, or otherwise endanger himself or other employees, you must take immediate steps to prevent this. The steps could be anything from moving his workplace to sending him home until he recovers.

If he really is on medication for a short-term illness:

Insist that Wally take sick time. Regardless how he feels about this, he's not able to perform his job satisfactorily. You're under no obligation to provide him a place to rest for a week or two.

If he doesn't want to take sick time, listen carefully to find out his reasons. Unless they're very good, insist that he take it. If he still refuses, follow whatever procedures your company has to put him on some form of absence until he's able to do a day's work again.

If the illness appears to be a long-term one:

You can't let Wally continue to work in his condition. You could send him home on sick time and hope for things to improve

in a few weeks. If he's willing, that might be an acceptable place
to start.

If there's no change, you'll have to take a more serious step.
If Wally qualifies for Social Security and/or an early retirement
based on disability, suggest that he seriously consider doing so. If
he's qualified but won't retire voluntarily, you may need to take
steps to retire him. (Your personnel office can explain what's involved.)

If he isn't qualified to retire, you might want to investigate
the possibilities of a reassignment to a more suitable job. (If his
drowsiness is bad, of course, this isn't an option.)

If nothing else will work, you may have to separate him based
on disability. States and cities offer some assistance for the disabled,
and he may qualify for assistance through Social Security. Talk with
your personnel office about the assistance available to Wally and
know what his options are before you talk with him.

You can find more on this situation in Problem 1 of this chapter.

If the illness is making him drowsy:

While this is different from either situation above, you treat
it the same way you would one of them—depending on whether it's
short term or long term.

There may be one other option: a medication which will counter-
act the drowsiness and make it possible for him to continue working.
You'll want to ensure that this option isn't practical before taking
any other action.

If he is abusing a drug:

Explore this alternative carefully and make sure that it's the
right one. If it is—act. See Problem 2-6 for specific suggestions on
what to do.

And If This Doesn't Quite Fit Your Situation . . .

If emotional instability is the problem (or part of it), see Problem 3-2. If there's a deterioration in the employee's performance

but no overt signs of illness or substance abuse, see Chapters 4, 5, and 6—which deal with specific performance problems.

Use Checklist 2 to develop a cure of your own.

—— **3-8** —— 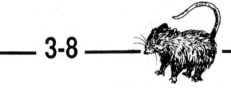 ——

The Problem: One of your employees has borrowed money from several other employees and hasn't paid them back.

The Scene

As you walked through the office a couple of days ago, you heard Liz and Pat arguing—not too loudly, but enough that you could hear snatches of the tiff:

"Well, if I can't trust you in such a little thing, how do I know you'll come through on this contracting assignment?" Liz snarled at Pat.

"You'll get it. You'll get it," reassured Pat.

"Yeah, sure," was the curt rejoinder.

Later, you asked a trusted coworker if he knew what was going on. "Oh, that," he remarked. "Pat's hit up almost everybody here for a loan one time or another. Most of us just write it off. We know we'll never see that money again. But Liz has taken it to heart. She's decided that 'once a deadbeat, always a deadbeat,' so now she's cut Pat out of that contracting assignment—and the trip to Phoenix!"

Possible Causes

Lots of offices have them—the freeloaders who think no one will notice if they borrow a dollar here, a dollar there, and then "forget" to pay it back. But people *do* notice. And many, like Liz, will interpret the behavior as a sign of general untrustworthiness—and react accordingly. When that happens, and the freeloading begins to affect work relationships, then it's time for you to step in.

Few jobs operate in isolation. Most of us depend on other people to accomplish our work, and they, in turn, depend on us. Jobs get done because employees establish relationships and work cooperatively within those relationships to meet some goal. When new employees come into the organization, it's often not the "technical" part of the job that takes longest to learn. It's the interpersonal part—who you go to for one thing or another, who your allies are, and everybody's various idiosyncrasies. Establishing and nurturing those relationships is a part of every employee's responsibility. Failing to nurture them or, worse, acting to destroy them, is the organizational equivalent of mortal sin.

Cures

Most freeloaders don't realize the larger implications of their irritating behavior. And they also don't usually need the money, so don't worry that you're stealing food from the mouth of some starving urchin! It's usually just an annoying habit the employee's fallen into.

So your aim in curing this behavior should be, first, to make the employee aware of the effect of his or her behavior and, second, to help him restore his relationships within the work environment.

Let the employee know that you know about his habit of borrowing money without repaying, that it's inappropriate behavior, and that it's detracting from his effective performance on the job.

Advise him that you can't force him to repay the money, but you can measure the impact of his deteriorating work relationships on his performance—and you will! Then follow through.

If you have written standards of performance, consider adding a section to everyone's standards on establishing and maintaining effective relationships. Making these relationships a part of the record emphasizes the importance you attach to them and their impact on overall performance.

If the employee repays past debts and makes a sincere effort to change his behavior, support him. Acknowledge the steps he's taken and, at appropriate moments, encourage his coworkers to give him another chance.

Something to Think About

There's nothing wrong with one employee occasionally borrowing money from another (but see Problem 9-3). An employee who borrows regularly from others, however, is a potential problem. Unrepaid lenders may not be as angry as jilted lovers, but they can raise a lot of havoc. If you have an employee who's starting to borrow regularly from others, try to discourage him before he creates the kind of problem described in this section.

And If This Doesn't Quite Fit Your Situation . . .

Look at Problems 3-10 and 3-11 for instances of other annoying behaviors.
Use Checklist 2 to develop a cure of your own.

——— 3-9 ———

The Problem: An employee is a "loner" who separates himself from the group.

The Scene

As you walk out of your office for lunch, you see a group of employees grabbing their coats on their way out. As they pass Henry Matthew's desk, they ask him to join them.

"Thanks," he says, "but I brought my lunch today."

As you follow the group down the hall, you hear them remarking on "Weird Henry" and speculating that he thinks he's better than they are.

Possible Causes

Henry prefers to be alone. Some individuals aren't comfortable in groups or just don't choose to spend their time with others.

Henry feels like an outsider. He may not want to be a loner, but believes that the group doesn't really like him or want him to be part of their activities. This especially happens when the individual belongs to a different racial or ethnic group from the others, or is a different sex.

The group is uncomfortable with him. He feels like an outsider because that's how the group considers him. This is particularly common when the "outsider" is different in race, ethnic background, or sex.

The group is discriminating against him. There's a fine line between being "uncomfortable" with another and discriminating against him. It's important to know if that line's been crossed.

Hint: The fact that Henry doesn't "fit in" may be unfortunate, but in itself it's not a problem. Don't try to force him to participate with the others. As long as it doesn't interfere with his job performance, he has the right to be a loner.

Cures

No matter what the cause is:

It's always important to know and understand your employees—and this is one of the times that it's particularly important. You may not know Henry very well, but you should know all of the people who've been with you for months or years. You should have a good idea whether or not they're excluding Henry.

It wouldn't be a bad idea, though, to talk with one or two of your employees to find out how they see the situation. Have they really tried to get Henry to join them? Or are they waiting for him to come to them? When you know the answer to these questions, you'll be ready to handle the situation.

If Henry seems to prefer being alone:

Essentially, you don't have a problem. As long as Henry deals effectively enough with others to get his job done, his isolation isn't anything more than a minor inconvenience.

You can continue to encourage him to join in the group's activities, and encourage them to keep inviting him. It's important, though, that everyone understand you're merely encouraging them to do something, not *forcing* them.

If Henry appears to feel like an outsider:

Don't rush things. He may be very careful and cautious about the group, and want to be sure he really wants to be part of it. Even though he may want to belong, pushing him can have just the reverse effect from what you or he intend.

Get to know Henry well yourself. Your goal is simply to get to know him—but this will also help you understand why and how he feels like an outsider.

If Henry has certain mannerisms that separate him from the group, you can discuss them with him. And if there are things in the way the group acts that he doesn't understand, you can help him.

Stay in touch with the group and their feelings about Henry. When both they and Henry are ready to move closer together, help the process. You might want to suggest going to lunch together or stopping for a drink after work.

If the group seems uncomfortable with Henry:

Again, don't rush things. Again, get to know Henry better.

Listen to what your employees are saying about Henry. If necessary, ask several of them what they're uncomfortable with in Henry. They'll probably talk in generalities ("He's unfriendly," "He's just *different*"). Push them (gently) for specifics ("He never asks us to help him," "He's so *loud*").

Now, as you talk with Henry, help him understand how the group is and how they see him. Where possible, point out tactfully the mannerisms and habits that bother them. Don't push him to change; just help him understand how they see him. You're suggesting he may need to change, and that often makes people uncomfortable. He may get defensive; if he does, don't get defensive back. Just stay friendly and objective and help him understand.

As you get to know Henry better, help your other employees understand him. Encourage them to talk with him, to understand him better and help him understand them. Don't push anyone—just try quietly to help Henry and the others become comfortable with one another. When the time is ripe, you might want to suggest a group activity that will include Henry.

If they are genuinely discriminating against Henry:

Problem 2-8 will suggest actions to take.

Things to Think About

People vary widely in their need for contact with others. Some would be happy in a job where they didn't deal with another person the entire day. Others require human contact almost every moment. Most of us are in between.

When you select people for your unit, take account of these needs. If you manage a claims processing section with high production quotas, you probably don't want someone who needs to socialize constantly. And you don't want a customer-service person who's uncomfortable around people. If you select carefully, you'll have a minimum of problems caused by individuals who don't "fit" the organization.

And If This Doesn't Quite Fit Your Situation . . .

If an individual isn't just a loner but competes with others when he should cooperate, see Problem 1-2. If he's also a nonconformer who won't follow work procedures, see Problems 5-1 and 5-3.

Use Checklists 2 and 3 to develop a cure of your own.

____ 3-10 ____

The Problem: An employee has personal habits that irritate the other employees.

The Scene

"What seems to be the problem, Steve?" you asked recently in a "closed door" session. "I thought I asked you to go over last month's account receivables with Martha and show her why her ledgers didn't balance."

"I tried," replied Steve. "I really did. But I just can't stand to be around that woman for more than a few minutes at a time. She smells, and looks, like she hasn't taken a bath in months. Not too much of that and I begin to feel sick—and I'm not normally a squeamish person."

Possible Causes

This scenario could have taken any one of a hundred different forms—bad breath, humming, knuckle cracking, teasing, messy work area, loud talking, bad jokes, no sense of humor. Every one of us—employees, bosses, the authors of this book, and even you—has some personal habit (or habits) that irritate other people. Sometimes the habits are just irritating, other times they interfere with work performance. But regardless of their impact, whenever an employee comes to you to complain about another employee, you need to pay attention, because one of two things is happening:

- *Martha's habit really is interfering with her relationships in the work environment.* As we've discussed before, a significant part of most jobs is establishing and maintaining effective relationships with customers and coworkers. When personal habits, whatever they may be, interfere with those necessary relationships, something has to change.

- *Steve is really concerned about something else, but has used the irritating habit as an excuse.* Sometimes, the thing that's really bothering the complaining employee is something he's reluctant to discuss. Especially when the complaint seems terribly trivial, you should at least consider the possibility that the real problem is something deeper.

Cures

If Martha's habit really is interfering with work relationships:

Talk to her and tell her what the objectionable behavior is. (If it's a habit of long standing, she probably doesn't even realize she's doing it or that it's objectionable to others.)

Explain the impact of the objectionable behavior on her work performance and the significance of relationships to her overall effectiveness.

See Problem 3-9 for other specific actions to take.

If Steve is really concerned about something else:

Try to find out what Steve's true motivation is. Is Martha a threat to him in some way? Is this a way of discrediting someone else who is perceived as a threat? Is the matter Steve is really concerned about something that he thinks you won't act on, an area in which you're likely to protect Martha, an objectionable behavior that you and Martha share (so that when he criticizes Martha, you may think Steve is criticizing you)?

If you can find out what the real irritant is, then, of course, you should act on that. If you can't, then deal with the stated problem as well as you can. If the complaint seems particularly trivial or irrelevant to the work situation, you may have to respond by telling Steve that this isn't an issue you think it appropriate to do something about. If there really is another agenda, that response may result in Steve revealing the true issue.

If you resolve the stated problem, but Steve still is dissatisfied, you then have an excellent opportunity to probe deeper to see what the real issue is. Remind Steve that you can't deal with problems you don't know about. But don't get discouraged; you may never find out what the problem is.

Things to Think About

Just as every organization has its share of employees with annoying habits, every organization also has its share of complainers. Before you're in any job for very long, you'll find out just who those complainers are.

Frequently, they're employees who are dissatisfied with themselves or have a low level of self-esteem and who mistakenly attempt to bolster their own self-image by putting down others. But not always. Some people just seem to enjoy complaining, the way you or I might enjoy fishing or reading or shopping.

If you have one of these "recreational complainers" on your hands, you might remind him that constant complaining can be every bit as annoying as the behaviors he's complaining about. Don't expect any big changes though, and don't worry about it. (Ultimately, people are responsible for their own happiness—you aren't.)

And If This Doesn't Quite Fit Your Situation . . .

Look at the next problem (3-11) and Problem 3-8 for discussions of other annoying behaviors.
Use Checklists 2 and 3 to develop a cure of your own.

___ 3-11 ___

The Problem: An employee is a "know-it-all."

The Scene

You grin wryly to yourself as you walk past the small group. Edna and Lorraine are trying to explain to Donna why her input isn't working. But she won't listen to them. "I know all about these things," she says emphatically. "There's something wrong with the system." Donna seems capable—but because she's so sure she knows everything, it's taking forever for her to learn how your unit does its job.

Possible Causes

Donna is new and trying to establish herself in the unit. New employees often feel they have to prove themselves. Sometimes they do this by refusing to admit they have to learn.

Donna is overeducated or overexperienced for her job. When someone believes that their job is "beneath" them, they often refuse to admit they need help from the other people who do the job.

She sees herself as a very competent person who never needs help. We all have ideas about ourselves that help us maintain our self-esteem. One of Donna's ideas may be that she's very good—which means she gives help, not receives it.

Hints: Don't react to Donna by showing her that's she's wrong (as emotionally satisfying as that might be!). Stay cool. If you (and the others) react defensively, that will probably make her insist even more strongly that she doesn't need your help.

Problem 4-5 is very similar to this. Unless one of the situations described here fits exactly, you might want to look at this problem before deciding what to do.

Cures

If she seems to be trying to establish herself with the other employees:

See Problem 4-5, which deals with this situation.

If she's overeducated or overexperienced:

It's often hard for people who have more experience or education than others in a work unit to accept help from these others. In turn, they may feel that the person feels "too good for them." Then everyone gets irritated.

Talk to your employees and try to help them appreciate Donna's point of view. Let us warn you, though—this may be very hard. It's often difficult to get people to "understand" others who seem more fortunate than they are ("Feel sorry for *her*? Nobody put me through college!").

Most of your work is going to have to be done with Donna. If you listen to her and help her talk about her feelings about the job, she may start to change. At the very least, having someone listen without judging her will help her to be more comfortable with the situation.

This may not be enough. You may have to talk very directly with her. No matter how understanding you may be, you can't afford to have an employee with this kind of attitude. Be just as plain-spoken as necessary.

If it's realistic, there's one more effective step you can take. Point out to her the promotion possibilities in the organization. Make a deal with her: if she does a good job, you'll help her move into a job that uses her qualifications better. That gives her a clear goal to work for and helps her think of more than just the present job.

If she seems to think she never needs help:

Now we're not talking about a temporary reaction to a situation but a personality trait. This is how Donna is in general, at least at work. You know by now that getting someone to change a trait is very, very difficult.

Decide whether her "know-it-all" attitude is really interfering with her work and that of the others. If it isn't, you can take your time dealing with the problem. If it is, but you can rearrange tasks to minimize it, you also have time. If she's interfering with effective work practices and you can't shift the work, you need to deal with the situation right away.

If you have time, you can talk with her over weeks or months to try to get her to loosen up. If she knows you think well of her even if she's not always right, perhaps she can afford to accept help more easily.

If you don't have time and her attitude is affecting her and/or others' performance—you've no choice but to be direct. Stay objective about it; you're interested in getting performance, not in remaking her personality. Outline for her how she's creating a problem and what you expect her to do about it. She will probably argue with you; after all, she's not going to like it. Listen to her. If you should change any of your requirements because of what she says, do so. Then establish a plan, with regular counseling sessions to evaluate how she's doing. Insist that she follow the plan, and give her plenty of praise when she does.

If she won't change and her actions are clearly affecting performance, take action based on that performance.

Something to Think About

You can have a very similar problem with someone who takes too much time helping others—whether they want it or not—and not enough on his own duties. The causes and the cures are just about the same as in the situation above.

And If This Doesn't Quite Fit Your Situation . . .

If the employee refuses to change the way she does things, see Problem 5-4, and possibly Problem 6-9. If the employee's attitude is good but she still can't produce, see Problem 6-2.

Use Checklists 2 and 3 to develop a cure of your own.

4

Troubleshooting Problems Caused by the Current Performance of an Employee

—— 4-1 —— 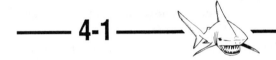 ——————

The Problem: An employee has angered a key supplier by his offensive manner.

The Scene

"Charlie, I can't believe I have anyone who would pull a dumb stunt like that. I can absolutely, certainly promise you it won't happen again. My God, I'm mortified!"

And you are. You slam the receiver down and start for the door. You've known that Art Mayfield wasn't the greatest in the world at dealing with people—but yelling at the manager of Eastern Manufacturing and then hanging up on him is too much!

Possible Causes

Charlie (or someone else at Eastern) did something that provoked Art. So far, you've only heard one side of the story.

Bad blood has been building between Art and Eastern. It may be that this is a "last straw" encounter.

Art really did "blow his stack" without reason.

Hint: What Art did was wrong, regardless of its cause. The question isn't whether to take strong corrective action. The question is whether you can remedy the situation short of firing Art.

Cures

No matter what the cause is:

Make sure that your own anger is under control. This is going to be a rough situation—and you need a clear head to deal with it. That doesn't mean you shouldn't be mad. You should, and Art should know it from the word go. But it should be controlled anger. If it isn't, take a walk, kick some file cabinets—do whatever you have to do to get back in control.

Then call Art in. Tell him exactly what you've heard. Don't exaggerate or pull punches. Let him see how angry the call made you. He needs to know that he's in trouble.

Now, here comes the really hard part. Give him every chance to explain his side—and listen, listen, listen. This is hard to do, but in this serious a situation it's absolutely necessary. If the encounter gets too emotional, break it off and get back with Art later.

If someone at Eastern really did provoke Art:

Consider Art's record with the company. If he's been a good worker, and this is the first time something like this has happened, give him the benefit of the doubt. If possible, let him get back with Charlie and mend the situation. You keep close tabs on it, though—both to support Art and to make sure that he's doing what needs to be done.

If Art can restore the relationship effectively, go lightly on him. Perhaps a short, clear chewing out will be enough. But he needs to understand clearly that—regardless of what anyone at Eastern did—his conduct can't be tolerated. If he understands, leave him working with Eastern.

If Art is too involved in the situation, or lacks the skills, you get back with Eastern, and Charlie, quickly. If you can do it in person, that's the first choice. If not, get on the phone. See if Charlie realizes the contribution he made to the problem. If he's calmed down and is willing to cooperate, see if you can get him to talk with Art. If they can smooth out their relationship, fine. If they can't, move Art and get someone else to work with Eastern.

If Art won't face the problem and/or can't help you solve it, take strong action. Just what's best will depend on your firm's policies. Suspension without pay, cut in pay, reassignment—any of these might be appropriate.

If bad blood has been building between Art and Eastern:

Art has helped create an extremely serious situation. He should have informed you of what was happening long ago. His not doing so is just as critical as the incident.

Again, take prompt action with Eastern. Try to work with Charlie or anyone else at Eastern to find out what went wrong and remedy it. At this point, you do whatever you have to do to resolve the situation. If Art can be any help, use him—but carefully.

Evaluate your options with Art. Unless there were mitigating circumstances—*very* mitigating circumstances—you can't trust him to deal with suppliers again. If you can find a position where his skills can be used without the danger of alienating others, do so.

Take strong disciplinary action. Regardless of his past record, what he did is indefensible. Your action should communicate that to him, clearly and unambiguously. Whatever happens, he should have the definite feeling that he just barely avoided disaster.

If Art lost his temper and alienated Eastern without reason:

Forget Art for the moment and get back with Charlie. Do *whatever* you must to reassure Eastern that this was an isolated incident, one that won't happen again. Assure them that they won't have to deal with Art again. If necessary, cry real tears and promise them your firstborn as a hostage.

Then take care of Art. The basic question is: Has he been so good an employee in the past, and is he apt to be so valuable in the future that he shouldn't be fired?

If you can answer "yes," take forceful action just short of firing him. The action should include moving him into another job, probably one at lower pay.

If the answer isn't "yes," fire him. That may sound inhumane, but it's necessary.

Things to Think About

A great deal has been made—and justly so—about pleasing customers. Maintaining good relationships with suppliers is only slightly less important. You cannot tolerate employees who do anything less than deal effectively with the firms you depend on for your raw materials.

But suppose you hadn't made this clear to Art? Suppose *you* didn't take the relationship with Eastern seriously enough? In that case, slack off on Art—he's not the main culprit. Then go look in the mirror and decide what kind of action's necessary to shape up the person you see there.

And If This Doesn't Quite Fit Your Situation . . .

Look at Problems 1-1, 1-5, and 1-9 if Art is just one of many employees in the unit who're performing poorly. If there may have been a racial overtone to the situation, see Problem 2-8. If Art's behavior may have reflected an emotional problem or use of alcohol or drugs on the job, see Problems 2-6, 3-2, and 3-3. If part of the problem might be that Art is a "know-it-all," see Problem 3-11. The problems in Chapters 4, 5, and 6 all deal with performance problems; one of them may be similar to your situation.

Use Checklist 1 to develop a cure of your own.

—— 4-2 ——

The Problem: A worker is new to the work group and properly qualified, but is very poorly motivated.

The Scene

"I just don't understand about Janine," you remark to Harry at lunch. "Loretta over in Stock Accounting said she was her top producer, and Ruben in Inventory Control thought she was great. But as soon as she was transferred over to my shop, she just sat down on the job. She's developing an "attitude" too. I don't need another problem like that, but I also don't know what I can do to get her motivated here."

"Sorry, I can't help you with this one," responds Harry. "But it sounds like if you don't think of something, things will only get worse."

Possible Causes

Janine may not like the work in her new assignment. She may have interests or aspirations in another direction and not be interested in the work she's doing now.

She may have been comfortable in her old job and be fearful that she won't perform well for you. That kind of anxiety drives some people to work harder, but for some people (Janine may be one of them), the normal response is to admit defeat immediately and give up trying.

She may not know how to do the work. Many people equate ignorance (which is simply not knowing something) with stupidity (or the inability to learn). Fearful that they will appear stupid if they admit they don't know how to do the work, they never tell you what the real problem is. So lack of knowledge *appears* to be lack of motivation.

Hint: Whenever an employee is not fulfilling your expectations for performance in a job, it's very tempting to blame his or her lack of motivation. But many times, apparent lack of motivation masks the real cause. Before you place all the blame for poor performance on the employee, consider what else could be contributing to the problem. Then do what you can to remove those impediments. Your efforts don't let the employee off the hook for improving his or her own work, but they will improve his or her chances of success. And it's much better to salvage a current employee than it is to start all over again with a new, and unknown, worker.

Cures

If Janine doesn't like the work:

Talk to her to find out what kind of work she's most interested in and point out to her those parts of her new job that are most similar to the things she likes to do.

Let Janine know that if she does well in her current assignments, you'll try to arrange for more of the work she finds interesting or help her find a job that's closer to what she's looking for.

Make it clear to Janine that your offers to help her don't substitute for her hard work and diligence in her current job. Be sure she understands that the responsibility for good performance is hers and that she'll still be held accountable for what she does (or doesn't do) in the job she has now, whether she likes it or not.

If Janine is afraid she won't do a good job in her new position:

Talk with her to let her know that you don't expect her to know how to do everything exactly right when she first walks into a new job. Express your confidence in her skills, pointing out that she wouldn't have been placed in the job if you, or your Personnel Department, didn't think she was qualified.

Make sure Janine gets to know everyone in the new office and has a special introduction to people in other organizations with whom she may have to interact in the course of her assignments.

Encourage her to come to you if there are parts of her job she's not sure how to handle, or identify a coworker who can be a good resource person (especially if you think she feels threatened by having to admit her imperfections to her boss).

Try to structure the job so that Janine's first few assignments are fairly simple ones that will give her an idea of what her job is and how to get things done in your organization without overwhelming her.

Most important of all, give Janine some time. You've told her you don't expect her to know everything right away, so don't act as if every mistake is a major failing. Let her know when she could have done better, but be patient!

If Janine doesn't know how to do the work:

Find out from Janine's previous supervisors, from the Personnel Department's files, and from Janine herself what kind of work she's done in the past and any training she's had that would equip her to do your job. Identify the skill deficiencies she has that interfere with her performance. To do that, you'll need to keep records of what she does right and what she does wrong. Fairly soon a pattern should emerge that will point to specific areas where she needs improvement.

Check with your Personnel Department to see if there are any formal classes available that will teach the skills Janine needs. Formal classroom training, if it's directly related to what happens back on the job, is frequently the fastest way to gain knowledge or skills.

Try to identify a "mentor" for Janine to whom she can go when she has questions or problems and who can check her work and help her correct her errors. It's better if the mentor is someone in the organization other than her supervisor or leader so she can feel free to admit problems without feeling threatened.

If there are several parts of the job Janine will need to learn, parcel out some of the work to several other employees and give to Janine first the few things that are *essential* to the job. As she masters those, you can add in the rest later.

Encourage Janine and give her all the positive feedback you can. At the same time, let her know that you expect her to pick up on the job and that doing well is ultimately her responsibility, regardless of the amount of assistance you're able to give her.

Something to Think About

Note that every cure we've discussed starts out with a direction like "Talk with Janine . . ." *Whenever* you have a problem with an employee, performance or otherwise, one of your first actions should be to talk to the employee. You may find that the answer is simpler than you'd thought!

And If This Doesn't Quite Fit Your Situation . . .

Look at Problems 4-5, 4-8, 5-5, 5-6, 5-9, 6-3 and 6-10 for other problems with new or apparently unmotivated workers.

Use Checklist 1 to develop a cure of your own.

4-3

The Problem: An employee has been an average performer but is slipping to the point that he's now unacceptable.

The Scene

"Boss, I hate to complain—but I just can't live with this!"

Ellen Wegner has just dumped Ollie Berlin's latest run on your desk. Once again, a high percentage of the sheets are smeared or out of register. Once again, Ollie is going to have to do a job over.

In the last couple of months, Ollie's work has clearly slipped from average to unacceptable. You've been living with it and hoping it would improve. But now you've run out of hope; it's time to do something.

Possible Causes

Ollie has a personal problem that's distracting him from his work. Some painful situation outside work may be worrying him to the point that he can't concentrate on work.

Ollie may have a physical problem which is preventing him from doing work correctly.

Ollie may be abusing alcohol or another drug, and it's gotten bad enough that he can no longer perform effectively.

Ollie may be "burned out" on his job. He just doesn't care any more.

Hint: While the cause of Ollie's poor performance is important, you need to focus your action on the performance itself.

Cures

No matter what the cause is:

You're going to have to talk with Ollie, of course. First, though, you might want to talk with Ellen and other employees who work with him. Anything you can learn from them about Ollie's performance and its deterioration will help.

Then talk with Ollie. Deal with the performance, and be very straightforward with him. You can't accept this level of performance, and he needs to know it. But don't attack him, or be angry with him for it, or threaten him. Just start with the bare fact that his performance isn't satisfactory.

Give him every chance to reply and listen carefully. The more he can tell you about why he's slipping, the better. The reverse is also true: if he evades the problem or can't come up with any reason for it, or if he just makes promises to do better without explaining it—the situation's going to be harder to deal with.

If Ollie seems to have a distracting personal problem:

We deal with these problems in several places, especially in Problem 3-4. Turn to it for suggestions on how to deal helpfully with Ollie.

If Ollie seems have a physical problem that's interfering with his performance:

We also deal with physical problems, particularly in Problems 3-1 and 3-7. One of these will give you the information you need to deal with Ollie's situation.

If Ollie appears to be abusing alcohol or another drug:

You'll find guidance for this situation in Problems 2-6, 3-3, and 3-5.

In this case, whether Ollie drinks or uses drugs on the job is only one aspect of the problem. No matter when he's using them, his performance is suffering. You have the right to require him to do whatever is necessary to improve his performance—or else.

If Ollie owns up to his drug abuse problem, work through your employee assistance program coordinator to develop a plan for Ollie. Every firm has a slightly different approach, and you want to follow yours.

Suppose your company doesn't have a formal program, and there's no one to help you? Many hospitals have rehabilitation units, and someone there will probably be happy to work with you. If the problem is drinking, talk to someone in a local chapter of Alcoholics

Anonymous. Somewhere in the community there will be people who can help.

Wherever help comes from, remember this: insist that Ollie perform satisfactorily—starting now, and without relapse. If he doesn't, "keep book" on him. Document his poor performance. Keep putting pressure on him. The worst thing you can do with an addict of any kind is to make his addiction less painful for him. Keep the pressure up without relief. It's the kindest action you can take.

If Ollie is burned out on the job:

This may be the hardest situation of all to deal with effectively. Job burnout probably happens to most of us at some time or another. But you can't accept it as a continuing reason for poor performance.

Don't deal with job burnout by blaming Ollie or by trying to "motivate" him out of it. Neither will work very well. You might see some improvement for a little while—and then things will be back just like they were.

One of the first solutions to think of, if it's available, is finding another job that Ollie could be reassigned to. Of course, it would have to be a job that he'd be motivated to do; reassigning him to another job that's equally as boring to him won't help for long.

Another solution might be to add extra duties—more interesting ones—to Ollie's job. This should be done as a reward; he gets to do them only if he performs his basic duties well. The result might be both that Ollie performs acceptably and that he produces more work.

Another solution is more demanding, but might be the best one. Do your employees often burn out on their jobs? Are several of the jobs the kind of boring, dead-end ones that produce burnout? If so, can you reorganize your work so that each employee does a greater variety of the duties? If the work is done piecemeal, can you rearrange it so that each employee does all of the steps necessary to produce a final product?

This last approach is called "job enrichment." We don't have room to go into it in greater detail here, but it's produced excellent results in some companies. If it sounds like it might work for you, find out more about it.

Something to Think About

It's easy to react emotionally to the *causes* of poor performance, to get angry at an employee who drinks too much or feel sad for one with serious problems at home. As a manager, though, you need to keep focused objectively on the poor performance itself, and to deal with it. In the long run, that's the way you're most helpful to the company *and to the employee.*

And If This Doesn't Quite Fit Your Situation . . .

If performance in your work unit (or the unit as a whole) is slipping, look at Problems 1-1, 1-2, 1-5, and 1-6. Problem 4-4 deals with a good employee who has fouled up an important job. Problem 4-8 describes an employee near retirement who is performing poorly. If the performance failure seems to be intentional, look at Chapter 5.

Use Checklist 1 to develop a cure of your own.

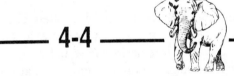

—— 4-4 ——

The Problem: A worker who usually does outstanding work has just fouled up an important job.

The Scene

"I can't believe this!" you exclaim with dismay. "Clark usually does such a great job on everything I give him. He's the one person I can count on to do things right when no one else knows how. And now this, this, this . . ."

Words fail you. A report due to your boss tomorrow, and what Clark has given you is *garbage.* The immediate problem is to get this fixed so you can present it on time. But . . . what do to about Clark?

Possible Causes

Clark may not have understood what you wanted in the assignment. Especially if Clark is usually a good worker on whom you can rely, you need at least to consider that part of the problem was a failure to communicate.

Clark may not have set his priorities effectively. He may have had a number of tasks and didn't give this one enough priority to get it done well on schedule.

Clark may have had personal issues that distracted him from performing this assignment as well as the others he's done in the past. He may have a sick child, marital problems, worries about finances. He may be getting ready to leave for a long-awaited vacation. Your best employees may be able to put those distractions out of mind to concentrate on the job at hand. But not everyone can, and no one can *all* the time.

Clark's performance in general may be slipping, with this foul up just the first sign you've noticed. Think about the other things he's done recently. They may not have been this dramatically awful, but have they been up to Clark's usual standard? If not, consider that this may not be a single incident of poor performance, but may be the start of a trend.

Hints: This list doesn't even begin to cover all that could be wrong. Clark could have had too little time to devote to this assignment; he may not have wanted the assignment and saw this as a way to "get back" at you; or there could be even more causes. One thing you can be sure of, though—when an otherwise good employee delivers a substandard product, you need to get to the bottom of the situation fast!

In each case, you have two distinct, and distinctly different, problems. The first is the substandard report. The second is the conditions that led Clark to produce it. Each needs to be dealt with— but the underlying conditions are almost certainly more important and more serious than the report itself.

Cures

If Clark misunderstood what you wanted in the assignment:

Ask Clark to tell you what he thought he was assigned to do in this project. Note the areas that differ between his ideas of what the assignment encompassed and what you intended.

For each area of misunderstanding, identify for Clark how the overall assignment would have come out differently if he had done things the way you intended.

Then, for each area of misunderstanding, try to find out from Clark what he thinks you said to him. If you can figure out what you said (or what he thought he heard) that caused the misunderstanding, you'll be better able to avoid a repetition.

If Clark didn't set his priorities effectively:

There are actually two problems here. First, he didn't set the right priorities. Second, he didn't tell you he couldn't produce a quality report by the deadline you set. Both have to be dealt with.

Deal with his failure to set priorities right by reviewing his work with him regularly and helping him readjust his priorities as necessary. Don't redo the priorities for him. Help him go through them and develop the judgment necessary to set them effectively for himself. (If you set them for him, you may have found yourself a job for life!) These sessions should be fairly frequent at first, then farther and farther apart—until they become unnecessary.

Clark's failure to tell you he couldn't produce a quality report on time is a separate problem, and one that's just as serious. Every employee should know that he or she has to let you know *in advance* if a deadline can't be met. No exceptions! Enforce this. But also make sure you listen when they tell you they can't meet a deadline, and help them readjust the deadline (or their other priorities). It takes *both* a firm requirement and a willingness to listen.

Give him back his work product and set the priority it should have. Meet with him as frequently as necessary to see that he gets it done.

If Clark had personal problems that detracted from his performance:

Discuss with Clark his *performance* deficiencies. If he offers the personal problems as a reason for his failure on this assignment, offer him your understanding and your help in getting outside counseling or assistance (if he needs it).

Let Clark know that, because he's been such a good employee in the past, you'll stick with him through the tough times too. But let him know also that there are limits to how much the organization can handle and that you expect him to take responsibility for working his personal problems out so that he can resume his productive role in the company.

Then follow up. If things get better, let Clark know that you've noticed and give him a pat on the back. If things don't get better, make sure Clark knows the consequences of continued poor performance, continue to counsel him, and take action if necessary.

If Clark's overall performance is slipping:

There are a lot of reasons why Clark's overall performance could be deteriorating. See Problems 4-3, 6-2, 6-3, 6-6, and 6-9 for possible solutions.

Something to Think About

Performance problems can have many causes. This scenario and discussion illustrate several of the most common ones: misunderstanding requirements, lack of knowledge, and personal problems. If you really want to save a good worker, you'll probably need to help him/her identify what's causing the poor performance. Many times workers themselves don't know what the problem is because they're too close to it. But especially if an employee has been a good worker and begins to have problems, it's important to step in as soon as you see that there is a problem. The more times an employee fails, particularly if he or she doesn't know *why* the failure occurred, the more likely he or she is to get frustrated and give up.

And If This Doesn't Quite Fit Your Situation . . .

Look at Chapters 4, 5, and 6 for lots of discussions about various manifestations of performance problems, their underlying causes and cures.

Use Checklist 1 to develop a cure of your own.

4-5

The Problem: An employee is new and not doing well, but won't accept help at doing better.

The Scene

Abel Resnick came to your outfit right out of technical college. He has a two-year degree in drafting, and he seems plenty sharp enough to do the job. He's been with you for almost four months now, though, and he hasn't learned as much about the job as he should. The big problem is that he insists on learning it on his own; he won't let anyone else help him.

Possible Causes

Abel is trying to establish himself in the unit. New employees often feel they have to prove themselves. Sometimes they do this by refusing to admit they have to learn.

Abel has always had to learn on his own and doesn't know how to accept help gracefully.

The way that the others are trying to help him isn't effective. They may (or may not) mean to be helpful, but don't do it very well.

Hint: Problem 3-11 is similar to this one. Unless one of the solutions here is exactly right, you might want to look at Problem 3-11 before deciding what to do.

Cures

No matter what the cause is:

As in so many of the situations a supervisor encounters, you need to talk with Abel and try to find out how he sees the situation. Since he's a new employee, though, he may be very defensive about his behavior. If he is, don't get angry; just deal with him calmly and learn all you can.

You also need to talk with your other employees. How do they see it? Just as important, how do they feel about it?

One other point. In each situation below, there's a choice to be made. You can always take responsibility for helping Abel. That may solve that problem; Abel may be willing to accept help from you because you're the supervisor. He may feel less threatened by getting assistance from you—or he may simply feel that he can't refuse it. This isn't normally an acceptable solution for very long; you want him to get used to working with other employees to solve his problems. But it may help him and the group get over an initial impasse.

If Abel is evidently just trying to establish himself in the unit:

Help your other employees understand what's happening. They may feel that Abel "ought" to want help from them. If they do, explain how hard it is for him to ask for it and accept it—and why.

Help them become more skilled at offering help in a way he might accept. Offering effective assistance requires interpersonal skills as well as technical ones. They may be doing fine on the technical level but need some coaching to develop their own coaching skills. (The last "cure" in this section has more ideas on this.)

At the same time, try to build up Abel's self-confidence. Assure him that he will be accepted by the group. Suggest gently to him that it's all right to admit he needs help while he's learning the work of the unit.

If Abel has evidently had to learn on his own and doesn't know how to accept help gracefully.

This may seem strange, but it happens. His parents may have felt that he would learn best on his own, or not been available to help him. He's always learned by himself. He may even feel that it's wrong or a sign of weakness to have to accept help.

You probably can't change Abel's approach quickly. He's had a long time to develop this trait, and it will change slowly. But it will change, if you and your unit have the skills to help him.

Put your attention on the group. Help them develop a very "low-pressure" approach to helping Abel. If one of your employees is particularly good at this, you might want to let him or her offer most of the help. Remind them that it will take time, but that they probably will see results.

If the group is trying to help him in ineffective ways:

The group may not have the interpersonal or communication skills they need. They may feel that it's Abel's "place" to let them help him, or expect him to ask them. Then, when he won't accept help, they get angry. They may even feel that their own expertise is being challenged.

Obviously, you need to help them deal with these feelings. If they're upset with Abel, they play a part in creating a vicious cycle that has nowhere to go but down. You need to work with both Abel and them to reverse this vicious cycle.

All of the ideas in the "cures" above may be useful here. But you may need some others. Here are some possibilities:

- Get training for some or all of your employees in how to do on-the-job training. (Get it for yourself, too, if you need it.)

- Help them remember how it was when they were new. If they really understand Abel's anxieties, it will help them be more patient.

- Get them training in communications skills. Maintaining effective communication in a stressful situation is difficult for everyone. Training can help.

Things to Think About

Your main job here is to help everyone "stay cool" and not overreact to the situation. If everybody accepts the situation without getting emotional, it'll be far easier to resolve.

All the suggestions above assume that Abel shows the basic skills and attitudes he needs to be a good employee. In that circumstance, it's best to be patient and help him develop. If he's seems to lack the necessary skills and attitudes, though, much less patience is called for. Try to understand him, try to help him—but insist that he put forth the effort to become a good employee. If he doesn't, take action to reassign him to a more suitable job or help him find a job elsewhere. (Problem 4-6 may be helpful if Abel's having trouble learning the job.)

And If This Doesn't Quite Fit Your Situation . . .

If Abel seems to be having difficulty learning parts of the job, see the next problem (4-6). If he appears to be poorly motivated, see Problem 2-3. If his problem is an unintentional failure to perform, see Chapter 6. If it's willful failure to perform or willful misbehavior, see chapters 5 and 7.

Use Checklist 1 to develop a cure of your own.

4-6

The Problem: A worker is new and can't seem to learn the harder parts of the job.

The Scene

Rosemarie came to work for you about six months ago. She's a good worker, dependable, friendly, and cooperative, but she consistently messes up your unit's time and attendance records. It shouldn't be that hard—just a few simple arithmetic computations and entries in an automated system—but for some reason Rosemarie just can't get it right. You don't want to have to fire her, but things can't go on like this much longer. Last week two employees were short on pay because of her mistakes.

Possible Causes

Rosemarie may lack basic skills she needs to learn the job. She may not know basic arithmetic or may lack keyboard skills or knowledge of the automated system. These skills are prerequisite to learning the more complicated time and attendance system, and she'll need the basic skills first.

The tools you're using to teach Rosemarie may not be appropriate for her learning style. If you're using a manual or written instructions, they may be hard for her to understand. If another employee is teaching her, that employee's explanations may not be meaningful to Rosemarie. You may need to find another way to get the message across.

Rosemarie may not be able to learn this particular task. She may have a learning problem that interferes with her ability to learn the arithmetic skills or with other parts of the job.

Cures

If Rosemarie lacks basic skills she needs to learn the job:

Identify what the skills are that she's lacking. What does she consistently do wrong? For a while, check each step in the process as she completes it. Does she do the arithmetic right? Does she make mistakes entering the information into the automated system?

Once you've identified Rosemarie's specific skill deficiencies, decide the best way to train her in those areas. Your company may have classes in basic arithmetic and keyboard skills or you may have arrangements with a local school for remedial training. Software vendors often provide training on the systems they sell. You may decide that the knowledge Rosemarie lacks is so specific that you can best train her right on the job.

After you've completed the basic skills training, review again how the whole job assignment is to be performed so she can see how her new skills fit in.

Follow up. Continue to check Rosemarie's work to see if she still has problems. If the work is not performed very often, she may lose the skills for lack of practice. Consider a job aid she can use to walk her through the process each time she performs. If training and job aids don't help, then look at some of the other possible causes.

If the training method you're using doesn't work with Rosemarie:

Consider some alternative ways of presenting the information. If she's been reading a manual, then do some one-on-one tutoring. If she's been working with another employee, listen to that employee explain the process to you. See if he or she is explaining it well enough that someone not already familiar with the work can understand. Put together a step-by-step instruction sheet. Some people learn better by *seeing* what they're learning; others learn better by *hearing* it. Try to match the learning method to the learner.

If your company has a training department, ask the professionals there to help you figure out the best way to organize and present the material Rosemarie has to learn.

If Rosemarie is finally unable to learn this part of her job:

Decide how important this task is to successful performance in the job as a whole. Is this something you could assign elsewhere without detriment to the job or the efficiency of the organization? If so, consider giving the work to someone else and assigning Rosemarie work where she can make valuable contributions.

If the task is integral to Rosemarie's position, then decide how important Rosemarie is to the company. Is there another job she could be assigned where she could work productively (even at a lower pay rate)? If so, and Rosemarie is someone who's valuable to the company, offer her the other assignment. If she refuses, or if she's not that valuable, then her poor performance warrants termination.

As tactfully and sensitively as you can, explain to Rosemarie why she's being fired. Let her know that you appreciate the good work she's done for the organization and explain why her performance deficiencies require that you terminate her. If she really has been a good, hard-working employee who just couldn't learn the job, offer her the opportunity to resign and work out with her what you'll tell any prospective employers who contact you for a reference.

And If This Doesn't Quite Fit Your Situation . . .

Look at Chapter 6, particularly Problems 6-2, 6-6, and 6-9 for discussions of employees whose performance problems are unintentional and seemingly beyond their own control.
Use Checklist 1.

4-7

The Problem: An employee met a deadline by producing a substandard report.

The Scene

You told Edwina Ellis you wanted the report today—and you got it today. Lot of good that did you—it's going to have to be redone. Superficially it looks good, but the organization is poor and the conclusions aren't well supported. Edwina isn't your strongest employee, but she usually does better than this! So what do you do now?

Possible Causes

Edwina is beginning to slip from acceptable performance to substandard performance. This may be a result of personal problems, health problems, substance abuse, job burnout—any of a wide variety of conditions.

The deadline didn't give her enough time. She did her best, but it wasn't possible to get out a quality product in the time she had.

She didn't set priorities effectively. She may have had a number of tasks and didn't give this one enough priority to get it done well on schedule.

She's angry at you about the deadline, and this is her way of showing you. She's just waiting for you to complain so she can tell you just how unfair (or dumb, or rigid) you were when you forced the deadline on her.

You weren't clear about what you wanted. All too often, employees produce the wrong product because they didn't understand clearly what was wanted.

Hints: This list doesn't even begin to cover all that could be wrong, though it covers the most likely candidates. One thing you can be sure of, though—when an otherwise good employee delivers something substandard like this just to meet a deadline, you need to get to the bottom of the situation fast!

In each case, you have two distinct, and distinctly different, problems. The first is the substandard report. The second is the conditions that led Edwina to produce it. Each needs to be dealt with—but the underlying conditions are almost certainly more important and more serious than the report itself.

Cures

No matter what the cause is:

If you're angry, get over it. Then call Edwina in, tell her how dissatisfied you are, and ask for an explanation. Don't be judgmental or accusing.

If she feels she has an explanation, listen carefully to it. If she doesn't have a ready explanation, probe a little bit. If the explanation is too glib, probe a little bit. Keep digging, if necessary, until you have a "feel" for the situation.

If she may be beginning to slip into substandard performance:

Look back at Problem 4-3, and at the other problems to which it refers you. They'll give you the information you need to deal with this situation.

If the deadline didn't give her enough time:

Here the underlying problem is lack of communication, lack of trust, or both. The first question to be answered is *why* she didn't have enough time. Did you impose the deadline without listening to her objections? Were you afraid she was "padding" her estimate? Did she know she didn't have enough time, but was afraid to say so? It's critical to find the answer.

Once you find the answer, there's much work to be done. You both need to agree that you won't repeat the actions that led to the bad deadline. Then you need to stick to your agreement. The next time you assign work with a deadline, you need to help each other live up to the agreement.

Give the report back to her, set a mutually acceptable deadline, and expect a fully acceptable product by the deadline.

If she didn't set her priorities effectively:

This *isn't* the same problem as the one above. In that case, she did what she should but didn't have time. In this case, she put her time on the wrong projects.

There are actually two problems here. First, she didn't set the right priorities. Second, she didn't tell you she couldn't produce a quality report by the deadline you set.

Deal with her failure to set priorities right by reviewing her work with her regularly and helping her readjust her priorities. Don't redo the priorities for her. Help her go through them and develop the judgment to set them effectively for herself. (If you set them, you may have found yourself a job for life!) These sessions should be fairly frequent at first, then farther and farther apart—until they become unnecessary.

Her failure to tell you she couldn't produce a quality report on time is a separate problem, and one that's just as serious. Every employee should know that he or she has to let you know *in advance* if a deadline can't be met. No exceptions! Enforce this. But also make sure you listen when they tell you they can't meet a deadline and help them readjust the deadline (or their other priorities). It takes *both* a firm requirement and a willingness to listen.

Return the report to her and set the priority it should have. Meet with her as frequently as necessary to see that she gets it done.

If she's angry at you about the deadline:

This may be based on any of the situations we've already described. Realistically, she may not have had enough time. Or she may not have handled her priorities well. Deal with that situation. But that's not enough.

The question that most needs answering is: *Why* was she so angry that she chose to set both you and herself up for failure this way? Is she so frustrated because you won't listen to her that she's decided to do this in hopes it will get your attention? Is it because of a completely unrelated grudge she has with you? Is she simply acting in this manner because she didn't get her way with the deadline in the first place?

Spend the time you need to find out just why she was angry and what the two of you need to do about it.

If this action got her anger off her chest, give her back the report and agree on a time when she'll finish it. If she's still angry, you may want to give the report to someone else to finish. If so, make it clear to Edwina that—regardless of the cause—this was a performance failure on her part. If necessary, write her up formally on this.

If you weren't clear about what you wanted:

One reason you need to listen carefully to Edwina's reasons for the poor report is that this may very well be one of them. Actually, this isn't just one failure. It may reflect one or several of these:

- You don't explain projects carefully to employees. If you get back many projects that aren't done as you want, this is probably one of the major causes.

- You don't ask effective questions to see if the employee understands what you want.

- The employee doesn't know to ask for clarification, or is afraid to do so. She may not think that you want her to. Just saying the words isn't enough; you have to communicate in your response that you want her to ask.

- You don't trust the employee, so you discourage her from asking questions. Or she doesn't trust you enough to ask. (This is very much like the one just above—but when lack of trust is a cause, the problem is more serious.)

Spend however much time you need to understand just what's happening and start to correct it. If you and the employee can't agree at the beginning on just what's wanted, you will both lose at the end.

Something to Think About

When a good employee stumbles on one product, it's easy to overlook the stumble. That's a judgment call. Remember, though, that every problem is easier to solve if it's caught quickly and dealt with quickly. Most of the time, the best course of action is to face the problem calmly and objectively as quickly as possible.

And If This Doesn't Quite Fit Your Situation . . .

Look at Problems 1-1 and 1-6 if employees in your unit often produce substandard work. If Edwina's work as a whole is slipping, see Problem 4-3. Edwina may be poorly organized (Problem 6-1) or may generally produce low-quality work (Problem 6-5). If she normally produces high-quality work only in small amounts, see Problem 6-6.

Use Checklist 1 to develop a cure of your own.

—— 4-8 ——

The Problem: A worker is near retirement and is starting to perform poorly.

The Scene

Charley O'Daid was never a great worker, but he's always been OK—dependable, reasonably conscientious, a good solid worker who's carried his share of the load. In the past few weeks, though, you've noticed more errors and less work coming from his desk. There doesn't seem to be anything you can really point to—no new assignments or changes in procedures, no personal or health problems that you know of.

You've heard from a couple of people that Charley intends to retire in a few more months. He hasn't said anything to you yet, but could these mistakes and work slowdown be a little "early retirement"? And is it really worth doing anything about if he's leaving anyway?

Possible Causes

Charley may really be getting ready to retire and so is losing interest in the job. As he plans for his retirement, the work he's been doing may be less and less meaningful to him.

Charley may be losing interest in the job—but without any plans to retire. Some workers believe that after they've spent a lot of years on the job the company "owes" them some time off—on the job.

Charley may have personal or health problems not obvious to you that are affecting his performance. Many employees have very strong needs for privacy, and so personal difficulties may not be apparent to you or the other workers in your unit.

Hint: This is one situation (probably the only one) where you can choose not to take any action in response to poor performance. You can't ignore the problem; you must at least consider how it affects the work you're responsible for and the other employees in your unit. But you may consciously decide not to take any specific action. The choice is yours.

Cures

If Charley is getting ready to retire and losing interest in work:

Take into account the severity of Charley's performance deterioration, its effect on the work of the unit and the other workers, and the length of time until Charley's retirement. Then decide whether you're going to take any action to correct the problem. If Charley's plans are firm and he's retiring in the next few months, any attempts to correct his performance will probably be futile and engender bad feelings in his last few months on the job.

If you decide that the problems are severe enough that you must deal with them, be as sensitive to Charley's situation as you can. He's planning a whole new way of life; the transition from work to retirement is one of the most traumatic periods anyone faces—particularly if the employee has been working for a long time.

If Charley is losing interest in work, but isn't retiring soon:

Deal with this problem as you would with any other instance of deteriorating performance. Chapters 4, 5, and 6 contain a variety of situations of poor performance and their solutions.

If Charley has personal or health problems:

Discuss with Charley the performance problems you've observed being as specific and detailed as you can. Tell Charley exactly what he has to do to improve his performance and identify what acceptable performance is for the tasks he's been assigned.

If Charley tells you that he has a personal or health problem that's affecting his performance, then accommodate his problems to the greatest extent that you can, referring him for help if he needs or wants it. Problem 3-1 discusses in detail methods for dealing with employees who have health problems that impact on their work.

And If This Doesn't Quite Fit Your Situation . . .

Problem 6-2 deals with another problem of poor motivation. Use Checklist 1 to develop a cure of your own.

5

---

*Troubleshooting Problems
Caused by the Continuing,
Intentional Performance
of an Employee*

5-1

The Problem: An employee is a poor worker because she won't follow work procedures.

The Scene

Carlotta did it again! She handled that problem with Mrs. Woods beautifully—with tact, deference, and just the right note of urgency. She can charm suppliers out of almost anything. But when it was all over and Carlotta hung up the phone, did she document the call and let the shop floor know when they could expect the next shipment of supplies? No, she did not! She went on to make another call, so now no one knows when the material is due. And when someone else calls the supplier, not knowing that Carlotta already has, they're likely to get angry and not send anything. She *could* be such a good worker, if only she'd follow procedures.

Possible Causes

Carlotta may not see any value in doing things your way. Particularly if there's no negative consequence to her for not following instructions, and plenty of positive consequences for *not* following them (like positive experiences with the suppliers), Carlotta may view the established procedures as a waste of her time.

Carlotta may not know how to perform the particular procedures you're concerned about. She may know a lot about how to wheel and deal on the telephone, but may have problems with the paperwork. In that case, she's most likely to do the things she knows well and skip the things with which she's less comfortable.

Carlotta may see herself as a free spirit who can't be bothered with your petty requirements. She may consider that her failure to follow procedures "makes a statement" and sets her apart from her fellow workers—which it certainly does, but not in a positive way.

Cures

If Carlotta doesn't see any value in doing things your way:

Explain to her the importance of the procedures you've established and how her failure to perform them impacts the rest of the unit.

Walk Carlotta through the other parts of your operation so she can see for herself how her failure to follow procedures makes it harder for other people.

Look at the way you've organized the work and the consequences to Carlotta of not following procedures. Wherever possible, arrange positive consequences for following the procedures and negative ones for not following them. At the very least, you can make sure that following procedures is an item that's specifically addressed in performance reviews.

Make sure Carlotta knows the consequences of failing to follow procedures (e.g., poor performance appraisals, low (or no) raises, possible reassignment, or termination).

If Carlotta doesn't know how to perform the procedures:

Talk to Carlotta to try to find out what parts of the job she's having problems with. Keep in mind that she may not tell you. She may prefer to disguise her lack of knowledge as a *refusal* to follow instructions rather than an *inability*. In that case, treat the situation as if she doesn't see the value in doing things your way (as described above). Let her know the serious consequences of her continued failure to follow procedures, and encourage her to tell you about any parts of the job she's having trouble performing.

If through your discussions with Carlotta or through your own observations you're able to identify specific areas where she needs help, find the best way to teach her those skills. There may be formal courses that will teach her the skills she lacks (particularly for things like basic literacy skills or keyboard skills). Or it may be better for her to work with an experienced employee who can coach her through the process until she gets it right.

Follow up with Carlotta. Congratulate her on her successes, and continue to identify and help her overcome her difficulties. Be sure she understands, though, that the ultimate responsibility for doing a good job is hers.

If Carlotta sees herself as a free thinker who can't be bothered with following your bureaucratic requirements:

This cause is somewhat like the first one, but not exactly. In this case, Carlotta may objectively understand the value to the organization of following procedures, but may not see their applicability to her.

Review with her the reasons for establishing the procedures and their importance to her job and to the rest of the organization. Try as much as possible to describe the effect of failure to perform on other *employees* rather than on the organization. Oftentimes, the object of a rebel's actions is the impersonal bureaucracy; pointing out the harm her actions do to *people* may help Carlotta to see the procedural requirements in a new light.

Emphasize to Carlotta the personal consequences to her of her failure to perform, including poor performance reviews and possible termination. She may still see her "cause" as more important and make a conscious decision not to follow your instructions. In that case, be prepared to follow through with the consequences you've outlined. If the procedures and employees' willingness to be team players are important to your organization, then, for the sake of the organization, you will have to "make a statement" of your own—by terminating Carlotta if necessary.

Things to Think About

In many ways, intentional poor performance is harder to deal with than is poor performance that results from employees not knowing how to do the work or from their being unable to do the work. If someone doesn't know how, you teach them. If, after training, they are still unable to do the work, you find something else for them to do or terminate them. Intentional poor performance is particularly troublesome because employees may *sometimes* perform as you want them to—but you can't predict when. And since the problem is one of *willingness* to do the work, there's nothing you can do to *make* someone want to do things your way.

If all of this sounds terribly discouraging, just remember that you are not ultimately responsible for your employees' performance. They are. You can coach, encourage, exhort, praise, reward, and correct them. But eventually, your responsibility ends. Not every employee will work out. Congratulate yourself on the successes. But don't beat yourself up about the failures. In the end, it's all up to the employee.

And If This Doesn't Quite Fit Your Situation . . .

Look at the next three problems (5-2, 5-3 and 5-4) for related cases of intentional failure to perform. Problem 5-9 deals with an employee who handles potential performance failure by getting someone else to do his work.

Use Checklists 1 and 2 to develop a cure of your own.

5-2

The Problem: An employee gives priority to the work she likes, not what needs to be done.

The Scene

When you passed Marybeth's desk, you couldn't help but look at what she was working on. Sure enough, it was the new office layout. She's doing it again! You've told her at least three times that the end-of-month reports need to be done before anyone works on office improvement. What do you have to do to get her to follow the right priorities?

Possible Causes

Marybeth honestly believes that the office layout is more important than the reports. This doesn't make her right, but at least she's being conscientious.

Marybeth is getting burned out on her regular duties. She'll turn to anything that will relieve the boredom of them.

She's undisciplined and sets her priorities by what interests her.

Hint: One of the basic skills of a fully competent employee is the ability to set appropriate priorities. When an employee can't do this, you (the manager) can't fully delegate work to her.

Cures

No matter what the situation is:

If you've lost your temper, wait until you cool down. Then call Marybeth in. Tell her you saw what she's working on; don't play games.

Be sure you give her the opportunity to explain her side of the situation. While it might not seem so, the time it's most important to listen carefully to an employee is when you believe she's in the wrong.

If she honestly believes that the layout is more important than the reports:

This requires skillful listening. You told her to set other priorities, but she believes she should do the layout instead—why? If you don't listen carefully to her, you may end up seeming arbitrary to her, which will probably make her angry and the problem even harder to solve.

If she convinces you she's right, agree with her. Work out a satisfactory set of priorities for the reports and the layouts and agree that she'll follow them.

If she set her own priorities because you wouldn't listen to her, assure her that you'll listen next time—and do so. But counsel her that she's not to go her own way again.

Suppose she had the chance to persuade you but couldn't, and then set her own priorities regardless of what you said? Counsel her clearly and firmly; that's not acceptable behavior. Warn her that if it happens again, you will discipline her. (Then, if it does happen again, be as good as your word.)

There's one more option. She disagreed with you but didn't say anything. What now? Would you have listened if she had said something? Are you sure? If you're sure, counsel her strongly that you won't put up with that again. If you wouldn't have listened, or give people the impression that you wouldn't—that's something you need to work on.

If she's getting burned out on her regular duties:

She may want to do what you told her, she may even think the reports are more important, but they've gotten so boring and empty for her that she'll do almost anything else instead.

In Problem 4-3, we discussed how to deal with an employee who's burned out on the job. Look at it for some suggestions that might apply to Marybeth's situation.

There's one other point to consider. Is Marybeth a relatively new employee? If so, a basic problem may be that she isn't cut out for the job she's doing. Perhaps you can reassign her, or help her get reassigned to a job that fits better. At the least, you should show her how—*if she does her current job well*—she might get promoted to more interesting work.

If she sets priorities by what interests her:

This may be a good characteristic for an inventor or tinkerer, but it's a sign of immaturity and lack of discipline in most other jobs.

It's not really necessary to know why Marybeth is this way, but it may help to know. Is she just young and inexperienced? Has she been working for an ineffective supervisor who let her do what she wanted? Or is she simply so hard to deal with that no one has wanted to tangle with her?

Whatever the situation, you do need to exercise some care—especially if she's a good worker (or potentially so). Her preference for the layout work may indicate that she's in the wrong job or doesn't do well at some of the duties. When the immediate problem is solved, you need to see if job changes are warranted (as in the "cure" immediately above).

Now that we've said all that, the problem is that Marybeth isn't doing what she needs to be doing, and what you told her to do. You need to call her in and explain clearly that you expect her to follow the priorities you set. If she complains about the work or disagrees with your priorities, offer to discuss that further with her—*after* she completes the reports. Make it clear that you expect her to follow the priorities you set, and that you will discipline her if she doesn't.

After this situation is settled, you may need to have one more talk with Marybeth. If you think she'd be receptive, you need to explain to her the problems she'll create for herself if she gets the reputation of wanting to work only on jobs she finds interesting. Show her that from a manager's point of view the best and most promotable employees are those willing to do whatever the organization needs done.

Something to Think About

In the long run, workers (including you and us) are happiest and most productive doing duties they like. One of the fundamental tasks of management is to get the right people in the right jobs. But this has to be balanced against the immediate need to get the work out, whether it's interesting or not. A good manager needs to keep both short-run and long-run factors in mind in all his dealings with his employees.

And If This Doesn't Quite Fit Your Situation . . .

Problem 6-10 deals with an employee who doesn't like his job in general. If the employee is avoiding work because it involves new technology or requires her to change, see Problems 5-4 and 6-9. If her refusal to do assigned work involved publicly refusing to follow an order, see Problem 8-1.

Use Checklists 1 and 2 to develop a cure of your own.

—— 5-3 ——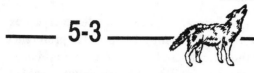

The Problem: A good worker consistently violates company rules to get his work done.

The Scene

Monday morning finds you on your way to an important meeting in the farthest section of the warehouse. As you stroll briskly through the busy sections, you see Tim whip around a corner on his forklift—narrowly missing the corner of the stacks *and* another worker.

Tim always gets the job done—often faster than others—and has never had an accident. But he's had several near-misses. It doesn't seem to matter how many times you stress safety rules in your staff meetings, Tim just ignores them and does his work his way.

Possible Causes and Cures

This situation is a lot like that described in Problem 5-1. The main difference is that Carlotta is a poor worker *because* she won't follow the rules, while Tim is a good worker *in spite of* the fact that he won't follow the rules.

The causes and cures for the two problems are about the same, with these differences:

It is less likely in this case that Tim doesn't follow the procedures because he doesn't know how. If he's a good worker who ignores rules to get his work done, chances are that it's because he sees a positive benefit (reaching his production goals) in not meeting your requirements and sees no benefit in doing things your way.

In Carlotta's case, there is a clear consequence of her failure to follow the rules (her poor performance). In Tim's case, there is no demonstrable result. He gets his work done, and he hasn't had any accidents. So the sole issue here is the violation of company rules. Decide how important it is that Tim follow the rules. While he may be able to ignore safety requirements without having an accident, does his behavior set a bad example for other workers who may not be as skilled as he is? Does the nature of the work itself require that employees follow rules without question, even ones they don't agree with (as for example, when you're dealing with hazardous materials, security items, or in other sensitive situations)?

If you decide that it is critical that Tim follow the rules, then first explain to him your rationale. Acknowledge his good performance, stressing that truly good performance requires not only that the end product be right, but also that the procedures be followed correctly. Invite him to tell you if following the rules prevents him from meeting his production requirements and to suggest ways to rearrange assignments so that the rules don't get in the way.

Explain also that, regardless of how well he's performing, following company rules is also a bottom-line issue. Remind him that violation of the rules may result in disciplinary action against him—even termination. Express your confidence in his ability to get the work out within the rules and point out examples of employees who manage to accomplish a lot without violations.

Then follow up. If Tim changes his behavior, congratulate him. If the rules really interfere with production, then overlook for a time slight performance slippages that may occur as he readjusts his mode of operation. If he fails to conform to the rules, remind him again— then take whatever corrective action is warranted (a notation in his file, a disciplinary action, or termination).

Something to Think About

You always have a problem when a worker—good or poor—refuses to follow work rules. If the rules are inefficient, change them; if they aren't, explain and enforce them. In short, have as few rules as possible, and then see that they're followed by everyone.

And If This Doesn't Quite Fit Your Situation . . .

Look at Problems 5-1 and 5-2 for similar cases of intentional nonperformance. Problem 8-1 addresses a public refusal to follow your direction.

Use Checklist 1 to develop a cure of your own.

5-4

The Problem: An employee refuses to use new work procedures or technology.

The Scene

"Mac, you don't seem to be using your new personal computer very much."

"Nah—it just doesn't do that much for me. I still get all my work done, just like always."

Mac does get his work done—but only because Marty, your office clerk, knows how to turn his sketchy handwritten notes into contracts. Mac is the only one left that Marty has to do this for, and before long she's not going to be available to help him. How do you get him to start using his computer so there won't be a blowup when that happens?

Possible Causes

Mac thinks the new technology is demeaning. For him, actually "typing" the contracts is clerical work that's beneath him.

He thinks that it will make his job less interesting. Many people associate new technology, especially automation, with boring jobs.

He thinks it may make him unnecessary. It's hard to get someone to be enthusiastic about new equipment that may replace him.

He may simply be afraid he can't learn it. If he doesn't try, he doesn't have to face the embarrassment of failure.

Hints: In Problem 1-8 we dealt with the problem of a work unit that didn't want to change. What applies to groups of employees also applies to individuals: people will change only when they believe that (1) the change will help them, (2) they can successfully produce the change, and (3) the change is worth the effort it will take.

Whenever you want someone to change, you need to show him that the change will help him, is practical, and is worth it. When you do that, he'll usually change.

Cures

If Mac thinks the new technology is demeaning:

For many people, using computers or fax machines or other office technology means doing their own "clerical" work. This is particularly true when they have to use a keyboard. Many of us were brought up to believe that only clerks use typewriters. When someone puts a computer with a keyboard on our desk, it looks like they want to make clerks out of us.

If that's how Mac looks at the situation, your first objective is to see that he understands the difference between using a personal computer and doing typing. A personal computer lets him do more of his job; it really means that *no one* does the clerical work.

You may also have to see that he has the skills necessary to use the new technology. No matter how he feels about computers in general, Mac may be uncomfortable because he doesn't have good keyboarding skills. Getting him self-paced training in keyboarding or sending him to a class (made up of other nonclerical employees!) will help.

If the problem is attitude, though, skills training alone won't solve it. You need to explain to Mac how personal computers can make it easier for *everyone* to do their job. Perhaps you need to have another employee, one whom Mac trusts, show him how useful it can be. If he understands that his using his computer will help Marty move up to a better job, that may help, too.

If he thinks it will make his job less interesting:

Unfortunately, organizations have often used computers in ways that *do* make jobs less interesting. Most of us have seen rooms full of data input clerks, punching data into terminals hour after hour. It's easy to believe that a computer on our desktop will do the same thing to us.

What you have to do is show Mac that this isn't the case. If you have another employee who's using a computer effectively, have him show Mac how helpful it is. Perhaps there's even a training course available which shows how to use personal computers effectively.

In general, personal computers make jobs easier and, often, more interesting. You just need to see that Mac understands this. Once you can get him actually using it, he'll probably find it out for himself.

If he thinks he may be replaced by the new technology:

This is a very common reaction to new technology, since technology is so often justified as a way of reducing the work force.

If your company is intending to reduce workers because of this new equipment, you need to be honest with your employees about it. See if the company has a program for retraining and reassignment inside for displaced workers. If not, see if they at least have an effective outplacement program. They may also be planning to offer early retirement, and Mac might qualify for that. If there's nothing else, explain to Mac that learning to use the new technology will make him more employable elsewhere.

Normally, new office technology *won't* reduce workers. If this is the case, see that Mac—and each other employee—knows it. He may still think it's demeaning or will make his job less interesting, but this will relieve him enough to let you work out the other problems with him.

If he doesn't want to try because he's afraid he can't learn it:

"You can't lose if you don't play." Many people avoid new and challenging situations to avoid the possibility of failure. Perhaps that's what Mac is doing.

If his fear is relatively mild, the combination of a little pressure and a lot of reassurance may be enough to get him to try the new technology. Other workers might help him, and apply a little bit of peer pressure, too.

If his fear is strong, his avoidance of new challenges is probably a deep-seated character trait by now. Look at the second "cure" in Problem 6-9 for some ideas on how to deal with that.

Something to Think About

A situation like Mac's may require a manager to walk a fine line. On the one hand, you need to accommodate each employee's personality and preferred way of working. On the other, you can't do this to the extent that it disrupts the production of other employees. Finding the right balance is often difficult, but always rewarding.

And If This Doesn't Quite Fit Your Situation . . .

If many individual in your unit are resisting change, look at Problem 1-8. If the individual is resisting change in general, see Problem 6-9.

Use Checklists 1 and 2 to develop a cure of your own.

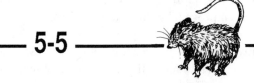

——— 5-5 ———

The Problem: An employee is talented, but only produces so-so work.

The Scene

You're having a hard time figuring out what the problem is with Adam. It's obvious from your discussions with him that he has a quick mind, a good grasp of the technical aspects of the job, and can express himself well. Some of his work products are great—models you'd like to show to other employees. But he's so inconsistent! Just as soon as you've decided he's got real potential, he'll invariably turn in for his next assignment something so awful you can't believe it came from the same person. Just what's his problem?

Possible Causes

He may not like the work. It simply may not interest him or be in areas where he feels his talents lie.

He may have "poor work habits." This expression covers a multitude of problems, but generally means that he doesn't organize and prioritize his assignments well to produce good work.

He may see no incentive to produce better work. If he is able to "get along" by doing so-so work, and if high levels of accomplishment at work are not important to him, he may be content to do whatever he can get by with.

He may be bored. It's unfortunately true that many of the most talented people don't do well in organizations because the very talents they have (creativity, for instance) are not valued in bureaucratic organizations. If Adam can't use his strengths, he will get bored and "tune out" the work.

Hint: Try to structure the work of your organization to let people do the things they're most interested in. If others in the company know that you have an employee who's particularly talented in an area, you may even be able to attract more of that kind of work to your organization. But that kind of restructuring can only go so far. Your unit was set up to accomplish a specific mission. As long as you can accommodate employees' individual preferences and still accomplish that mission, you're probably free to do both. But when accommodating employees means you can't get your basic work done, you have to draw the line. It's a fact of life in the American organization that the mission comes first.

Cures

If Adam doesn't like the work:

Talk to him to find out what kind of work he's most interested in and point out to him the parts of his assignment that are most similar to the work he likes. Also identify work in the organization that is not currently assigned to him that matches his preferences.

Let Adam know that if he does well in his current assignments, you'll try to arrange for more of the work he finds interesting or help him find a job that's closer to what he's looking for.

Make it clear to Adam that your offers to help him don't substitute for his hard work in his current job. Be sure he understands that good performance is his responsibility and that you're disappointed that his products haven't been better since he has such obvious talents.

If he has poor work habits:

Observe the way Adam accomplishes work. Follow through an assignment with him step by step to see if you can identify what he's not doing as efficiently as he could. If he's always been able, in school or previous jobs, to get all his work done with time and energy to spare, he may never have had to learn the skills of organizing and prioritizing that enable the rest of us to cope.

Once you've identified specifically where Adam's weaknesses lie, determine the best way to teach him the necessary skills. There are a number of commercial courses available that help people learn how to organize and prioritize work. You can do a lot by coaching Adam, helping him get started, and then following up periodically to see if he's beginning to have problems again.

Make sure you let Adam know specifically and in detail the things about his work products that you're dissatisfied about. Give him back work that doesn't meet your expectations and have *him* do it over until it's acceptable. Problem 6-1 has more tips on dealing with a specific case of poor work habits—the disorganized worker.

Adam may accuse you of expecting more of him than of other employees—and maybe you are. If so, and you're convinced he can handle the extra demands, admit your greater expectations of him. But also reassure him that he'll get greater rewards (in the form of pay raises, promotions, or bonuses). Then if he begins to deliver to your expectations, make sure you follow through on your promises.

If he sees no incentive to produce better work:

Examine your own pay and reward systems to see if it pays off well for good performance and poorly for poor performance. If not, do as much as is within your immediate authority to change the relationship between rewards and production. If there are issues that you can't deal with at your level, let your supervisor or personnel department know about your concerns and suggestions for improvement.

Make sure Adam is aware of your expectations of him and of the consequences of good and poor performance. Let him know you appreciate the skills he has to offer and you're disappointed in his performance so far. Encourage him to work to his full potential both for his own satisfaction and for the benefit of the company.

Keep in mind that this is a situation in which you may not be able to effect much change in Adam's performance. As long as what he's producing is "good enough," there's not a whole lot you can do. Threats obviously won't work, and the incentives you have to offer may simply not be things that Adam finds motivating. It's undeniably frustrating, but different people value different things. For some people, the job just isn't that important except as a way to earn a living.

If Adam is bored:

Talk with Adam to find out what kind of work he'd rather be doing or how you could change the nature of his assignments to use his creativity. If his job requires him to research cases and precedents, expand his responsibility to include recommending solutions. If he's responsible for promotions or recruiting, ask him to help design campaigns. Whenever possible, include him on committees that will work out new procedures or methods or come up with new ideas. Even if the subject is not in his specific area of expertise, he may have valuable insights to offer.

If it's obvious that Adam's talents are wasted in your unit and that there's no satisfactory way to utilize him, give him your support in finding a job (in the company if possible) that will use his talents.

And If This Doesn't Quite Fit Your Situation . . .

If the employee is new, look at Problem 4-2. If the problem is that the employee does what he's told, see the next problem (5-6).

Use Checklist 1 to develop a cure of your own.

—— 5-6 ——

The Problem: An employee does what he's told, but no more.

The Scene

"Nancy, don't you have anything to do?"

"No, Ms. Mason."

"Do you think that Edna or Tommy might have some work you could help them with?

"I don't know."

"Well, do you think you could ask them and see?"

"I guess so. Do you want me to?"

"Yes—that would be good," you say—and then turn away so you won't yell "AND DO IT NOW!" at her. It happens this way every time. If you don't specifically tell her to do something, she'll sit at her desk and read magazines all afternoon!

Possible Causes

Nancy believes her only responsibility is to do the work specifically assigned to her. She thinks she's doing exactly what she's supposed to.

She has very little initiative or assertiveness. She may wait for someone to tell her what to do at home, too.

Nancy is lazy. She intends to get away with as little work as possible.

Hint: It's easy to jump to the conclusion that Nancy is lazy, or uncooperative on purpose. Don't reach this conclusion, though, until you've made sure that neither of the first two causes is true.

Cures

If she believes her job is to do only the work specifically assigned to her:

If Nancy is an inexperienced worker, she may think that all she needs to do is to accomplish the work that's assigned to her. (And being inexperienced doesn't necessarily mean that she's young; many older women have very little experience in a job and may not have a clear understanding of what's generally expected.) She may also have come from a job where employees were responsible only for work specifically assigned to them.

This may be the easiest problem to solve. Talk with Nancy, and explain to her that you expect her to work with the others and help them with their work load when hers is done. You may need to reassure her that they'll also be willing to help her. Then keep watching her, reminding her of your discussion if she's sitting without work and praising her when you find her helping with someone else's work.

She may get angry. She may feel that it's not fair for her to have to help the others: "I do my work—why can't they do theirs?!" This is much harder; now she may think you're expecting an unfair amount of work from her. She may think, in short, that you're being unfair.

While you need to counsel her on the need for everyone to work together, that's not going to be enough. You need also to take steps to build more of a team feeling between Edna, Tommy, and her. You might want to seat them closer together, or perhaps have them exchange jobs for a few days or weeks. You could even consider having work given to the three of them as a group, with each one taking the next job regardless of whose it is.

Depending on Nancy's age and background, you may want to be especially patient and considerate with her. But you can't tolerate someone who won't work as a member of the team. You also probably aren't so overstaffed that you can put up with someone who spends several hours a week not working. Keep the pressure on, and if there's no other solution give her the choice of becoming part of the team or leaving.

If she shows very little initiative:

In some ethnic groups and in some families of any background, individual children or (particularly) girls may be expected *not* to be assertive and want to do things. Nancy may believe that it's "right" for her to wait until someone tells her what to do, and "wrong" if she were to show initiative.

If this is the case, you'll need a lot of patience—but the result will probably more than justify it. Nancy needs to learn that it's all right for her to show initiative, that people will even like her better and appreciate her if she does. This won't necessarily be easy; she may still be expected to be passive at home. But if you and the other employees involved are kind and guide her toward being more assertive, she'll probably open up and begin to change.

If Nancy is simply lazy:

As we said above, don't jump to this as a conclusion. Check the other alternatives out first.

If this does turn out to be the case, deal with it quickly and firmly. Sit down with Nancy and make clear that you expect her to share the work load with the others. If your organization uses position descriptions, you may want to change hers to show that she helps the others. You might want to put her in another job with more work or assign more work to her.

Don't expect it to be easy. She may well decide that she doesn't want to do that much work, no matter what. If that's the case, make it clear to her what the consequences will be if she refuses to do additional work. Then, if she continues to refuse, let her go.

Things to Think About

This is a good place to make a point that's important in many circumstances. You may put in the time with Nancy and get her to start changing. When you see her changing, you may be tempted to slack up and leave her on her own. Don't. When you're trying to get someone to change, it's important to keep guiding, pushing or forcing them until the change is completely made. If you ease back when you're only half way there, the person will generally go back to behaving the way they were. If you get fired up again and try to get them to change, it will be doubly difficult the second time.

The moral is simple. Think before you decide you want to get someone to change. If you decide you do, stay with it until the person has changed *and* the new behavior has become habitual.

And If This Doesn't Quite Fit Your Situation . . .

If Nancy is new and poorly motivated, see Problem 4-2. If she won't accept help or can't seem to learn the harder parts of her job, see Problems 4-5 and 4-6. If she's poorly organized, see Problem 6-1. You may also find some suggestions in the problem just before this one (Problem 5-5).

Use Checklists 1 and 2 to develop a cure of your own.

5-7

The Problem: An employee argues with you when she disagrees with your decisions.

The Scene

You dread Tuesday morning staff meetings with the team chiefs. Every time you make a decision, Judy has some objection. Nothing you do is ever right, and she shows no hesitation in letting you know. And, what's worse, she never lets go of a point. Once she's decided you're doing something stupid, she comes up with 6,000 reasons why you shouldn't do it—one right after the other, so that sometimes you just cave in from sheer exhaustion.

Doesn't being the boss mean you get your way at least *some* of the time? Obviously not to Judy!

Possible Causes

Judy may think she's impressing you with her insight and reasoning. She may be under the impression that challenging the boss is a good way to show how much she knows—not to make life difficult for you.

On the other hand, she may want to make your life miserable, because of some slight you've given her, real or imaginary. She may correctly perceive that she's wearing you down and feel that she's somehow "paying you back" for something you've done to her.

She may just be a generally contentious person who gets personal enjoyment from others' discomfiture. Arguing with you may be no different to her than arguing with her coworkers, her friends, or her family.

Hint: This kind of carping by subordinates is usually no more than a minor irritant—except in two cases: where the employee embarrasses you publicly and where the arguing ends in the employee refusing to abide by your decision. Public criticism of you as a supervisor is discussed in Problem 8-4. Refusal to follow your instructions is a kind of insubordination and is covered in Problem

8-1. If either of those conditions occurs, you have a serious problem that, left uncorrected, will undermine your authority. Petty carping such as we're discussing here, even in the presence of trusted peers, is more annoying than harmful—but it can still make life unpleasant.

Cures

If Judy is "showing off" when she challenges your decisions:

Talk to her and explain, gently but firmly, how irritating you find her behavior. Reassure her that you appreciate her ability to analyze and critique.

At the same time, remind Judy that some things just aren't worth arguing about and that, even for the things that are, at some point you have to stop talking and make a decision. Make sure she understands that you're not just being arbitrary when you cut her off and take a final stand, but that it's part of your job as the supervisor to make decisions—even unpopular ones.

Let Judy know that you are sincerely interested in her ideas and comments, particularly about those things where she has unique insights. Invite her to come to you early in the discussion and "thinking" stages of the planning process so she can have input *before* decisions are made.

If Judy is trying to "get back" at you for something:

Try to figure out what Judy's grievance is. Can you remember something you did to her (particularly something that may have embarrassed her)? Talk to Judy to see if she'll tell you what the problem is. But she very likely won't. She'll only tell you if she trusts you—and if she trusted you she probably would have come to you in the first place rather than sniping at you.

Whether or not you can figure out what Judy's upset about, talk to her to tell her how irritating you find her behavior. Explain what your supervisory decision-making responsibilities are, and make sure she understands how close she is to real insubordination in continually haggling over your instructions. As above, offer her the opportunity to give you her input before decisions are made so she won't have cause to second-guess you afterward.

If Judy is just an argumentative person:

There's probably not a lot you can do to change her. Make sure she understands how irritating you find her behavior and describe for her more appropriate ways of expressing disagreement. Explain too how her effectiveness as an employee can be damaged by the way she interacts with others in such an argumentative way. But if Judy is basically a good employee and her personal style doesn't interfere with her (and others') performance appreciably, you may just have to put up with her annoying habit.

And If This Doesn't Quite Fit Your Situation . . .

If Judy seems to be a "know-it-all," see Problem 3-11. If the problem is that she gets defensive, see the next problem (5-8). Problems 3-8, 3-10, and 3-11 discuss other irritating behaviors.

Use Checklist 2 to develop a cure of your own.

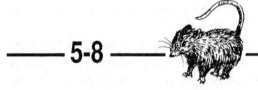

—— 5-8 ——

The Problem: An employee gets defensive when told how he could have done something better.

The Scene

"I do perfectly good work, and you're always criticizing it! I don't know why you keep picking on me. I do the best job I can every day—isn't that enough?!"

It's happening again! Every time you try to suggest to Steve that he could have done a project more effectively, he gets angry and defensive. He's a good worker, but he'd be even better if he'd just listen.

Possible Causes

When an employee reacts defensively to suggestions or criticism, it's because he *feels like* he's being attacked. There may be any combination of three reasons why he feels this way.

The person doing the criticism is being judgmental, not objective and helpful. How often have you heard "suggestions" that were really attacks? We've heard them a lot.

The employee being criticized is insecure in his job. When an employee is afraid of what others think of his performance, he has a very low tolerance for criticism of it.

The employee may be a "perfectionist." Some people come to believe that they must do everything just right or else. It's too painful for them to accept that they might not have.

Hint: In situations like this, it's tempting to play amateur psychologist: "Steve has an inferiority complex," or "Steve must have had a very demanding father." *Don't!* Get to know Steve, and all of your other employees, well enough to treat them as individuals—and leave it at that.

Cures

If you don't give criticism helpfully and objectively:

First, don't *you* get defensive about this. It takes real skill to present criticism helpfully. If you don't have the skill, you can learn it.

It starts with the decision that you want to be helpful. This isn't always as simple as it sounds. It's very easy to feel you should "shape up" employees. As a manager it is your job to tell employees how they can improve; you need to do that. You'll do it best, though, if you begin with the assumption that each employee wants to do a good job—and you're just helping them.

You've probably heard this a dozen times, but we're going to repeat it: combine the criticism with honest praise for his work. Don't do it mechanically; don't rush through a half-hearted good word or two and then "get down to business." Take time to identify what's good about the performance, then present your ideas as a way it could be even better.

You may have read that you should always praise first, then criticize. In our experience, it's not that simple. You should present both praise and criticism honestly, straightforwardly—and in the order that's most appropriate for the situation.

If you're not used to giving criticism in a really helpful and objective way, you won't learn to do it overnight. But you can learn to do it—and you'll be amazed at the difference it can make in your employees' response to your attempts to help them.

A final point: always criticize the behavior, *never the employee*. There's a world of difference between "You're careless" and "You're a good worker, but you made a number of careless mistakes on this."

If Steven is insecure in his job:

He may be a new and inexperienced worker, or new to your work unit. He may have made several mistakes lately and be worried about what you think of him. There may be rumors of layoffs, and he's afraid for his job. Or any of a dozen other reasons.

Get to know him well enough to understand the reason(s), and then do your best to reassure him. If he's new, you can explain that it's only normal for inexperienced workers to make mistakes—and that the important point is to learn from them. If there may be a layoff, deal with that honestly. If he can improve his chances of staying by improving his performance, point that out to him.

It may be helpful to develop specific performance improvement objectives with him. If his work is organized poorly, for instance, he might set a goal to improve his organizational skills in stages over the next few months. Developing and focusing on a realistic goal emphasizes your belief that he *can* do better. It also gets both of you looking at the positive side of the situation, not the negative.

Steve may need a great deal of reassurance along with any suggestions for improvement. Give it to him. And make it a point to give him positive recognition whenever he accepts criticism and uses it.

If he's a perfectionist who can't stand criticism:

Don't reach this conclusion until you've explored both of the alternatives above. It's all too easy to dismiss someone as a "perfectionist," when the problem is really the manager or the work situation.

There are individuals who believe they must always do the best possible job. For some of them, this means seeking criticism, so they can improve. For others, though, it means doing so well that no one can ever find a flaw in their work. If someone does appear to criticize something they've done, it means to them that they've failed.

This is a heavy burden, both for the individual and for the people who work with him. And you're not going to change the situation quickly or easily. In fact, you may not be able to change it at all.

If this is how Steve is, be sure you continually recognize the good work he does. If you regularly use performance improvement objectives in your unit, you may be able to get Steve to set a performance objective or two. And keep your eyes open to another phenomenon: Steve may reject the criticism on the spot, but then accept it and use it later on.

Something to Think About

Actually, this is something to avoid. Don't make a point to your employees as a whole that you mean for one individual. It can be tempting. You have to say something to Steve that you know he won't like. Instead of telling him, you call everyone together and say it to the whole group—hoping that Steve will get the message. Forget it! He may not get the point. If he does, he'll probably get angry because you didn't come out and say it to him. And the other employees will be confused and perhaps angry. If you have something to say to an employee, say it to him or don't say it at all.

And If This Doesn't Quite Fit Your Situation . . .

Look at Problem 3-11 if the root problem is that the employee is a "know-it-all," or the immediately preceding problem (5-7) if he argues with you. If Steve is new and won't accept help, see Problem 4-5. If his defensiveness may be because he can't learn the harder parts of his job, see Problem 4-6.

Use Checklist 2 to develop a cure of your own.

5-9

The Problem: An employee consistently gets others to do his work.

The Scene

Fred has just handed you another report and, as usual, it looks fine. But as you examine it more closely, parts of it look suspiciously like Penny's writing—certain phrases and sentence structures that are typical of Penny, but not typical of Fred at all. Did he get her to do another assignment for him? It seems like every product Fred gives you should really be credited to someone else. Doesn't he do any of his own work?

Possible Causes

Fred may have little confidence in his own abilities. He may get other people whom he trusts to help him because he doubts the worth of the products he prepares personally.

Fred may have helped other workers out with their work and occasionally "calls in" favors. While it may appear that others are helping Fred write all his assignments, he may, in turn, have helped them with research, or computations, or other areas where his skills are better.

Fred may be imposing on his coworkers to get out of work himself. If this is the cause, you'll probably find out fairly soon as those coworkers begin to file into your office to register their complaints at being taken advantage of.

Hint: The main problem here is not the quality of Fred's work—what he's turning in is quite acceptable. The problem is that you have no idea of how much *Fred* is capable of because, as far as you can tell, you don't often see original products of his. As a result, you can't be sure how far you can push him, how much of a load he can carry, or how he'll do when the pressure is on and there's no one in the office to help him out. Of course, if he's imposing on other workers, you have another problem too—bad feelings among the staff, toward Fred for imposing on them, and possibly also toward you for not noticing and doing something about it!

Cures

If Fred lacks confidence in his own abilities:

Let Fred know that it's important to you, and to him, to find out just what he's capable of doing. Then give him a series of one- or two-step assignments with instructions that he's to perform them entirely on his own and report directly to you when they're completed. Express your confidence in his ability to complete them satisfactorily.

Review the assignments with Fred as he turns them in to you. Emphasize the parts he did well and identify those specific areas where he needs help.

If you do identify particular performance deficiencies, arrange for training opportunities so that Fred can gain the necessary skills.

Make sure Fred understands why it's important that he do his work himself. Get his agreement to check with you before asking coworkers to help out with any significant portions of his assignments.

Congratulate Fred on those assignments he performs well by himself, giving him formal recognition and bonuses when it's appropriate as an additional incentive to continue to do his own work.

If Fred's agreed with his coworkers on a reciprocal arrangement for completing assignments:

Talk with Fred and the other employees involved about the arrangements they've made. If the distribution of work is satisfactory to you, with no one carrying too much or too little of the burden, you may decide to approve their agreement officially.

Before you approve this arrangement, however, consider how important it is to the organization to have several people with the same basic skills to whom you can assign work. Fred's arrangement is likely to make specialists of your staff—allowing employees to do primarily the work they like or are especially good at and to avoid the things they don't like or don't do as well. If flexibility and keeping a broad range of skills distributed throughout the organization are important to you, then Fred's arrangement won't work. But if you're going to disapprove this assignment of responsibilities, make sure Fred and the other employees know why.

If Fred is taking advantage of his co-workers:

Explain to him, in firm tones, why his behavior is unacceptable. Warn him that you'll be reviewing his products very carefully to be sure that he doesn't impose on the rest of the staff and that you'll take whatever action is necessary to ensure that he doesn't impose on them again.

Let your other employees know too that, while you normally would applaud their willingness to help out a fellow employee, in this situation they should refuse to help Fred unless you have explicitly approved their participation in advance. That will ensure that Fred is forced to do his own work. It also gets your other employees out of the position of being "bad guys" when they refuse to assist.

Then follow up. Review Fred's assignments in detail—both to see if they're really his work and to see just how good a job he does on his own. If Fred continues to impose on the others, take appropriate disciplinary action for disobeying your direct order. If Fred begins to do the work on his own, but submits substandard products, talk to him about his performance deficiencies, arrange training where it's likely to help, and follow through as you would for any other performance difficulty.

And If This Doesn't Quite Fit Your Situation . . .

If he tries to get others to do his work because of clear performance deficiencies of his own, look at the other problems in this chapter and those described in Chapter 6.

Use Checklists 1 and 2 to develop a cure of your own.

6

Troubleshooting Problems Caused by the Continuing, Unintentional Performance of an Employee

—— 6-1 —— 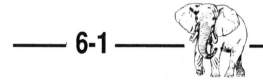 ————————

The Problem: An employee is poorly organized and consistently misses deadlines.

The Scene

"Gladys, do you mean to tell me that you're going to be late with the newsletter again this month?!"

"I'm sorry, Mr. Cuzak, I really am. I took the material home with me every night this week and worked on it—but I just can't seem to get it together. If you could just get someone to help me. . . ."

You sigh. Gladys doesn't need someone to help her. She needs to get herself organized and quit spinning her wheels. But how to do it?

Possible Causes

*Gladys may not realize that she's **not** organized.* Perhaps she's never worked with anyone who was really well organized.

She may never have had to learn how to organize herself. In her previous jobs she may never have had to do anything but get the work done as it came to her.

She may not believe that it's important to organize herself. It may seem too trivial for her to spend time on.

Hints: As you're probably realized already, none of the causes exclude the others. She may not believe it's important to organize herself because she's never had to *and* never worked around anyone who did it well. One of the critical steps here is knowing just where to start.

Remember, organizing your time and your work is a *learned* skill. Because of their past history, and perhaps their personalities, some people are better at it than others will ever be. But everyone can learn to organize themselves well enough to do what has to be done.

Cures

No matter what the cause is:

Spend some time observing Gladys and talking with her. Your goal is to find out how she's disorganized. Does she put things off until the very last minute? Does she spend too much time on the unimportant parts of the job? Does she start on something, work on it for a little while, and then leave it unfinished while she goes on to something else? It's important to get a feel for the specific ways that she's not being efficient.

If she doesn't realize that she's not organized:

This is good news and it's bad news. The good news is that once she realizes she's not organized, she'll probably want to learn how to get organized. The bad news is that it may be difficult for her to see that she's not organized.

The easiest, least-threatening way for her to learn she's not well organized is to work with someone who is. Can you arrange a joint task that she and one of your best-organized workers can do together? (The other worker also needs to be one who can be helpful and not get frustrated.)

If you're good at organization, and there's no one else to work with her, you can do it. (You're the second choice because it's going to be harder for her to relax and learn from you, her supervisor.) You may just need to tell her what to do—but you'll be more effective if you can ask questions and make suggestions.

Once she realizes that she doesn't have the self-organization skills she needs, she'll probably be happy to have you or someone else help her gain them. It would probably be a good idea to send her to a formal course on work organization, too.

If she's never had to learn to organize herself:

She may have had jobs before where she wasn't required to do much organizing, so she never learned how.

This may not be as difficult as the situation above. If you can explain the difference between the work she did and her current work, with some examples, she may see the difference quickly. Having her work jointly with a well-organized worker can also help her to see the difference.

Once she sees the difference, having another worker help her and/or sending her to a formal course should get her going in the right direction.

If she doesn't think that organizing herself is important:

If this is the case, it's helpful to understand why she thinks this way. Does she see herself as a "creative" person and believe that being organized would only get in her way? Does she think that "organizing" is something that only clerks and secretaries do? Or does she just not realize that she's disorganized (back to cause 1).

If she insists that she's as organized as she needs to be, deal with her performance. Instead of talking about being organized, insist that she get her work done on schedule. If she feels pushed enough, she may ask someone else to help her get organized.

Having a person who's organized work with her is also a good idea here—particularly if she begins to feel pressure to meet deadlines. Once she sees that someone else can handle the same kind of work more easily and skillfully, she'll probably want to learn the skills.

When she accepts the need to organize herself, see that she gets the on-the-job and/or formal training she needs.

What if she still refuses to learn how to get organized? Deal with the problem as a performance problem and take whatever steps are necessary. See Problem 6-9 for suggestions.

Things to Think About

Everything in this problem assumes that *you* are organized. Be sure that's the case. If it's not, your disorganization may be spilling over onto Gladys and other employees. You may actually be making it harder for them to organize themselves. You can figure out what the solution is to that, can't you?

Have you been accepting it when employees are late with assignments? Do you fuss and fume a little, then give up and take the assignment when you can get it? If so, *you're* a major part of the problem. See problem 3 in this chapter for suggestion on how to handle this.

It's important in this case, and in so many others, for the employee to believe that there really is a better way. As long as Gladys thinks her problem is just overwork—or lack of ability—she's stuck in it. Once she sees that she can get out of the situation by learning some new skills, the battle is almost won.

And If This Doesn't Quite Fit Your Situation . . .

Problems 6-2 through 6-6 also deal with employees who have problems producing. Failure to be organized can also be a factor in most problems in Chapter 5.

Use Checklist 1 to develop a cure of your own.

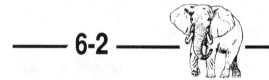

—— 6-2 ——

The Problem: An employee has a tremendous attitude, but just isn't producing satisfactory work.

The Scene

Glenda did it again—gave you a report you couldn't use. You thought you had done everything right: You called her in to explain exactly what you wanted, where the numbers came from, how to compute the percentages, the way to format the columns. She nodded in all the right places and even asked a couple of questions that sounded as if she understood what you were talking about. "Right away, Dan," she had said as she left your office.

But the report she gave you is nothing like what you had in mind! Glenda tries so hard—but it's just not working out.

Possible Causes

Glenda may not understand what you want. Especially if she is obviously trying very hard to do a good job, she may just not know what it is you're looking for.

She may not know how to do the work. Even if she understands what you want, she may not know how to get there. This is particularly likely if she's recently been assigned new duties or is new to the organization and if what's she's doing now doesn't bear much resemblance to the work she's done in the past.

Glenda may be the sort of person who starts out well, but then doesn't deliver. You may think she has a great attitude because of her apparent enthusiasm when you give her assignments. But that enthusiasm may be feigned to get you off her back so she can go back to whatever it is she really wants to be doing.

Hint: If you decide that Glenda's intentions are good, but she's still having trouble producing, then it's important that you help her solve her performance problem. An unfortunate consequence of repeated failure is that even employees who want to do a good job eventually get beaten down so badly that they give up, don't care anymore, or become resentful and hard to manage. By stepping in as soon as you discover the difficulties, you may be able to overcome them in time to avoid the demoralizing effect of continued unsuccessful performance.

Cures

If Glenda doesn't understand what you want:

Talk with her about your expectations. Her lack of understanding may stem from one of two causes: either she's been misinterpreting your instructions or you've been unclear in explaining what you need. In either case, your first step should be to have Glenda tell you what she thinks you told her to do.

In those areas where Glenda's interpretation and your expectations don't match, identify for her what she should have done differently. Show her some examples of work that's been completed to your expectations and how it compares with the products she's submitted.

Try to put Glenda's work in context. Show her who the customer is for her products and how her work affects other people's performance. By learning how her work is used by others, she'll be better able to identify the things it's critical that she do well and the parts that are just "nice-to-haves."

Review Glenda's work closely for a while. Look at her work each time she turns in an assignment, or sample her products every day or two if they're things that don't normally flow through you on their way to the customer. Identify the things she's doing correctly and the areas that still need work.

An even better idea is to have Glenda work with another employee who can review her work and give her pointers on how to do things better. She may be more willing to go to a peer for advice than to you, since she may believe that you'll hold her lack of knowledge against her at appraisal time.

After you've given Glenda what ought to be sufficient opportunity and assistance to improve her performance, review her progress to decide if she's showing satisfactory improvement. She probably won't get better all at once, but you should begin fairly soon to see signs that she's catching on to what you want. If not, you'll need to make some hard decisions. Not only is it not fair to the organization and your other workers to carry Glenda in a job she can't perform; it's not fair to her either. Try to find her another position in which she can perform satisfactorily, but, failing that, you must be prepared to terminate her as tactfully and sensitively as you can. Your personnel department should be available to help you and Glenda get through both the paperwork and the emotional upheaval.

If Glenda doesn't know how to do the work:

Identify the specific areas in which she makes mistakes to isolate those parts of the job where she needs help. Decide what kind of training is best to give her the knowledge or expertise she needs (e.g., formal classroom training, on-the-job training) and arrange for her to get it.

Work with her closely for some time to review each product and to identify the things she's doing correctly and the areas that still need improvement.

Encourage Glenda and let her know that you have confidence in her ability to learn the work. At the same time, make sure she understands that it's her responsibility to do well, regardless of the amount of assistance you're able to give her.

As above, be optimistic but realistic. If, after your best attempts to teach Glenda the job, she still doesn't improve, be prepared to remove her from your organization or to help her find another position. That doesn't mean you've failed. No worker is equally good at every job.

If Glenda starts out enthusiastically, but then doesn't deliver:

See Problem 6-3 for help in dealing with an employee who doesn't deliver what he or she promised.

And If This Doesn't Quite Fit Your Situation . . .

See Problems 4-4 and 4-6 for situations where well-motivated employees are having performance difficulties.

Use Checklist 1 to develop a cure of your own.

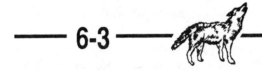

6-3

The Problem: An employee doesn't deliver what he promised.

The Scene

"R.B., this is just a summary of the overdue accounts. You told me you'd have me an analysis of them by today."

"I really meant to—but you know how busy we've been lately. I'm sure I can do the analysis by Wednesday."

"You'd better!" you fume as you walk off. Will R.B. *ever* come through on time?

Possible Causes

R.B. is disorganized. He means well but can't produce.

You accept it when employees don't deliver what they promise. If this is the case, you've got to change yourself before you can change them.

R.B. worked for another supervisor who accepted it. You haven't caused the problem—you've inherited it.

R.B. makes promises to "get people off his back," whether he can deliver or not.

Hint: Unless the problem is R.B.'s lack of organization, you have a serious problem here of work discipline. Don't confuse this with "discipline" for misconduct. Work discipline is simply what good workers make it a point to do, *always*. And good workers always deliver what they promise, when they promise it—or they let you know in advance.

Cures

If R.B. is disorganized:

Look back at the first problem in this chapter for suggestions.

If you accept it when employees don't deliver:

First, accept something else: *you're* the cause of their failure to come through for you. If you don't care about promises and deadlines, why should they?

There's a simple way to deal with this: Stop! Now! Get your employees together, explain the change—and then enforce it.

You'll probably get a great deal of static at first. Employees will say that you're being unfair and expecting too much. Change is painful; you can accept that. But *don't* accept work that isn't done as promised, when promised. You may have to counsel them a little, perhaps even write an employee or two up for not delivering. Do it. They'll get the word. And your unit will start to run considerably better.

Don't go to the other extreme and insist that they deliver no matter what. Something may happen which genuinely has a higher priority or that causes an unavoidable delay. If this happens, if the employee can't produce on schedule—he lets you know *as soon as he knows*. Then the two of you work out a realistic new schedule.

If R.B. worked for another supervisor who accepted it when he didn't deliver:

First, make sure you really don't have the same problem (see above).

Then have a talk with R.B. Say to him essentially what we suggested you say to all employees in the situation above. Make it clear that your standards are different from those of his former supervisor.

R.B. may feel that you're being unfair to him. If you've set clear standards and enforced them, though, your other employees will set him straight quickly. They deliver, and they'll expect him to deliver. (Yes, it usually is just that simple.)

If R.B. makes promises to keep people from pressuring him:

Unfortunately, all too many employees (and their managers) fall into this trap. Somebody pushes them, so they promise anything to get the pressure off. Then the day comes to deliver what was promised, and the individual who did the promising is in trouble.

If the cause seems to be one of the other ones above, keep your eyes open to see if this is also the case. Employees who'll promise anything to get out of a tight spot feel right at home with supervisors who don't insist that commitments be kept.

This problem will probably take a bit more time and attention. First, make your position clear to R.B. Then be equally clear that you won't force unrealistic commitments on him—and that you don't want him to let others do it, either. (There's a good chance that he won't believe this, so be prepared to have him test you on it.)

Follow up to ensure that he stops making unrealistic commitments—and that he keeps those he makes. When he makes a commitment and delivers, praise him for it. If he doesn't deliver, counsel him. Be patient, but be firm. It may take a few times, but he'll get the message.

Things to Think About

It's worth repeating: if your employees don't deliver what's promised, when it's promised—*you're* the culprit. Be realistic about what you expect from them and insist that they're realistic about it, too. Then expect that they deliver or tell you in advance why they can't. With no exceptions.

There's a very simple truth at work here. Most employees will produce what their supervisor will settle for. Even good employees will get sloppy if the supervisor has sloppy standards or (the same thing) has high standards but doesn't enforce them. Enough?

And If This Doesn't Quite Fit Your Situation . . .

If the problem is more that he fouled up an important job, see Problem 4-4. If his failure to deliver is part of a general slippage in his performance, see Problem 4-3. If his failure may result from his refusing to use new technology or to change the way he does his job, see Problems 5-4 and 6-9.

Use Checklist 1 to develop a cure of your own.

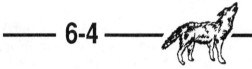

6-4

The Problem: A good performer goes to pieces under pressure.

The Scene

"What's wrong with Brendan?" asked Sally. "He's normally so calm and easygoing. But today, we've had complaints from three different people who said he gave them bad information and didn't seem to know what he was talking about. I know the line out at the reception desk is getting longer by the minute, and Keith said he'd help out as soon as he finishes with this client. But Brendan's just going to have to hold on until we can get somebody else out there!"

"I guess this isn't really a new problem," you reply ruefully. "Brendan falls apart whenever the going gets rough. He's such a good worker most of the time, I hate to get on his back about something that doesn't come up that often. But, unfortunately, when it does, he makes a bad situation even worse."

Possible Causes

Brendan may not have the skills to deal with stress and pressure. He may know the job itself well enough, but not have learned coping strategies to keep from panicking when the pressure's on.

Brendan may not be that good at the work he's assigned. He may be able to get along all right when he has plenty of time to figure out what to do, but, when things move along too quickly, he gets lost.

Brendan may have learned to fall apart under pressure to get himself out of an unpleasant situation. If falling apart under stress in the past has resulted in people feeling sorry for him and bailing him out, he's likely to repeat the behavior in similar situations. Your job is to help him unlearn that behavior.

Hint: There are very few jobs that don't require the ability to work under pressure at least some of the time. Brendan may be a very good worker when he has little stress to contend with. You can try to structure his environment so that the pressures are reduced or so that they occur very infrequently, but sooner or later it's almost inevitable that he'll be asked to perform under some kind of pressure—whether from deadlines, or an angry client or co-worker, or the boss looking over his shoulder on an important project. So regardless of how infrequently the situation occurs, it's in both his and your best interests to help him prepare ahead of time—not in the middle of the crisis.

Cures

If Brendan hasn't developed his own mechanisms for coping with stress:

Start by talking to Brendan and explaining why it's important that he not let the pressure get to him. Make sure he understands the impact on other people when he falls to pieces—that he's not just getting himself worked up but others, too, and that his lack of coping skills only makes tense situations worse.

Find a good commercially available course on stress reduction that includes not only relaxation techniques but also specific tactics for planning around stressful situations. Send Brendan, then ask for his feedback—both on the content of the course and what he plans to do to put the things he learned into practice.

Take some time to work out scenarios with Brendan in which you describe some of the kinds of pressure he's likely to encounter in his job (like having 16 people lined up at the reception desk, all of whom want answers *now*). If you're both comfortable with the technique, roleplay the situations with him until he's practiced in dealing constructively with the pressure. If you're not comfortable with role playing, at least have him describe to you how he would handle the situation. Go over similar situations in several different sessions until you're confident that his appropriate response has become well ingrained.

If Brendan's work skills aren't strong enough for him to operate effectively under pressure:

Talk with Brendan to find out what skills require his unstressed time and attention. Then have him practice those skills over and over again until he can perform them to mastery.

NOTE: Mastery requires that he be able to perform the task both *accurately* and *quickly*. If he has learned the tasks to mastery, he is less likely to fall apart under pressure since mastery is reached only when the responses become semiautomatic.

If it's appropriate, you may want to see that Brendan gets some remedial training or you may want to review, step by step, what's involved in his assignments. He may know how to perform each individual task, but get muddled when he has to sequence steps rapidly.

If falling to pieces is a learned response to get him out of stressful situations:

Explain to Brendan, tactfully but firmly, why you have to count on him when the pressure's on and how his inability to cope hurts others in the organization. Let him know that you'll do whatever you can to help him develop coping strategies (including the actions we discussed above), but that you need his cooperation.

Give Brendan some time to come to terms with your requirements. Send him to stress reduction courses and work out ways of coping with the stresses he's likely to encounter, as we mentioned before.

The next time a stressful situation occurs, don't rush in to help him out. Give Brendan a chance to use the techniques he's learned. Once he sees how you're counting on him, he may do fine. If not, and you have to step in, be sure to do a "postmortem" with him to review how he handled the situation and what he could have done differently.

If Brendan improves his ability to perform under pressure, no matter how slowly, congratulate him on his improvement and stick with him. If he seems not to be improving, you can try a referral to your Employee Assistance Program or another counseling service for more individual professional attention. You may be able to restructure the job to minimize the pressure. Or you may want to help him find another job where ability to deal with pressure isn't so critical.

While termination is always a possibility when employees don't perform to your expectations, it's less likely to be necessary in this situation. If the ability to work under pressure is a real necessity in Brendan's position, and if he continues not to cope well, chances are good that he himself will be uncomfortable enough that he'll look for another job.

And If This Doesn't Quite Fit Your Situation . . .

Look at Problems 4-4 and 6-3 for cases of nonperformance that are caused by factors other than stress.

Use Checklist 1 to develop a cure of your own.

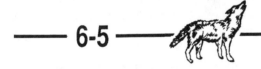

6-5

The Problem: An employee produces a high volume of low-quality work.

The Scene

"Sarah, I see that Emile is your top producer again this month. Is he still making bunches of mistakes?

"Barrels of mistakes is more like it! I've spoken to him about it several times, but he just points out how much he produces. He won't listen to me, because I'm not his supervisor. I need you to take care of it."

Possible Causes

You set low standards. Alternatively, you set high standards but don't insist that people meet them.

Emile learned how to work fast but not accurately. He's continuing to do what he knows how to do best.

The real rewards are for quantity, not quality. In many organizations, quantity is what's tracked and paid for.

Hint: On the surface, this is an individual problem. If you let Emile get away with fast, sloppy work, though, others may start copying him. (This is particularly apt to happen if the pay system stresses quantity at the expense of quality.) Now you have an additional reason to act quickly and effectively.

Cures

If you set low standards (or high ones you don't enforce):

Let's be realistic here. What really counts in your company? In your division? In your unit? Is quality critical, or important, or an also-ran to quantity? Yes, "quality" is still a buzz-word—but that doesn't mean that it's what is wanted, fought for and rewarded.

If quality is a low priority for your company, your problem is much bigger than Emile. He may be producing exactly what the organization rewards. See the last "cure" for this problem to get some ideas on this.

Suppose the company wants quality but you concentrate on quantity instead? The first question, of course, is why your boss lets you get away with sloppy work. Perhaps we'd better talk with him.

Since we can't, we'll just have to suggest that you get your act together. There's not room to talk about it in this book, but there's broad agreement that the best way to get high productivity is to do the things that lead to high quality first.

We can give you this: in a well-run organization, everything is done right the first time—*everything*. If you believe, live, support and reward this, most of the sloppy work will vanish. Then it will be easy to deal with the occasional employee who hasn't gotten the word.

If Emile learned how to work fast but not accurately:

He's doing what most of us do—what we know how to do. In fact, even if he slows to half speed he may still make just as many errors.

What sounds like the sensible thing to do? Retrain him. Retraining is always harder than training, but it can be done. If Emile doesn't see the need for it, refuse to accept sloppy work and make him redo all of it. Make it crystal clear that you expect the work done right the first time.

That should get him in the right frame of mind to do some relearning. This is when you need to be patient, because he may have to begin over almost from the beginning. He'll have to establish new work habits—and they'll be difficult at first. Keep insisting, keep encouraging, and keep persisting.

One other thing: make sure he understands that he can work just as fast without errors. Sound too good to be true? It's not. If he's trained properly, that's what will happen.

If the real rewards are for quantity, not quality:

Anyone who's worked for very long in an average American firm has run into the dilemma. The company advocates quality and encourages its employees to produce quality. Then, when the dust has cleared, the people who get the rewards are those who meet or exceed their quantity targets—without regard for quality. (Just in case you haven't noticed, the time it takes to produce something is out in the open and measured; the time it takes to redo it is usually hidden.)

If this is your situation, you're caught in a real bind. Unlike the first cause above, you're not the reason for the sloppy work. If the firm pays for quantity at the expense of quality, you probably can't change that.

Does this mean there's nothing you can do? No. You can encourage Emile and others to produce quality work—which may help a little. If you have some discretion over bonuses or the amount of pay increases, announce that you'll give them for quality, not quantity. Then do it.

Make sure your boss knows how of the company's preference for quantity over quality is affecting your unit. Perhaps you can enlist his help. Sooner or later, maybe managers like you and she can change the company's compensation policies.

Things to Think About

In some organizations, inspectors, senior workers, or leaders review everyone's work and redo any of the work that's substandard. Don't, *DON'T, DON'T* ever fall into this trap. Every individual should be responsible for his own work; if it wasn't done right, he redoes it. If he has to do the rework and it detracts from the bonus he or the group gets—watch how quickly the rework will drop off.

Some companies still think you get productivity by emphasizing quantity—at the expense of quality, if necessary. That's been proven wrong. The way you get productivity is by organizing for quality. When your people and your processes get it right the first time, then you'll get quality and quantity.

And If This Doesn't Quite Fit Your Situation . . .

If Emile has the reverse problem (high-quality work, but too little of it) see Problem 6-6. If he produces poor work because he won't follow the proper procedures, see Problem 5-1. If his poor quality work may result from lack of organization, see Problem 6-1.

Use Checklist 1 to develop a cure of your own.

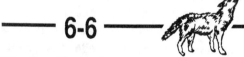

6-6

The Problem: An employee produces high-quality work, but too little of it.

The Scene

Camille is one worker you can always depend on—slow and steady. Very, very steady—and very, very slow. In the three years she's been packing here, she's never had a package returned for breakage, or incorrect address, or falling apart in shipping. But as slowly as she goes, she might as well be wrapping fancy Christmas presents. The wrapping has to be just so, and the tape, and the filler, and the label, and everything else! You admire her meticulousness, but she takes twice as long as she should. How can you hurry her up?

Possible Causes

Camille may lack confidence in her abilities. She may fear that if she goes any faster, she'll begin to make mistakes (whether that's true or not).

Camille's skills may not be well developed enough to allow her to go faster without making errors. She may do fine as long as she goes slowly, but may begin to make mistakes once she speeds up.

Camille may have a mental or physical disability that makes it impossible for her to go any faster.

Hint: If you're not sure whether Camille will begin to make mistakes when she speeds up or just thinks she'll make mistakes, the only way to find out for sure is to test her. Tell her exactly what you're doing (finding out how fast she can go without increasing her error rate) and why (because her current production isn't satisfactory). Then instruct her to pack as many boxes, start to finish, as she can in a given amount of time (half an hour, an hour, two or three hours—whatever seems reasonable in your situation). Stand nearby during the test, giving her encouragement (and checking to make sure she really is increasing her speed). Then measure her production and error rates at the end of the specified period.

Cures

If Camille lacks confidence:

Encourage her as much as you can. Let her know that you appreciate her attention to the quality of the product, but stress that quality also means on-time production—and the company won't be on time if everyone works at her rate.

Help Camille set goals for incrementally increasing her rate. If you want her eventually to pack 8 boxes an hour and she's now at

4 or 5, begin by increasing her requirement to 6, then 7, and finally 8. Congratulate her on each success, and reassure her of your confidence that she can make the next increment at the same high quality rate.

Make sure your incentive system rewards production rate as well as quality, if that's what's really important in this job. Camille may not lack confidence as much as she lacks incentive to go any faster. If pay and rewards are based on error rates exclusively, then there's no good reason, from Camille's standpoint, to go any faster—especially if her errors are likely to increase.

If Camille lacks the skills to go any faster:

Observe her as she packs several different kinds of items. Are there particular areas where she seems to have some trouble, where she hesitates or seems to have to think about each step as she completes it?

Wherever you find those hesitations or problem areas, isolate those tasks and teach them specifically. This is an area where you can probably delegate the teaching and practice monitoring to one of your better workers. Have Camille practice the tasks to mastery, that is, until she can complete them both accurately and rapidly. Once she's mastered those isolated tasks, then she can begin to combine them with the other steps in the process to speed up her overall rate.

Don't stop when she's mastered the individual steps, however. She may still have problems when she tries to put them together. In that case, you can combine the individual tasks into larger and larger units, until she has the whole process down. You may find, as you observe her combining the individual steps into a whole process, that there are parts of the job that aren't organized as well as they could be. Are all the steps in the most logical sequence? Does she have to "undo" things she's already completed to complete another step? Are the materials she needs organized so she can get to them when she needs them, or are they in the way of something else? As you observe Camille, you may find that her production problems are simply an exaggeration of difficulties everybody's having!

If Camille has a mental or physical condition that prevents her from working faster:

Decide how important speed is to the success of the operation. Can you afford to let Camille continue at her slower pace? Does her lack of errors compensate for her lower production level?

If the organization will suffer by allowing Camille to continue at her current production rate, you must look at alternatives. Can she be assigned to some other work where speed isn't as important, or where her condition won't interfere with her production? Does your company have an employment program for handicapped employees that would allow Camille to remain in your unit, working at her own speed, but that would give you some relief from work quotas?

If you cannot accommodate Camille within the company, be as tactful and sensitive as you can in terminating her. Explain to her exactly why you are taking the action, and offer her as much assistance as possible in outplacement efforts.

And If This Doesn't Quite Fit Your Situation . . .

Look at Problem 6-5 for the reverse problem. Problems 4-6 and 6-2 contain discussions of similar performance difficulties.

Use Checklist 1 to develop a cure of your own.

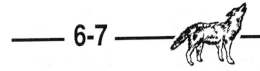

6-7

The Problem: An employee is technically your best worker but constantly disrupts the other employees.

The Scene

Paula wasn't exaggerating when she told you how disruptive Maury is. He's consistently one of your top two or three producers—but it's no wonder the others don't keep up with him. He talks constantly and—there's no other way to put it—he's loud! You're going to have to do something to put an end to it.

Possible Causes

Maury doesn't realize he's being disruptive. Sounds too simple, but it may be true. No one may have ever said anything to him about his talking.

He simply doesn't care about the others. If his pay is based on his individual production, he may not see any reason to worry about their reaction.

He's a "compulsive talker." This is how he is all the time.

Cures

No matter what the cause is:

Now that you've seen the problem for yourself, talk to Maury. Be as tactful as possible, but point out to him the effect he's having on others. Then see what his reaction is.

If he doesn't realize he's being disruptive:

Pointing out the problem may be most of what you need to do to solve it. He may be a little offended by what you say, but he'll probably begin to control himself on his own.

If he tries but has difficulties, this may be a good time to set some objectives. Can he reduce his talking to short conversations, with several minutes of silence between them? Is there any other way he can begin cutting down? Find a step he can take, then follow it with another step and another one.

Make sure that both you and the other employees notice any improvement and stroke him for it. If you don't, he may conclude no one really cares and go back to talking constantly.

If he doesn't care about his effect on others:

Most employees are sensitive to other employees' reactions and want their approval. But not all employees. Some will do what rewards them, with little or no thought for others. This is particularly true if the individual is a "loner," or someone the group doesn't particularly like.

The best cure is to base at least some of everyone's pay on the amount they produce. This will motivate the rest of the employees to deal with Maury themselves; you probably won't have to worry about the problem again. The same thing will happen if you base some of the individuals' pay on the group's performance.

What if you can't do this? Then you attack the problem head on. Make it clear to Maury how disruptive he is; make it just as clear that you're unwilling to put up with it. If he persists, warn him again and then begin applying discipline. His behavior causes a real performance problem, and you have every right to get him to stop it.

Here again, make sure that you and the other workers notice and stroke any improvement he makes. Even if he doesn't particularly want to change, this may encourage him to.

If he's a "compulsive talker":

As we've said before, don't play amateur psychologist. Talk with Maury and try to get him to stop. If he appears genuinely to want to stop but just can't seem to, he's probably going to want to keep talking, no matter what.

Before you accept this, see if the other employees can help the situation. If they're a close group and good at working together, they may be able to at least slow Maury down. Ask them to help and then see what they can accomplish.

If this fails, or if it's not practical, look for other alternatives. Perhaps you can separate Maury from the others, or put a partition around him. Perhaps he'd be willing to see a counselor and try to overcome the problem. Perhaps there's another job he could be reassigned to where his talking wouldn't matter so much (like putting him with another "talker").

If none of these work, you've arrived at the moment of truth. Be as kind and gentle as you can, but make it clear to Maury that he needs to change or else. The prospect may be enough to get him to change. Or he may get another job on his own. Or you might offer to help him find another job. If none of these work, take the appropriate action to remove him from the job.

Something to Think About

What if you don't believe Maury is really as disruptive as Paula claims? If the problem is that he's a loner, or a member of a minority group, see those problems for suggestions. But you must do something. When an employee complains to you about another, you must respond. You get the choice of how to respond: support the complainer, support the person being complained about, counsel them both—whatever is appropriate. But your worst choice is to dismiss the complaint out of hand, or listen to it and then drop it.

And If This Doesn't Quite Fit Your Situation . . .

If several people concentrate on their own productivity to the detriment of the productivity of the whole group, see Problem 1-2. If Maury may be disruptive because he is emotionally disturbed, see Problem 3-2. If his behavior may be a symptom of substance abuse, see Problem 3-3.

Use Checklist 1 to develop a cure of your own.

6-8

The Problem: An employee is a marginal performer, but an informal leader in the group.

The Scene

Gretchen is a real challenge. She's hardly one of your best workers—in fact, she's marginal at best. But people listen to her. She's never admitted to you that she's unhappy about anything, but the rest of the staff have certainly heard enough about it! And, unfortunately, they listen to her. She's stirred up resentment about your overtime schedule, and your project assignments, and your travel procedures—and probably a lot of other things you haven't even heard about yet. Not everyone pays attention when she complains, but enough do to cause you trouble. So how can you deal with her marginal performance without causing more discontent in the ranks?

Possible Causes

Neither the cause of Gretchen's marginal performance nor the source of her influence with the work group are of particular concern here. We've discussed the causes and cures of poor performance, intentional and unintentional, elsewhere. (See Chapters 4 and 6 particularly.) And it doesn't matter *why* the rest of your staff are willing to listen to Gretchen's complaints; the fact is that they do, and that's causing you problems.

Your intention here is twofold. You want to help Gretchen improve her performance and you want to stop her negative influence with your staff. This is *not* a situation where you can take the justified, but entirely ineffective, step of dealing with the performance difficulties while ignoring Gretchen's leadership role in the work group. That approach will just result in Gretchen's complaining more to her peers about your "unreasonable" demands and will do nothing to improve her performance. You *must* deal with both the performance and the influence at the same time.

This is a tough situation, and it's not one in which we can give you a neat set of steps to follow that, if performed correctly, will solve the problem successfully. What we *can* do is offer a number of suggestions, some of which will apply to your problem, some of which won't. Consider them in light of the specific characteristics of your "Gretchen" and your workforce, use the ones that you think will work, disregard the ones you think won't—and good luck!

Cures

If your other workers are not aware of the quality of Gretchen's work:

They may accept her leadership more readily than they would if they had little respect for her technical competence. In that case, it may be very effective to let your other employees see for themselves the kind of work Gretchen does. It's unlikely that they will have much faith in her critical remarks if they perceive them as a cover for her own lack of production.

NOTE: Your intention here is *not* to discredit Gretchen; that's underhanded, unworthy of you as a manager, and likely to backfire. Your intention is to structure opportunities for your staff to work with Gretchen and make their own informed decisions about her ability to form objective opinions about you and your management of the office.

To the degree that it's possible, given the kind of work your unit performs, assign some work to teams rather than to individuals. Make sure Gretchen is a part of the team and that one or two of your best workers is too. Make your expectations clear to the team members, both in terms of the product you expect at the completion of the assignment and in terms of the level of participation you expect from each of the team members. If Gretchen isn't carrying her fair share, the team will discover that very quickly.

Again to the degree possible in your particular work situation, let some decisions be made by teams rather than by individuals or by you. If your unit is supposed to develop schedules (e.g., for inventorying, for review of other units' work, for customer visits), assign a team to develop those schedules—and make sure Gretchen is part of it. The degree of cooperation she exhibits in her dealings with you will probably be reflected also in her interactions with the team members.

Establish a peer review system. Instead of checking all your employees' work yourself, set up a system in which workers review each others' products. Include Gretchen as part of the peer review group. When you set up the system, establish regular rotation dates so that employees do not become so accustomed to reviewing the work of specific individuals that they lose their objectivity. Rotating review assignments also ensures that every employee gets the chance to review and evaluate the worth of every other employee's contributions (including Gretchen's).

If Gretchen is a marginal employee in a group made up largely of marginal workers, your challenge is a very different one.

The group itself will probably not be able to see that Gretchen's contributions aren't all that great, because they're all performing at about the same level. Problems 1-1, 1-6, and 1-7 all discuss variations on the same basic theme of *organizational* productivity problems. In correcting the organization's performance deficiencies and improving their overall morale, you may solve your specific problem with Gretchen. If the rest of the group responds to your efforts, but Gretchen does not, then the steps outlined above may help *after* you've improved the productivity of the majority of your staff.

If Gretchen's performance and attitude problems stem from a dislike of the job:

Her perception of your management style and decisions will be distorted by her own unhappiness. That doesn't mean that other employees are less likely to listen to her. On the contrary, she is more likely to be listened to if she's bright and articulate and talented, but simply misplaced in her current assignment. Problem 10 in this chapter discusses steps you can take when an employee clearly doesn't like the job.

Things to Think About

An employee who is unhappy can make life miserable for you and the rest of your staff. When that employee requires correction, either because of poor performance or unacceptable conduct, the "noise" level is almost invariably going to increase, and everyone will be even more discontented. But both the unhappiness and the performance or conduct issue are problems that you can't ignore. They won't go away; they'll only get worse.

Your first approach should be to reduce the level of influence the employee has with the rest of the work group. Then, when you deal with the performance or conduct problem, the employee's attempts to stir up the work group against you won't meet with much success.

If you can't reduce the employee's negative influence, you still will have to address the performance or conduct problem. You may precipitate a crisis. But if you're being fair and reasonable, and have ensured the support of your superiors, both you and the organization will survive—a little bruised perhaps, but ready to forge ahead.

And If This Doesn't Quite Fit Your Situation . . .

Look at Problem 8-5 if the problem is the employee's friendship with your boss or Problem 8-6 if he tries to sabotage you with other employees.

Use Checklist 1 to develop a cure of your own.

6-9

The Problem: An employee is excellent but rigid and won't change with the times.

The Scene

You've finally gotten the money to put your people through a course in how to develop training systematically. All of your trainers love the method—at least all of them except Martha.

Despite all your encouragement, she hasn't tried the new method even once. Martha has always been one of your best trainers, but now she's being left behind. The new method really is better.

What do you do?

Possible Causes

Martha doesn't understand how the new methods can help her. Since she doesn't know how it could be useful, she has no motive to learn to use it.

She just doesn't want to change the ways she does things. People differ from one another. Some of us like to find a way to do something and then do it that way, period.

Hint: People have very different reasons for not wanting to change. Be sure you look and listen carefully before reaching a conclusion about Martha.

Cures

If she doesn't understand how the new methods can be helpful:

There are probably two facts you and Martha both know about "new ways of doing things." First, there are a lot of them—a sort of "fad of the quarter" or so. Second, most of them don't turn out to be that good and fade away when the next fad comes along. Before you push Martha, make sure either that this really is an improvement— and one that will last—or that it's mandated by the organization and neither you nor she have a choice whether to use it or not.

If it is a real improvement, the basic solution for Martha's reluctance is plain: get her to use the new method. If there's a formal course which will help her understand the benefits of the new methods, you may want to send her. Or you may want to have an employee who likes the methods explain their advantages to Martha.

It's important to get Martha actually using these procedures. Can you get her to work on a joint project with another employee who's good at them and likes them? This is the best kind of training, since it gets Martha actually using the new methods.

What if it's mandated, and the benefits aren't so clear? It may be more painful for Martha, and she may never like it—but she still has to adapt. You'll probably have to apply the motivation; then the training will help.

Another question: do the new procedures mean that employees have to organize their jobs in a different way? Does Martha have to plan her lessons differently, or develop them in a different sequence? If so, that may be the problem—not the new procedures themselves.

If she just doesn't want to change the way she's always done things:

While some people find changing exciting, for others it's uncomfortable, even threatening. Martha may be in the latter group. She just plain doesn't like to change.

This is a very different situation from the other. You ought not conclude that this is the case until you've made sure Martha's resistance isn't from another, more specific cause. If there doesn't seem to be another cause, though, it may be that change itself is painful for Martha.

Here, your options may be limited. If Martha is still producing satisfactorily, it's probably best to let her continue to do it her way. However, if "her way" starts to interfere with others' production, you need to act.

What you have to do may depend on Martha's situation in the work unit. If others are willing to spend some time supporting her, and it doesn't significantly interfere with their work, she may be able to keep doing her job the same old way. If she's very close to retirement, the best solution may be for everyone to adjust to her for a few months.

And if none of these is true? Then the time has come for a very frank talk with Martha. Tell her that as of such-and-such a date you'll expect her to be using the new methods, and using them proficiently. Give her enough advance warning for her to start changing, if she chooses to do so.

This may be a very emotional time for her. Be empathetic and considerate—but be firm. When she sees that you mean it she'll probably conclude that changing is advantageous, practical, and worthwhile. In other words, she'll change.

If she doesn't, if the day comes and she's not ready for it, you'll need to take action. Perhaps she can be reassigned to another position in the organization that will suit her better. in. As a last resort, you may simply have to let her go. But that is the very, very last resort—particularly if she's been a good worker and a good producer.

Things to Think About

The problem of employees (and managers) who don't want to change is getting more acute all the time. New technology and new methods and procedures are being implemented constantly. Your best defense against employees who cling rigidly to the way they've always done things it to keep them from always doing the same thing. Vary their jobs, reassign them to different jobs—do whatever you have to do to keep them (and yourself) from getting in a rut.

There's one other point. There are lots of fads today in the business world. We're getting close to the "fad-of-the-quarter" level. You may not be able to control the fad changes that higher management imposes on you. You can certainly do your best not to add to them. Think through the changes you want carefully, limit yourself to the ones that are practical, and then stick with them until they work.

And If This Doesn't Quite Fit Your Situation . . .

Problems 1-8 and 5-4 describe similar situations in which employees don't want to change.

Use Checklist 1 to develop a cure of your own.

—— 6-10 ——

The Problem: An employee clearly doesn't like the job.

The Scene

It doesn't seem to matter what you do, Chuck just doesn't like his new assignment. He's never told you in so many words, and his work is acceptable, if not wonderful—but it's obvious from his lack of enthusiasm (and the fact that he's applying for other jobs as fast as he finds out about them) that he'd really rather be someplace else.

Possible Causes

Chuck may not feel comfortable with the assignment he has. He may be accustomed to being the "star" in the office—either because he's the best at what he does or because he has a unique role—and this assignment doesn't offer that opportunity. Chuck will either have to adjust to this new role or be miserable until he can find something else.

Chuck may not find the work interesting. It may just not be in a field that he has any interest in. It may be an administrative position—when Chuck's really a "people person." It may involve a lot of travel—when Chuck would rather be at home. Or it may just involve a subject area that Chuck doesn't care about—and so he's bored.

Chuck may not feel that he fits in with the rest of the staff. They may have different interests or styles of interaction than he's comfortable with. And so he separates himself from the group and tries to think of ways to get out.

Hint: This problem is only a Mouse as long as Chuck's dislike of the job isn't reflected in performance or conduct problems. While you may believe that employees are responsible for their own happiness or unhappiness (and they are), it is still in your best interest to help them adjust to the situation or find another job. An employee who doesn't like what he's doing 8 hours a day, 250-plus days a year, isn't likely to be very productive—and may develop performance or conduct problems over time.

Cures

If Chuck doesn't feel comfortable with his assignment:

Make sure he knows how to do the work. Problem 4-6 provides some tips on working with employees to be sure they learn what they need to know to do the job. If Chuck has been a "star" in the past and has the opportunity to learn the new assignment, he's got a good chance of being a star again.

Talk to Chuck about the aspects of the assignment he's not comfortable with. Think about how you can change the emphasis of the job a little to accommodate his specific goals. If it's not possible to restructure the position, let Chuck know up front, and help him in his efforts to find a more satisfactory assignment.

If Chuck isn't interested in the work:

See Problem 4-2 for steps to take when an employee is assigned work in which he's not interested. Offer your support to Chuck in finding an assignment that more closely matches his interests, but make it clear that you expect him to continue to do his best for you until the new job comes through.

If Chuck doesn't feel that he fits in with the rest of the staff:

See Problem 3-9, which offers advice on situations when an employee doesn't relate to the group. You'll be working with the rest of your unit as well as Chuck to try to help him become more a part of things.

Something to Think About

An individual may not fit a job for three different reasons:

- He may not have the native ability to do it.

- He may not want to do it.

- He may not have an affinity for that kind of work—that is, no matter how good he is or how hard he tries, the work just isn't satisfying to him.

When you have a real mismatch between a person and his or her job, your best bet is to help them get a job that fits them as soon as possible. Don't waste your time verbally beating on them or otherwise trying to "motivate" them.

And If This Doesn't Quite Fit Your Situation . . .

Look at Problems 4-2, 4-5, 4-6, 5-2, 5-5, 5-6, 5-9, and 6-3 for performance problems which could be a symptom of dislike of the job.

Use Checklist 1 to develop a cure of your own.

7

Troubleshooting Problems Caused by the Intentional Misbehavior of an Employee

— 7-1 —  —————

The Problem: An employee is one of your best workers but has lied under oath in an investigation.

The Scene

You stare sadly at the report lying open on your desk. It's all too clear that Jeremy Cook lied in the investigation. The report says that on at least two occasions Mike Murgaty, one of your subordinate supervisors, approached Jeremy to try to talk him into participating in his land development scheme. But Jeremy denied that Mike had ever discussed the subject with him. Jeremy's one of your best workers—reliable, hard-working, and trustworthy—or so you thought. But a lie is a lie, isn't it?

Possible Causes

A lie is a lie? Well, yes—and no. Any time an employee lies, it chips away at the bond of trust which is the basis of all of the relationships we form, at work and elsewhere. And the answer to that breach of trust is usually fairly automatic: An employee who lies is fired, since you never know, from now on, when you can believe him and when you can't.

But there are some extenuating circumstances that require that you at least consider an exception to that rule. You may still decide that you can't afford to keep the employee on the payroll any longer—either because you can't trust him or because you have to make a clear statement to the rest of the staff. But in certain situations, you owe it to the employee to at least consider some alternatives:

Jeremy may have believed he was expected to lie in the investigation. Particularly if the employee being investigated is in a sensitive or highly visible position, or if he's one of the company favorites, Jeremy may have thought that he was supposed to protect the employee and the organization. His dishonesty may actually have been misguided loyalty to the company.

Jeremy may have been pressured to lie. He may not have decided on his own that he was expected to lie, others in positions of influence over him may have fostered that impression. He may even have been threatened with loss of pay, or stature, or position—or with physical harm.

Jeremy may have lied to protect himself. This is the most likely situation, and the least forgivable. Jeremy may have been implicated in the wrongdoing being investigated, or in some other wrongdoing that is likely to be revealed in the course of the investigation. He may have lied simply to keep his own transgressions from being discovered.

Hint: In deciding on the appropriate action to take, you need to consider not only the employee's motivation, but also the effect of your decision on the company (including the rest of the staff). Your bottom line position must be that lying, or any action that undermines your trust in an employee, is intolerable. If it's well known in the company that the employee lied, then you have no choice but to take some corrective action. Regardless of the employee's misguided loyalty or perception of outside pressure, you must make it clear to the rest of the staff that you expect them to be open, honest, and trustworthy. If your staff can't trust one another, you can't expect customers to trust you either.

Cures

If Jeremy believed he was expected to lie:

First, be sure that Jeremy really did believe he was expected to lie and that this isn't just an excuse for his unacceptable actions. Even if Jeremy has been entirely trustworthy in the past, remember that he has just broken that trust, so anything he says is suspect until he has proven himself again.

If you're convinced that Jeremy is being honest with you about his reasons, explain to him what you would have expected of him in this situation, and why his attempts to be a loyal employee were misguided. Make sure he knows that he can come to you if a similar situation arises for clarification of your expectations and support for his honest testimony.

Decide what corrective action is appropriate. If Jeremy lied about something relatively minor that had no material effect on the outcome of the investigation, if his false testimony is not a matter of public knowledge, and if it's clear that he gained *in no way* from his lie, you may be able to let him off with just a warning. If any of those conditions are not met, take corrective action in accordance with your company's disciplinary policies. Your Personnel Department will be able to help you decide on an appropriate penalty and work through the required procedures.

If Jeremy was pressured to lie:

You will need to do an investigation of your own here. Find out who Jeremy felt was pressuring him. Get names, dates, places, records of conversations. Have Jeremy document his contacts in writing. Talk to other witnesses in the original investigation who may have been pressured by the same person(s) to see if they were approached. If your company has an Investigations or Security division, ask for their help in following up. Your Personnel Department may also be able to help you investigate Jeremy's allegations. If, at any point, it looks like there is possible criminal activity involved, go immediately to your Legal Department or to the police in your location to report what you've discovered.

After you've collected all the information you can, make a decision about whether Jeremy had good reason to believe that he was being pressured to lie in the investigation. Remember, there are many kinds of pressure, some more subtle than others. It doesn't take a direct threat to convince an employee that he needs to listen, but you do need some reasonable basis for Jeremy's perception of outside pressure.

If it appears that Jeremy was pressured and reasonably expected some harm to come to him if he didn't lie, explain to him how you would have wanted him to handle the situation. Make it clear to him that he could have come to you, that you would have supported him and taken action against those who were pressuring him. Some minor corrective action may still be appropriate (e.g., a reprimand), but it could also be appropriate to let Jeremy off with a warning.

If Jeremy misperceived pressure where none existed, you will need to take stronger measures. Explain clearly and firmly to him the standards of honesty to which you expect your employees to adhere. Make sure Jeremy understands what it was that he did that was wrong and *why* it was wrong. To make sure other employees get the message, you may still need to take some disciplinary action against Jeremy—perhaps write up the incident for his personnel file.

Decide what corrective action is appropriate. If Jeremy has been a good employee and trustworthy until now, it may not be necessary to fire him. A suspension or a demotion to a position of lesser trust may be sufficient. But if there's any doubt about your ability to trust him in a similar situation again, terminating his employment is the appropriate action.

If Jeremy lied to protect himself:

The appropriate course here is clear. Make sure Jeremy knows what he did that was wrong and why it was wrong. Then separate him from your organization.

Let him know that his dishonesty is a matter of record and, subject to your company's policies, that you'll let his prospective employers know the reasons for his termination when they do reference checks.

Particularly if you work for a large company with multiple offices, make sure your Personnel Department has documentation to support the termination and a recommendation that Jeremy not be rehired within the company. Ask them to keep the records on file so that he isn't inadvertently rehired by another division who doesn't know his history with the organization.

Something to Think About

While it should go without saying that employees are expected to be honest and trustworthy, this might be a good time to issue a policy letter on the subject. Have it signed at as high a level in the company as you can, then present it to your employees with your own personal endorsement.

And If This Doesn't Quite Fit Your Situation . . .

See Problem 7-4 if the employee lied about completing work. If the problem is that your boss expects you to lie or commit other unethical acts, see Problems 9-1 and 9-2.

Use Checklist 2 to develop a cure of your own.

—— 7-2 ——

The Problem: An employee embarrassed you in front of your boss.

The Scene

You can't believe it! You assured your boss that everything was on track for the Smithson job, then called Joe Esch in to confirm it. Instead, Joe told you pointedly that he wasn't doing anything on it because you hadn't gotten him the spec sheets you promised. You got rid of Joe, mumbled the best excuse you could think of to your boss, and tried to look calm as he left. Now it's time to deal with Joe.

Possible Causes

Joe was just giving you an answer. For some reason, he didn't understand what its consequences would be.

Joe is angry because you're holding up a project you assigned him. Maybe he really has to have the spec sheets before he can go on.

Joe's been holding a grudge against you and this was his chance to "get" you. Sometimes employees have long memories.

Joe wants to get you replaced as his boss.

Hint: Watch your anger! This kind of situation really gets under the skin of most managers. That's okay—but don't take any action to resolve it until you've cooled down.

Cures

No matter what the cause is:

You guessed it—you begin by talking with Joe—after you've calmed down. Give him every chance to tell you why he did it.

Then, no matter why Joe did it, make it clear that he's not to do it again. How clear you have to be depends on the situation—but don't leave any question in his mind about what will happen if he repeats the behavior.

If Joe was just giving you an answer:

As painful as it is, this is the easiest situation to deal with. Explain to Joe just what his response caused, and how he should have handled it. Then make sure he knows not to do it again. Finally, explain that you're not angry with him, since he acted out of ignorance.

If Joe is angry because you're holding up his project:

Perhaps Joe is a conscientious worker. Perhaps you really emphasized the due date when you assigned it to him, and he wants to get it done on schedule. Whatever the cause, to Joe you're holding up his work.

You have two issues to deal with here. First, face up to your failure to give him the materials he needed. Perhaps he could have reminded you that you promised them—but if you made the commitment he has no responsibility to serve as your memory. You blew it. Give him the spec sheets, or tell him exactly when you'll have them for him.

Second, tell Joe clearly that he's not to do that to you again. This may make him angry, but stick to it. Explain how it hurts him as well as you.

If Joe's been holding a grudge against you:

You may have to probe a bit to find this out. But it's important that you do.

When you find out what caused the grudge, try to work it through. Is Joe unhappy over work assignments, or over a chewing out you gave him? This can be an opportunity to surface the issue and lay it to rest.

While you may not deal with it now, there's a question you need to ask: Does this point to a continuing problem in your relationship with Joe—and perhaps with others in your unit? If it does, take this incident as the occasion to deal with the underlying problem.

If Joe wants to get you replaced:

This specific incident is probably the least of your worries. But you have to deal with it. If what Joe did was really blatant, you may want to take some disciplinary action.

The deeper issue is Joe's wish to get rid of you. Is there something specific you did that offended him—and that you might be able to settle now? Sounds like you need to do it. Any manager who has employees working to get him removed has a serious problem—one worth every reasonable effort to resolve.

What if no resolution is possible? Hopefully, Joe is the only one who really wants you out of your job. If that's the case, you might want to see about getting him reassigned. (His behavior in front of your boss may help you get your boss's support for this.) If there's no realistic step you can take, just stay aware of the situation and be prepared. Joe may go too far, and then he may be the one who leaves—whether he wants to or not.

Suppose most of your employees would like to see you taken out of the job? Why? If it's because you're carrying out your boss's direction to "shape up" the unit, make sure they know that you have his support. If it's because your supervisory style creates unnecessary friction—well, do you have any good reasons not to change it?

Things to Think About

We've been concentrating on how you handle Joe—but there are two other issues you can't overlook. First, it's important to handle your boss. You can't undo the damage that Joe's comments did. You can make sure that you get the spec sheets to Joe, revise any dates that you have to—and then assure your boss that everything is okay. If Joe had an ulterior motive, mention it to your boss, but not as an attempt to get yourself off the hook. (By the way, is Joe behind, so that the project due date will have to slip? Don't let it; do whatever you have to do. Remember, you said it was on track—your credibility is at stake here.)

The other problem is you. *Why* didn't you get the spec sheets to Joe? You intended to but it just slipped your mind? Remember what good intentions pave the way to. Do what you have to do to see that this kind of thing doesn't happen again. From now on, when you make a commitment, keep it—period.

And If This Doesn't Quite Fit Your Situation . . .

If the cause of the problem was that Joe argues with you when he disagrees with your decisions, see Problem 5-7. If the problem was his unintentional or intentional failure to perform, see the problems in Chapters 4, 5 and 6 and Problem 7-4. If Joe criticized you in public, see Problem 8-4.

Use Checklist 2 to develop a cure of your own.

7-3

The Problem: An employee uses company property at home for his personal use.

The Scene

"Nice poster," you observed as you walked past the bulletin board. "I see Steve's neighborhood association is having a rummage sale next weekend."

But wait! That type style and those graphics look terribly familiar. Steve took the computer home to finish that design proposal a couple of nights ago; it looks like he finished something else while he was at it! That's not supposed to happen. One thing they're firm about here is company property for company use—only.

Possible Causes

Steve may not be aware of company policy. Especially if he's new to the company or if he just began taking the equipment home to work, he may not know what the rules are.

Steve may not agree with the rule. He may have made a conscious decision to violate this company policy.

Steve may have a disregard for rules and restrictions in general. This may not be an isolated incident, but Steve's usual mode of operation.

Hint: As with any suspected violation of company rules, it's critical that you get the facts before you act. Is the software that Steve used commercially available? Might he have bought software identical to what you're using at work for his own use? Can you prove that Steve used company property? Especially if he made an honest mistake or if he made a conscious decision to break the rule, he may just tell you. But you can't do anything until you know what the real situation is.

Cures

If Steve isn't aware of the company's policy:

A word of instruction is probably the only action you need to take in this situation. Tell Steve what the company's rules are and, as clearly as you can, explain why the rules exist. If you have any authority to make exceptions to the rules, explain what the limits of your authority are and how Steve should request an exception.

You might also take this opportunity to make sure everyone in your unit knows what the company's policies are—on this and maybe one or two other things that people seem to have trouble remembering. The rules may not be all that meaningful to the employees who have to follow them, so a friendly reminder now and again doesn't hurt.

If Steve doesn't agree with the rule:

Discuss with Steve his reasons for not following the company's policy. Explain the purpose of the rule and what it is intended to accomplish; listen to any ideas Steve has about how the same purpose could be accomplished differently. Let him know that you'll try to push for changes in those areas where his ideas show promise. (If your company has a formal suggestion program, encourage Steve to submit his ideas through that channel so he can get credit for them.)

At the same time that you're listening to Steve's criticisms and recommendations for improving the current system, remind him of his obligations as an employee. Regardless of his opinions about company rules and policies, as an employee of the organization he's expected to follow directions first and *then* question them. Make sure he understands that refusal to obey a company rule or policy is insubordination and is subject to severe penalties.

If this is the first time Steve's failed to follow the rule, your warning and explanation are probably sufficient. If this is a repetition of similar behavior, however, you'll need to take stronger disciplinary action. (See the cure described below.)

If Steve has a general disregard for rules and restrictions:

This is a serious problem. Organization without rules and limits is disorganization and only confuses and disturbs people—it doesn't "free" them from anything except a sense of purpose and order. If Steve does have a general disregard for rules and restrictions, chances are this isn't the first time he's exhibited it. You may even have warned or disciplined him in the past for similar behavior. Your specific actions in this case depend considerably on his history with the company.

If this is the first time you've personally had to deal with Steve in this kind of incident, and if this offense is relatively minor, a warning is appropriate—preferably one documented in his employee records, either in your office or in the Personnel Department.

If this is not the first problem of its kind you've had with Steve, harsher measures are necessary—a formal write-up in his personnel file, a suspension, or maybe even termination if this has happened several times before and lesser remedies haven't corrected the misconduct.

In any case where you have to warn or discipline an employee (whether for failing to follow rules or for something else), it's crucial that you explain why you're taking the action. The purpose of discipline is almost always to correct behavior rather than to "punish" employees. At the same time you impose the penalty, make sure Steve understands not only what he did wrong, but what behavior you expect in the future.

And If This Doesn't Quite Fit Your Situation . . .

Look at Problems 8-1, 8-2, and 8-7 for other cases where an employee doesn't follow rules or directions.
Use Checklist 2 to develop a cure of your own.

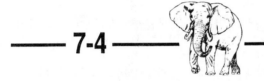

—— 7-4 ——

The Problem: An employee may have lied about having completed an assignment.

The Scene

"Charlene, are you sure you don't have the production report?"
"Weldon, I *know* what a production report looks like, and I can promise you it never got to us."
"Dammit! I specifically asked Vic if he'd finished it before he left yesterday—and he told me he had. I'd never have let him take the day off today if I'd known it wasn't done. I'll grab him as soon as he walks in tomorrow and get him to finish it."

Possible Causes

There's been a mistake somewhere. Vic finished the production report, but it didn't get to Charlene.
There was no mistake—Vic lied.
Vic may have lied. The situation looks suspicious, but . . .
Hint: This may seem like a small thing. After all, it was only one report, and it was only one day late. That's almost beside the point. Employees need to live up to their commitments, or you won't

be able to rely on them. You also don't want employees around whom you can't trust. This is serious, and Vic needs to understand how serious it is.

Cures

No matter what the cause is:

Once again, begin by calming down, then call Vic in and confront him with the situation. Give him every chance to explain, but ask the hard questions if you have to.

If there's been a mistake somewhere:

Find out what happened to the production report and get it to Charlene. Do whatever you have to do to see that the problem isn't repeated. (This could mean revising an office procedure.)

If the mistake happened because Vic was sloppy or didn't follow through, counsel him. The problem was embarrassing to you and to the unit—as well as to him—and he needs to make sure it never happens again.

If Vic lied:

The only serious question you're facing is whether to keep Vic or fire him. This may seem like a harsh approach to one small lie—but now you don't know how many times in the past Vic lied and you didn't catch it.

If Vic is a good employee and this is the first time anything like this ever happened, it may be enough to give him a couple of weeks off without pay. It's also possible—though not likely—that there were extenuating circumstances which might permit a lesser penalty. Be understanding, but don't forget how serious the offense was.

In this circumstance, you also have to remember the effect of your action on others. If you merely "slap Vic's wrist," it will communicate to the rest of your employees that you don't think lying is too serious. They may decide to try it—and then you and they will be in real trouble.

If Vic may have lied:

Suppose this is what happened. You're deeply suspicious of Vic, and no one can find the report. Then, three hours after he returns to work, he "discovers" the report in a desk drawer and immediately carries it to Charlene's unit. He apologies, explaining that he thought he'd put in the office mail but that it got stuck in some other material. Did he really misplace it, or did he rush and get it done as soon as he got back?

There's no way you can find out for sure—this time. You *can* talk with Vic, and you can make two points loudly and clearly:

- The situation looks extremely suspicious. Even if he did misplace the report, he's raised a question in everyone's mind. It will be that much harder for you and others to trust him the next time.

- Even if he's being completely honest, he dropped the ball. He knew finishing the report before he left was a condition of taking the day off. He should have made absolutely sure that either Charlene's unit or you had the report.

Whichever is the situation, he's put a question mark by his performance. Now it's up to him to perform so well that the question mark gets removed.

Things to Think About

Lying is an extremely serious offense. It not only destroys the trust between employee and manager, but it calls the whole past performance of the individual into question. It's effect is far beyond the immediate incident.

This works both ways. If you lie to your employees and get found out—and sooner or later you will get found out—it destroys your credibility and any trust they have in you. There's virtually nothing you can accomplish by lying that's worth that.

And If This Doesn't Quite Fit Your Situation . . .

Look at Problem 6-1 if Vic may have intended to produce the report but fouled it up because of poor organization. Problem 6-2 covers another situation where an employee doesn't deliver what he promised.

Use Checklist 2 to develop a cure of your own.

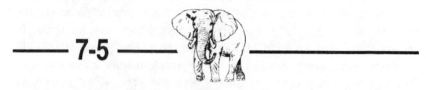

7-5

The Problem: An employee is trying to discredit a co-worker.

The Scene

"You'll never believe what Vivian just did," Ross confided at lunch yesterday. "She told the people on the Willenbacher account that she could get them a 20% price break if they signed a contract in 15 days! Can you believe it? That's the only reason she got that contract in so fast. She thinks she's "Queen of the Hill" right now—but *I*'d never stoop to a trick like that!"

Oh, no? You know why Vivian closed that deal so quickly; you've been working with her on it since the beginning. And there was nothing underhanded about it. So who does Ross think he's fooling? And why is he out to get Vivian?

Possible Causes

Ross may be jealous of the attention Vivian is getting. He may crave the same attention and think it's easier for him to shoot down someone else than to prove himself.

Ross may be trying to sabotage Vivian's chances for advancement—whether a promotion or some reward like a bonus or public recognition. This cause is related to the first, but the intent to harm is greater.

Ross may have misunderstood the facts. He may just be repeating a version of the story he heard from someone else. That version may have been distorted either intentionally or unintentionally farther up the line.

Hint: Unless Ross genuinely misunderstood the situation and is inadvertently passing on bad information, it doesn't make a lot of difference what his true intentions are. Just as the trust between supervisors and subordinates is critical to the operation of any group, the trust among the members of the group is also critical. Whenever you have a situation in which one of your employees is trying to discredit another, there are two things you need to accomplish: (1) You must make it clear to the employee at fault that you will not tolerate that behavior, and (2) you must do all you can to repair the damage to the offended worker's reputation.

Cures

If Ross intended to discredit Vivian, whether because he's jealous of the attention or because he wants to keep her from getting some benefit:

Let him know *immediately* that you're aware of what he's doing and order him to stop spreading the falsehoods.

If this is the first time he's engaged in this behavior and if the damage to Vivian is minimal, you may let him off with just a warning—preferably a documented one. Make sure that he understands that you consider his conduct unacceptable and that you will deal harshly with any repetition of this behavior.

If he has a history of similar conduct, or if Vivian has really been hurt by his rumors, you'll need to take much more severe action. Termination wouldn't be out of line, especially if yours is a business where cooperation and teamwork are essential. If competition among employees is encouraged in your line of work, lesser measures are appropriate. But even then, it's important that Ross learn from this experience the limits of acceptable behavior—that you can compete just as well, if not better in the long run, by improving yourself rather than by discrediting others.

If Ross was inadvertently passing on bad information:

Let Ross know that his information is incorrect, tell him the real story of how Vivian pulled off this brilliant feat, and enlist his help in undoing the damage he's done. Require that he talk again to people to whom he repeated the wrong story and give them the right version.

Give Ross a warning about trusting everything he hears "on the street." Especially if he's new or if yours is a competitive business, make sure he knows the dangers of turning into a dupe for someone else's plans to discredit others. Express your confidence in his own good intentions and his ability to learn to distinguish those sources he can trust from those he can't.

In either case:

You need to take some positive steps to restore Vivian's good reputation. You can begin by spreading the word among your staff of Vivian's good work—perhaps offering it as an example of a strategy others might want to copy.

You might consider also some public recognition of Vivian's achievement. If the circumstances are appropriate, your repetition of the true story and stated approval of Vivian's actions will go far in overcoming the negative effects of others' gossip.

And If This Doesn't Quite Fit Your Situation . . .

Look at Problem 8-6, which describes an employee who's trying to sabotage *you* rather than a co-worker.

Use Checklist 2 to develop a cure of your own.

7-6

The Problem: An employee is habitually late for work.

The Scene

As you walk through the work area, you notice that Chuck's desk is empty. You glance at your watch; it's already fifteen minutes past starting time. He didn't ask for any time off, so there's only one likely conclusion you can draw—he's late again. Sure enough, as you finish your errand and walk back, there's Chuck rushing in. This has got to stop!

Possible Causes

Chuck has family responsibilities that take time in the morning.

You've been letting him and others get away with being late and not saying anything. He's concluded it doesn't matter to you if he gets in late.

He's beginning to develop a bad habit.

This is the first sign of a serious personal problem. He may be drinking to excess, or abusing other drugs.

Hint: Just one employee coming in "a little late" may not seem like much. When this happens and you don't seem to care, it sends a message to other employees. The message may be that you don't care, or that you're a "weak" supervisor, or that you play favorites or . . . . All of the messages are bad ones.

Cures

No matter what the cause is:

Need we say it yet again? Begin by talking with Chuck—and don't put it off. The rest of the office is probably watching already, to see whether you're going to deal with the problem.

If you're really angry, though, put off talking with him long enough to cool down. It doesn't hurt for Chuck to know you're unhappy with him—but you want to be able to listen objectively to what he has to say for himself.

If Chuck has family responsibilities:

It wasn't too long ago that mothers were the ones who were late because they had to get kids off to school. Not any longer. Many husbands perform these chores, either because they want to or because the wife has to leave before they do. And it's not just kids anymore; more and more working people have to take care of aging parents.

If that's the situation, and Chuck is otherwise a good worker, make whatever accommodations you can to his situation. Will it help if he starts his workday later and then puts in a full day? Can he start a little late and make up the difference by taking a short lunch? Could you even consider "flexitime" for the entire unit?

The important point is that if Chuck has honest reasons for not getting to work at the normal time, it's proper to fit his work schedule to his personal schedule. If you can't, of course, then you have to deal with his tardiness as a performance problem (see Problem 6-9). But try very hard to avoid that.

There's one other important aspect of the problem. Why hasn't Chuck told you? He's been late several times—he should have taken the initiative to explain this to you. Even if his reasons for tardiness are the best and you do accommodate his situation, you need to counsel him on this point.

If you've been letting him (and perhaps others) get away with being late:

You've been sending them the message that it's okay to be "a little late"—whatever a little late is. Chuck figures that if you don't care, he doesn't care.

It's time to stop that foolishness—*your* foolishness—right away. That doesn't mean chew out Chuck and then ignore the problem again until it hits you in the face. It means having an honest talk with him, admitting that you've been getting lax, and then making it clear that you won't permit tardiness in the future. If you've been letting others get away with it, talk with them—either singly or in a group.

Chuck or one of the others will probably test you on this, quite possibly the next morning. Be ready for it. There's no point in getting mad; after all, you helped cause the problem. But confront the situation and be very firm about it. That will probably end the testing. If it doesn't, do some serious counseling, even writing up the offenders.

If Chuck is beginning to develop a bad habit:

He may have been a good worker, so you didn't want to push him the first time or two. But now his tardiness is turning into a habit—and it's time to stop it.

Talk to Chuck, make it clear what your standards are. If he makes excuses, brand them as excuses and reject them. If he has poor work habits, he may not think that tardiness is that important. Make it clear to him that it is.

Don't be surprised if he resents this and gets angry. Just accept it, but repeat that you won't tolerate the tardiness. Then, if he's tardy again, counsel him immediately. You'll probably want to write him up this time.

Keep the pressure on. If Chuck likes his job, he'll start getting there on time. If he doesn't, treat it as a performance problem and deal with it that way.

If this is the first sign of a serious personal problem:

Chuck may be drinking too much, so it's hard for him to get going in the morning. He might be producing the same result by abusing other drugs. Perhaps his home life is bad, so that it's emotionally difficult for him to start the day.

There are dozens of possible causes. If Chuck is a normally good worker who's suddenly starting to have bad work habits, or if the excuses he gives you don't hold up at all, he may well have this kind of problem.

Look at Problems 3-1, 3-2, 3-3 and 3-5 for suggestions on how to deal with an individual who has a serious personal problem.

Something to Think About

It's only natural to give a good worker some slack. If Chuck is a good worker, you don't want to hassle him just because he's late a time or two. No—but you don't want to let him set a pattern either. It's possible to talk about his tardiness without being angry. That's what you need to do, just as soon as you see it's not an isolated case.

And If This Doesn't Quite Fit Your Situation . . .

Look at Problem 1-10 if the problem is that several employees (or even all of your whole work unit) are late, take long lunch periods, etc. If Chuck is nearing retirement and his lateness may be connected to that, see Problem 4-8.

Use Checklist 2 to develop a cure of your own.

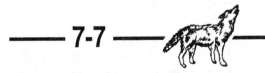

The Problem: An employee engages in horseplay and practical jokes on the job.

The Scene

Bill is such a clown! The trouble is that not everybody's laughing. He locked Sara out of her office last week—and then forgot where he hid the keys. He put glue on Chris' pen—right before a meeting with an important client. He's well-intentioned: He thinks the pressure of the job is getting to some of the group, and he's trying to lighten things up. But his efforts are backfiring. Instead of making people feel better, he's making them feel worse. This has got to stop!

Possible Causes

Bill may not realize that his behavior is inappropriate in this setting. He may honestly be trying just to lighten up the atmosphere.

Bill's practical jokes may mask real hostility towards his co-workers. He may not even recognize his true motives. But practical jokes and horseplay are often a way of "getting back" at other people without the stigma of more overtly hostile acts (like insults and fighting).

Hint: The degree to which horseplay and practical jokes can be tolerated in a work environment depends on the characteristics of the environment itself. In some, particularly blue-collar settings, the behavior may be fairly well accepted and even encouraged within specified limits. In white-collar environments and in industrial settings where security and safety are especially important, practical jokes and "horsing around" are generally not tolerated. It's your call, based on your knowledge of your own work setting and its norms of behavior, whether this is really a WOLF or a MOUSE.

Cures

If Bill doesn't realize that his behavior is inappropriate:

Take Bill aside and explain to him not only *that* his behavior is inappropriate but also *why* it's inappropriate. Make this as non-threatening, non-confrontational a session as you can. Let him know that you respect his intentions, and elicit his suggestions on other ways you and he could work to reduce the pressures the rest of the staff feel.

Try to channel Bill's concerns in more productive ways. Ask him to participate in team-building efforts or in planning office social events that might help bring people together and reduce tension.

If Bill's practical jokes are an outlet for masked hostilities:

Discuss with Bill what his real motives are in horsing around on the job. (He may or may not tell you, depending on how much he trusts you.) Try to find out if he's jealous of the attention other workers are getting, if he's insecure about his own standing in the company, if he perceives that the others are competing with him, or what other concerns might make him want to "get back" at other workers.

If you can identify the root cause, work through Bill's concerns with him. Where you can, explain how he may have misperceived situations or events. Discuss how he can cope more effectively with any real problems that exist and avoid conflicts in the future.

At the same time that you're working through the underlying relationship problems with Bill, make clear to him the unacceptability of his behavior. Explain the consequences of his practical jokes, both to the individual employees and to the organization. Chris' gluey pen may not only have lost him a client, but may also have lost the company (and Bill himself) later referrals.

Warn Bill that continued practical jokes and horsing around may result in harsher penalties in the future. Make it clear that you've had enough and that, if Bill doesn't cut out the joking on his own, he won't be laughing any more when he's being disciplined for it.

And If This Doesn't Quite Fit Your Situation . . .

Look at Problem 6-7 if the employee is otherwise a good worker but disrupts other workers. If it's his irritating personal habits that cause the problem, see Problem 3-10.

Use Checklist 2 to develop a cure of your own.

── 7-8 ──

The Problem: An employee is frequently absent during hunting season, always with a doctor's excuse.

The Scene

"I'm sorry I was out last Thursday and Friday," Harold says as he hands you the doctor's slip. "You can see that I had one of those viruses that's running around. Kept me in bed until last night."

You glance at the doctor's slip. Sure enough, it's the same doctor as the last two times. In ordinary circumstances, you'd probably wonder about his absences. Since they've come right in the middle of deer-hunting season, you don't wonder—you know. But how do you stop it?

Possible Causes

Harold really has been sick. The coincidence with hunting season really is just that—a coincidence.

Harold went hunting, and the doctor is willing to cover for him.

Cures

No matter what the cause is:

Do you start by talking with Harold? No, not this time. You start by sitting down and taking stock of the situation. How good a worker is Harold? Is he off sick a great deal, or just a few days during hunting season? Does his absence really handicap production, or can you spare him then? How do the other employees feel about his being off (if you know)?

What you do depends on the answers to these questions. If the answer to them is positive, if Harold is a good worker who's seldom off and doesn't hurt production—you're probably best off just to ignore the whole matter. If he's not that good, or if his absences affect productivity, you need to try to deal with it.

One last point. If Harold starts setting a trend, if others start being "sick" when they want a day or two off, it's time to deal with the situation. It doesn't matter whether Harold is a good worker, etc., etc.

If you decide to deal with the situation, brace yourself for a tough struggle. The odds are that this won't be an easy one.

If Harold really is sick:

How are you going to find out? Probably the best way is to level with Harold about your suspicions and see how he reacts. If he strongly protests his innocence, ask him to call his doctor and authorize him to talk to you about his illness. If Harold won't do this, you probably need to assume that his illness is just a cover and proceed accordingly.

If the doctor says he really was ill and satisfies you on that point, apologize to Harold. Hopefully, he'll take it graciously.

If Harold probably went hunting and the doctor is covering for him:

You have a sticky situation. If neither Harold nor the doctor is willing to cooperate with you, it's very difficult to get far.

Some companies expect supervisors to check up on "sick" employees in person, or they send a nurse to do so. We don't recommend this as a regular policy. We don't recommend it in special situations unless you're virtually certain the person is using sickness as an excuse to get time off. If you are certain, it may be the only way you can check up effectively.

If you do visit Harold's house and he's not home, you've no choice but to follow through to the finish. Give Harold any chance to explain—or to hang himself—when he comes back to work. Then, if he has no reasonable explanation, throw the book at him. (Remember, we said not to tackle the problem unless the situation really demanded it.)

Things to Think About

It's offensive to firms and managers to think that an employee can get away with something like this—but they can. One of us stood helplessly by in a situation where a doctor certified an employee as disabled so she could get her disability pension, then certified her as able to work so she could collect unemployment insurance. It's not easy to tell when to live with the situation and when to tackle it.

If a particular doctor regularly certifies what you believe are phony illnesses, see if your company permits you to get a second medical opinion. If so, routinely get this second opinion when that doctor certifies that an employee is unable to work.

You might also check with other supervisors. If they're having the same problem, the group of you may be able to work together to stop it. At this point, find a doctor you trust and ask him for advice. He may be able to suggest an effective approach to the problem.

And If This Doesn't Quite Fit Your Situaion . . .

If numerous employees are "sick" at suspicious times (football season, good golfing weather, etc.), you may have a problem with the morale and or discipline of the work unit. See Chapter 1 for suggestions, especially Problems 1-1, 1-5, 1-6, 1-7 and 1-9. If Harold doesn't deny that he misused sick time but brags that your boss won't let you do anything about him, see Problem 8-5.

Use Checklist 2 to develop a cure of your own.

8

Troubleshooting Problems Caused by an Employee Who Challenges Your Authority

8-1

The Problem: An employee publicly refuses to follow an order.

The Scene

"I don't care what you do, I *will not* touch that mess in the Collection Room. You get somebody else to do it, or you do it yourself." With that, Jolene stalked out of your office.

Possible Causes

Jolene may believe you've asked her to do something that's unsafe.

Jolene may believe that you're picking on her. As she sees it, you've singled her out for the job unfairly.

She may believe that what you want her to do is "beneath" her. She may see it as menial, humiliating work.

She simply may not like the work and isn't going to do it. Sometimes, people's reasons are no more complicated than that.

Hint: There are two distinct problems here. The first is Jolene and her motives. The second is the impact of her action on other employees. You have to consider both.

Cures

No matter what the cause is:

You may have a good idea of the cause, or you may not. Either way, wait until you and Jolene have both calmed down and then talk with her. Don't jump to the conclusion that she's wrong. Listen with an open mind, and give her every chance to explain what she did.

If Jolene honestly believes you asked her to do something unsafe:

This is sticky, but there's broad agreement in our society that an employee may refuse to carry out an order which she believes endangers her health or that of others, is illegal, or violates common moral standards. An employee is at risk whenever she refuses to obey an order, but if it's for one of these reasons, the disobedience may be justified.

It may be difficult to tell whether Jolene means this or is just using it to get off the hook. This is where skillful listening comes in handy.

If she genuinely believes what you told her to do was unsafe, then accept that as a sufficient reason for not doing it. But it doesn't answer everything. There are still questions like:

- Did she tell you she thought it was unsafe at the time? (And, if she did, why didn't you pay attention?)

- Did she ask you to let her explain? (And, if she did, did you refuse to let her?)

- Did she tell you *why* she thought it was unsafe? (Again, if she did, did you listen?)

If you were ready to listen to her, but she didn't give you a reason for disobeying—she didn't do what a conscientious employee should. Counsel her on that. Then make sure that the two of you agree on how you'll handle the situation (if it may reasonably come up again).

If Jolene believes that you're picking on her:

This is also sticky, but for different reasons. How do you tell if this is the case, or just a convenient excuse?

Here's where you have to be really clean with yourself. What is your relationship with Jolene? Were you trying to "show her who's boss," or force her to change a "poor attitude"? Were you angry with her before the situation came up? Or—we hate to ask, but we have to—were you influenced by the fact that Jolene is a woman or (perhaps) a minority?

If you're convinced you treated Jolene as you would have anyone else, you still have to deal with her feelings that you were picking on her. And you should deal with them—regardless of what else you do. As long as she feels that way, situations like this can occur at any time.

What if you may have picked on her? Discuss it openly. If it was based on her personal characteristics or traits, discuss these with her. Give her plenty of room to express herself. See if you can get the situation behind the both of you.

If she honestly believed you were picking on her, it's not really appropriate to discipline her—this time. Agree that if it comes up again, you'll call a halt in what's happening and go somewhere that you can talk it over.

Regardless of all this, make it clear that if she refuses to follow an order again, you will discipline her. Her honest feelings buy her one pardon—but only one. Make sure she understands the options open to her the next time such a situation occurs (see the last part of the preceding "cure.")

If she believes the work is "beneath" her:

Golly—another sticky one! This dances right on the border between excusability and lame excuse.

Here past practice may help you decide. If there's a clear practice that employees in Jolene's job do that kind of work, *and if she knows it,* she has no excuse. If they don't usually do it, or if she's never been told, what she did may not have been quite so bad. If there is no consistent practice—well, back to square one!

If employees in her job don't normally do this kind of work, both of you need to understand why you expected her to do it. If you've decided to change how things are done and just didn't tell anyone, you shouldn't be surprised that she reacted as she did.

Now, suppose employees in that job do regularly what you ordered her to do. Would she reasonably have known that? If she wouldn't have, make sure she knows now. If she should have, use the suggestions in the next cure.

Again, no matter the situation, use the suggestions at the end of the first "cure" to make sure the situation never happens again.

If she simply doesn't like the work and isn't going to do it:

She picked the wrong place and time to make her point. This is where you and she have a heart-to-heart talk about how much she wants to continue to have a job. It should be a *serious* talk; clear insubordination is one of the reasons for severe discipline—including termination—accepted by almost everyone.

If she's an otherwise good worker and appears to have learned, you may want to close off the situation by giving her a few days off without pay. If she's marginal, or she clearly has learned nothing, look into terminating her. (Sound cruel? Remember, the rest of your work unit is looking over your shoulder, waiting to see what you're going to do.)

Something to Think About

There are two reasons for firing an employee:

- He's demonstrated that he doesn't intend to follow workplace rules. In other words, he's past reasonable rehabilitation.

- He may or may not be salvageable, but you have to take the action to maintain discipline in the work unit. When an employee is openly insubordinate, just this reason may be a sufficient reason to fire him.

Always consider both reasons when you're faced with a serious offense.

And If This Doesn't Quite Fit Your Situation . . .

Look at Problems 8-3 and 8-5 in this chapter if Jolene goes over your head when you give her an order she doesn't like or brags that your boss won't let you do anything to her. If she tries to sabotage you with other employees, see Problem 8-6. If she accuses you of discrimination, refer to Problem 10-5.

Use Checklist 2 to develop a cure of your own.

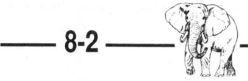

— 8-2 —

The Problem: An employee ignores your directions to co-operate with a manager that he doesn't like.

The Scene

"What's wrong with that Sartini woman on your staff?" Joe asks indignantly. "All I asked for was expedited handling of *one little supply requisition*, and you'd think I'd asked for the moon and the stars. I thought you told me you were stressing customer service to that group of yours upstairs!"

Well, actually you can empathize a little with Elaine Sartini; Joe's not the easiest manager to get along with. *On the other hand*, you explicitly told her to cooperate with him since you're trying to get *his* cooperation on something else. Wasn't she listening?"

Possible Causes

Elaine may have misunderstood your directions. She may not have meant to be uncooperative, but simply didn't know what you were asking her to do.

Elaine may not realize why it's important to cooperate with the other manager. Even if she knows why it's essential to keep customers satisfied, she may not have grasped the concept of "internal customer" or the importance of peer relationships.

Elaine may be deliberately ignoring your instructions. She may not agree with you, she may not respect your decision-making capabilities, she may have let her dislike of Joe interfere with her good judgment, or she may be out to get you. But regardless of her underlying motive, in this case she's clearly made a conscious decision *not* to follow your direct order.

Hint: As we'll discuss in more detail in a later chapter, good peer relationships are critical to a successful career. But that fact is often not obvious to your employees, who are most concerned about protecting their own parochial interests. Regardless of any individual employee's attempts to undermine your efforts to establish and maintain those relationships, it's important that your staff in general understand why they're important and what they can do to foster good relationships between units.

Cures

If Elaine didn't understand what you were asking her to do:

Review with her the limits of her authority—to bend the rules or to make other accommodations in response to "special requests." Make sure she understands which rules or procedures *may not* be violated and why, as well as those over which she exercises some discretion.

Then discuss with her the particular case with Joe. Explain what she could have done better and how. Rehearse with her how she should handle similar situations in the future—and how to decide whom she should make special efforts for.

Suggest that she consult with you the next time this kind of situation arises. And when she does, instead of *giving her* an answer, ask first how she thinks it should be handled. That way you'll foster her own independent resolution of cases, while ensuring that there are no more foul-ups while she's developing her judgment-making skills.

If Elaine doesn't understand why it's important to cooperate with the other manager:

Describe to her the relationship between Joe's unit and yours. Explain what benefits you get from him—either as a regular part of the work or because of special efforts he may make for you. You may have to go into considerable detail here, especially if Joe and his unit don't impact Elaine directly. In that case, you'll need to make sure that Elaine also learns something about the different functions of your unit and in particular the areas where Joe can help, or hurt.

If the message doesn't seem to be getting across, you might ask Elaine to list the people that she personally relies on to get her work accomplished. From there you should be able more easily to generalize to the interdependence among units—including yours and Joe's.

In the end, although it's better for you and Elaine if she understands why it's important to cooperate, your basic concern must be that she does it. If you can't convince her of the necessity of fostering good relationships with other units, then be as direct as you need to be to get your instructions across. You can't afford to let one employee's lack of understanding alienate an important ally.

If Elaine is deliberately ignoring your instructions:

Failing to follow an order is tantamount to refusing to follow it. Both are forms of insubordination. Problem 8-1 describes a blatant case of insubordination and describes appropriate responses.

Something to Think About

You can't assume that every incident in which an employee fails to follow a direction is a conscious attempt to undermine your authority. In at least some of the cases we've discussed here, there's a real possibility that the employee was trying to help out—that she thought you were mistaken and could save you by doing things differently. In dealing with failures to follow instructions, it's important to explain to employees as well as you can why you've made the decisions you have. Of course, they also need to know that it's not acceptable for them to substitute their judgment for yours when you've required a specific course of action. But you're much more likely to get their wholehearted cooperation in the future if your decisions appear to them to be the well-reasoned judgments they are—rather than capricious whims.

And If This Doesn't Quite Fit Your Situation . . .

Look at Problems 5-1, 5-2, and 5-3 for discussions of employees who do things the way they want to rather than the way you want them to. Problems 8-1 and 8-7 deal with other forms of insubordination.

Use Checklists 1 and 2 to develop a cure of your own.

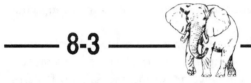

—— 8-3 ——

The Problem: An employee goes over your head when you give him an order he doesn't like.

The Scene

"Hello—this is Mrs. Wilkins."

"Eleanor, are you and Eddie Daniels having some sort of donnybrook?"

"I don't think so, Mr. Sugeno," you answer, with growing anxiety. "Why do you ask?"

"He came up her to see me—as a matter of fact, he just left. He was complaining about some work you assigned him; said you were loading him up and letting the others off."

"I really don't know what the story is, but I'll take care of it," you say—as bravely as you can.

"I expect you to."

"Damn!" you mutter to yourself as you hang up. You knew Eddie didn't like the assignment, but you hadn't expected him to run right to your boss.

Possible Causes

In Eddie's eyes, you're mistreating him so badly that he believes this is the only way he can get things straightened out. What he did was an act of desperation.

Eddie believes that what you told him to do is so bad that your boss ought to know about it.

He isn't getting what he wants, so he tried to "end-run" you.

When Eddie doesn't get what he wants, this is his habitual way of dealing with the situation. The difference from the one just above is that this is Eddie's *pattern* of dealing with these situation.

Hint: This is irritating, of course—but there's something more. You need to deal with this one quickly and effectively so that your authority doesn't start to erode. If other employees see that Eddie can get around you, well . . .

Cures

No matter what the cause is:

This is another situation where you wait until you have your anger well under control and then review the situation objectively. If you've contributed to the situation, you need to realize it up front.

Then have a very clear discussion with Eddie. You want to listen carefully to him, so you get a good feel for just what's going on.

If Eddie believes you're mistreating him and this is the only way he can deal with it:

Be very careful with this one. You need to listen carefully and be honest with yourself: are you mistreating him? Is this something he did only out of desperation?

If he apparently believes this in all honesty, deal with that problem. Why does he believe it? What have you done? What can you—and he—do to correct it? Do your best to get to the bottom of the situation and deal with his concerns. You want to lay them to rest if you can.

Did he voice his concerns to you before? If so, why didn't you listen? If not, why didn't he? Unless he had a good, realistic reason for not talking to you, counsel him strongly that you expect him to do so next time. If necessary, tell him that if he goes over your head without talking to you, you'll write him up, or even take more serious action.

You may have noticed this pattern in other problems: First make sure that you really listen when an employee comes to you with a

problem or complaint. Then make sure that he comes to you before
he talks to anyone else or takes any action. If you do the first, you
have every right to require the latter.

***If he believes what you told him to do is so bad your boss
should know about it:***

We don't need to tell you this is serious. Why would he believe
that? Again, look at the situation calmly. Did you tell him to do
something because you were angry or trying to prove a point? If so,
you need to apologize, get straight with yourself about why you did
it, and then not do it again.

If you really didn't, if the assignment was an acceptable one—
why did he react so strongly to it? There could be any number of
reasons for this; the burden of proof is on him to persuade you that
his was a legitimate one. (If it wasn't, see the next "cure" for suggestions.)

Your relationship with Eddie obviously needs some work. If he
believed that you told him to do something you shouldn't have, he's
telling you that the relationship isn't very good. What do you have
to do to correct that?

You also need to talk to Eddie about his responsibility to talk
with you first. Use the suggestions in the "cure" above.

If he tried to "end-run" you because he didn't get his way:

(The difference between this situation and the one below is that
in this one Eddie is pulling an end-run for the first time. In the one
below, it's an habitual way that he deals with not getting what he
wants.)

When you've established that this is the case, the mildest thing
you do is counsel Eddie in no uncertain terms not to repeat it. Then
promise him that if it happens again you'll take much stronger action.
You want to stop this before he starts to make a habit of it.

Your side of this action is to make sure that you haven't contributed to the problem. For instance, some employees—some very
good ones—have a highly developed sense of what's reasonable.
What looks to you like Eddie trying to get his way may seem to him

like an attempt to get around your "unreasonable" assignment. (This is akin to the "cure" right above, but not really the same thing.)

You also need to speak to Eddie about the importance of coming to you first; see the suggestions in the first "cure" above.

If this is the way Eddie habitually deals with not getting his way:

This is where you make crystal clear that you won't tolerate his behavior. You may not be able to discipline him formally this time, but you can certainly write him up now and then discipline him if he tries it again.

Why so strong an approach? If this is the way he usually reacts when things don't go his way, he'll keep on doing it. He won't change unless the cost of doing it becomes too high.

Keep this in mind: Eddie may be used to going around supervisors because he's had one or more who wouldn't listen to his problems and complaints. What you see is the habit; the frustration that drove him to it may not be so clear. It's worth probing for. If his action was based on frustration, you can try to show him that you'll listen to him and try to deal with his problems.

Things to Think About

We've left out an entire element in the situation: your boss. Once you get Eddie dealt with, you need to deal with your boss. If you and he have a good relationship, simply be honest about the situation. If not, put the best face on it that you can. You need to assure him that it was an isolated incident that you've dealt with firmly and fairly—and that it won't happen again.

Then make sure it *doesn't* happen again.

And If This Doesn't Quite Fit Your Situation . . .

If Eddie has simply refused to follow an order, see Problem 8-1 or 8-7. If he went over your head because of his friendship with your boss, see Problems 8-5 and 14-10.

Use Checklist 2 to develop a cure of your own.

8-4

The Problem: An employee publicly criticizes you.

The Scene

"Just who does she think she is?" grumbled Peggy to Mike in the hall outside the restroom. A group of workers began to gather as Peggy expounded her litany of grievances: "She couldn't find her office without a map and here she is telling *me* how to manage a project I've had for years. On top of that, she's *insisting* that I co-ordinate with Paul Preston next door. We'll never get anything done now, and all because the old bat has to have things her way!"

Possible Causes

It really doesn't matter why Peggy is criticizing you in front of the rest of the staff. This is an action designed specifically to undermine your authority. You cannot tolerate it—regardless of what provocation Peggy may have had or of how limited her influence is over her coworkers.

Cures

This is one situation where immediate action is important. You overheard Peggy's remarks, and your workers know it. If you ignore the situation or put off dealing with it, they'll interpret your inaction as a sign of weakness—and you'll add another nail to the coffin Peggy is working so hard to build for you.

At the same time, you cannot stoop to the tactics Peggy has employed. Public criticism is always out of line—barring a direct threat to human life or safety. It doesn't matter whether it's Peggy criticizing you or you criticizing Peggy. You cannot allow yourself to engage in the behavior for which you're about to chastise Peggy. But you can make it clear to the group at large that this a serious matter with which you're about to deal now.

Calmly but firmly disengage Peggy from the group. A clear, "Peggy, I'll see you in my office right now!" should convey the message.

Explain to Peggy exactly what she did that you consider inappropriate. She probably already knows, but it's important that you define the specific things she did that are unacceptable. Explain also why they're unacceptable. Nothing long or complicated is required here—just a short statement about the need for respect and courtesy for coworkers and for proper authority.

If this is the first time Peggy has publicly criticized you, warn her that you will not treat such behavior lightly and that repetitions of this incident will likely result in severe action, including termination. Make sure she understands the consequences of a "leaderless" organization and the confusion and lack of focus that result.

If Peggy has criticized you, or other supervisors, in public before or if this criticism is likely to result in real damage to your credibility or effectiveness, a warning is not sufficient. You should try to obtain a public retraction from Peggy, but, even after retraction, you may decide that Peggy has done enough irreparable damage that you can't afford to keep her on the staff.

Public retraction does not necessarily mean public apology. While it's certainly desirable to get Peggy to admit to her audience that her behavior was inappropriate, this is not an opportunity for you to exact revenge. Public retraction should be done as sensitively and tactfully as you can arrange it. It should not result in Peggy's humiliation.

Something to Think About

While public criticism is clearly inappropriate behavior, public disagreement is not. In fact, the best managers have a clear preference for open and honest disagreement on issues that arise. The difference between unacceptable criticism and acceptable disagreement lies in the setting and the manner of presentation. Public disagreement should be in a setting where both sides of the question are represented so that there can be real debate on the merits of each position. It should not be done behind your back or the backs of other employees who hold the opposite position. And acceptable public disagreement always focuses on the issues—never on personalities and never descending to insults or name-calling.

And If This Doesn't Quite Fit Your Situation . . .

Look at other problems throughout this chapter for discussions of employees' attempts to discredit you or undermine your authority.

Use Checklist 2 to develop a cure of your own.

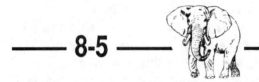

——— 8-5 ———

The Problem: An employee brags that you can't do anything to him because of his friendship with your boss.

The Scene

"Look, it doesn't really matter *what* you think I ought to do. I'm not going to do it, and there's nothing you can do about it! Elvin Eckart and I are old friends, and he'll do anything I ask—and if you push me one time more I'm going to ask him to get you off my back. Understand?"

With that, Andy turned and sauntered out—leaving you even more frustrated than before. How are you going to maintain discipline when an employee openly flaunts his friendship with your boss?

Possible Causes

Andy is bluffing. His friendship with Mr. Eckert is an exaggeration, or even a pure invention.

They are friends—but Eckert still expects Andy to produce like any other employee.

They are friends—and what Andy said is exactly right. Eckert cares more about the friendship than Andy's productivity or your work unit discipline.

Hint: It doesn't sound good, but don't panic yet.

Cures

No matter what the cause is:

We often begin with the recommendation that you talk with the employee. Not this time. This time you talk with your boss—Mr. Eckert.

Your goal is to find out just what the relationship is between him and Andy. You might start the conversation something like this:

"I understand you know Andy pretty well, and I was wondering if you could help me. I've been having some problems with his productivity and . . . ."

Listen carefully to Mr. Eckert's response. If he's honest with you, you'll know just what to do. But he may not be completely honest. If he says "I want you to treat him just like anyone else," he may or may not mean it. Be tactful, but try to probe for his real feelings.

If Andy is bluffing:

He just tried to play hardball and failed. Now it's your turn to play hardball. Call him in, make it perfectly clear you don't buy his "friendship" routine, and tell him what you expect. Then make sure that he delivers.

Needless to say, you don't take this course of action unless you're *sure* that Mr. Eckert has no interest in what happens with Andy.

If they are friends, but Eckert doesn't expect you to make exceptions for Andy:

Call Andy in. Explain that you just talked with Mr. Eckert and found that he expects the same thing you do—an honest day's work from Andy. Be tactful and reasonable, and be clear. When Andy leaves, he should have no doubts about what you expect from him.

Keep in mind that Andy will probably relay his version of the conversation to Eckert. You'll help accomplish your objectives if you take these two steps:

- When you talk with Eckert in the first place, explain to him the problem you're having and what you intend to tell Andy. If any of it troubles him, change it and get his okay before you leave.

- When you've talked with Andy, give Eckert a call. Tell him that you and Andy have had your conversation, and that he can expect a call or a visit from Andy. Depending on Eckert's response, you might want to summarize the conversation for him.

If they are friends, and Eckert will support Andy:

Don't conclude this until you've probed very carefully in your talk with Eckert. He probably won't ever tell you he'll side with Andy—but he may say something like "Oh, yes, he's a good man. I expect you to treat him well." A few statements like this, and you've got the picture.

If Andy can get Eckert to block you, your choices are very limited. Problem 14-10 discusses this situation at length.

Things to Think About

It's a good rule of thumb to treat employees as though they intend to do a good job. That prevents a lot of misunderstanding and helps you get the best from each of them.

There are exceptions, employees who really do intend to get away with everything they can, any way they can. When you've got one of those, take your kid gloves off. Don't do anything immoral or illegal; don't break the rules. Just be very smart and very tough.

By the way, this is where it really pays off to have good working relationships with your employees. If the group as a whole thinks well of you, they'll help you take care of the people who don't want to do their fair share.

And If This Doesn't Quite Fit Your Situation . . .

Look at Problem 8-1 if Andy publicly refused to follow your order or Problem 8-3 if the problem is simply that he goes over your head when he doesn't want to do what you tell him to. Problem 14-10 covers this problem from the point of view of your relationship with your boss.

Use Checklist 2 to develop a cure of your own.

8-6

The Problem: An employee tries to sabotage you with other employees.

The Scene

"Boss, I think you should know what's going on behind your back," offers Carolyn after staff meeting this morning. "Frank is running around the office trying to get people stirred up against you and your decision to take us off flexible hours for the next two months. Most of us know why you had to do it, and, while we're not thrilled, we're willing to go along with you. But Frank is talking about a slow-down—kind of a 'you can't make me if I don't wanna' trick. He thinks if he can make you look bad enough, he can drive you out of this unit!"

Possible Causes

Frank may believe that you're damaging the organization. He may feel so strongly that what you're doing is wrong and so powerless to change it by working through "channels," that he's willing to descend to guerilla tactics.

Frank may be out to get your job. He may see discrediting you as a way to get you out of the organization and open up chances for his own advancement.

Frank may just not like you. It may be not that he thinks you're doing a terrible job from which he has to save the organization or that he wants your position; he just wants you to be gone! Maybe you have a personality clash; maybe he doesn't like the way you dress, wear your hair, or talk. But for some reason, he just doesn't want you around anymore.

Hint: This situation, like most of the others in this chapter, involves overtly hostile acts toward you by your subordinates. Regardless of the motives, which may be essentially good, the methods are unacceptable. Organizations can't run without leaders; someone has to set directions and make decisions about policy and values. Undermining authority never solves a problem; it only creates additional ones.

Cures

If Frank believes you're hurting the organization:

His motives are basically sound, even though his methods are not. Before you talk to Frank, you need to get your own emotions under control. It's not pleasant to realize that someone's out to get you, no matter what the reason is. So think before you act. Try to find out from trusted coworkers what it is that Frank's concerned about. Then in confronting him, deal with the issues—not your own pain.

Let Frank know that you're aware of what he's been doing and that you disapprove strongly—not just because of the personal harm it's causing you, but also because of the damage he's doing to the organization. Sabotage only works when it's undiscovered; once it's out in the open, it's a useless tactic.

Give Frank a chance to explain why he believes you're harming the organization. Listen carefully. If he believes it that strongly, there may be something important in what he says. Tell him specifically what you intend to do to allay his concerns, and what *acceptable* redress is available to him if he's still not satisfied.

Explain to Frank how his efforts to sabotage you damage the organization at least as much as anything you may have done. Talk to him about why mutual respect and trust are so critical and how his actions have undermined both your respect for and trust in him.

If Frank wants your job:

As before, the best way to get Frank to stop his campaign against you is to let him (and others, as appropriate) know that you're aware of what's going on.

Because Frank's motives are not nearly so pure in this case, it's not so important to direct your efforts toward reestablishing the relationship. Frank has made it very clear that his ambition is paramount, and your reasonable, understanding approach is going to have no impact on him.

Confront Frank. Let him know that what he's done has destroyed the trust and confidence you had in him, and that you see no way for him to regain them.

He may apologize and offer to make amends. If so, it's your judgment call whether he's destroyed the relationship so thoroughly than it's unsalvageable or whether you're willing to give it another try. If you do decide to work with Frank, watch him carefully. He's betrayed you once, and he may again—especially if he really wants your job.

He may not offer to make amends, or he may offer and then step back into his old maneuvering. At this point, you have no choice but to offer him the door. As long as he's around to sabotage your efforts, your effectiveness will suffer.

If Frank just doesn't like you:

Once again, begin by bringing the covert behavior out into the open—but as unemotionally as you possibly can. At this point, you don't know whether the underlying cause is something you can work out with Frank or not.

Make sure Frank understands why his actions are unacceptable, and their impact on the trust and confidence you have in him. At the same time, explain that you know people don't always get along and offer to discuss with him things that the two of you can do to mend the relationship.

If Frank trusts *you*, he'll probably be willing to tell you what it is that bothers him. Then you can decide whether it's something that you can, and are willing to, change. If so, work out with Frank what you're willing to do and what you expect from him. Remind him that one of the things you expect is that he won't engage in sabotage against you again—and warn him of the consequences if he should.

If Frank won't talk to you about the underlying causes of his dislike of you, then you won't be able to salvage the relationship. He's already undermined your trust in him and now, in effect, has refused to do anything to fix things. Offer him a position in another part of the company if one's available and he's a worker you would otherwise want to keep. If not, let him go.

Something to Think About

If a number of the problems in this chapter sound familiar to you, you're probably working in an organization that is essentially sick. Disagreement and dissention among workers is not uncommon—particularly in organizations undergoing unusual stress or change. But deliberate attempts to undermine authority, overtly or covertly, are not that common. Individual workers may be dissatisfied, not know more constructive ways to accomplish what they want, and resort to these kinds of tactics. If you begin to see patterns of this kind of behavior, either within your unit or across organizational lines, you need to look hard at the company itself. Something is operating to make employees believe that this is a good way for them to get what they want. For the good of both the company and you, it's essential that you convince them otherwise.

And If This Doesn't Quite Fit Your Situation . . .

Look at Problems 7-1, 7-2, and 7-4 and others in this chapter for situations in which employees engage in behavior that undermines your respect and trust in them.

Use Checklists 2 and 3 to develop a cure of your own.

8-7

The Problem: An employee refuses to work emergency overtime.

The Scene

"Ms. Johansen, we can stand here and argue until quitting time and it won't change anything. I won't work until 9:00 tonight. May I go now?"

You nod. You really need for Bonnie to work late, and the example she's setting by refusing to do so may encourage other employees to refuse, too. Now what do you do?

Possible Causes

Bonnie has personal commitments that keep her from being flexible. She may have to get her children at a fixed time or go home to take care of elderly parents.

She may have special plans for this evening.
She's organized her life so she doesn't have any flexibility.
Bonnie has a second job. She starts work soon after she leaves this job.
She's simply not a flexible person.
Hint: Sorting out just what the situation is may be a challenge.

Cures

If she has personal commitments that keep her from being flexible:

In Problem 7-6 we looked at an employee who was late because of personal commitments. You might want to look at that problem for additional thoughts.

More and more people who work have demanding personal responsibilities. If Bonnie has to pick up an elderly parent from an "elder-care" facility and take him home, she may have to do it no matter what. There's no point in getting upset about it; she simply doesn't have flexibility.

Does this mean you simply let her refuse to work overtime? Perhaps. But there are other alternatives (though probably not for today). It may be she can make other arrangements if she gets advanced notice of the overtime. Perhaps she could come in early in the morning instead of staying late. The important point is for both of you to know what if any flexibility she has and then make your plans based on it.

There's a moral in this story: you should know what flexibility each of your workers has—before a situation like this comes up. That way, both your expectations and theirs will be realistic. You'll avoid these last-minute confrontations.

If she has special plans for this evening:

What you do depends more than anything else on the practices of your work unit. Is this the first time last-minute overtime has come up in months? Then it's reasonable for her to make plans like this. On the other hand, is last-minute overtime common—with the expectation that

employees will be available to work it? That's a different situation.
Also, did she tell you in advance she wouldn't be able to stay today?

In other words, there's a lot to take into account in this circumstance. If she knew from past practice that she was taking a gamble,
she should be counseled or even disciplined for refusing the overtime.
Otherwise, it's not reasonable to expect it from her.

Is the situation apt to arise again, with Bonnie or someone else?
Then you (and your employees, if possible) should establish a reasonable policy which gets the work done with the least disruption
to their personal lives.

If she's organized her life so she doesn't have flexibility:

Sometimes this is hard to tell from the first cause. She may be
locked into responsibilities after work, but she may have had the
option whether or not to do it that way. Does she have to pick up a
child from day care? She may have been able to get a neighbor to
do it for her. It's important to find out how much flexibility she
really has.

If she has made most of the decisions that have taken away her
flexibility, and you need her to work last-minute overtime periodically—then make it clear that you expect her to reorganize her life to
accommodate the overtime. This may take several discussions, and
you may have to help her think it through. If she can reasonably do
it, though, you have the right to expect her to.

If she has a second job:

Is this her primary job? If the answer is "yes," then this is the
job she owes her primary allegiance to. You have the right to expect
her not to refuse reasonable requests for overtime.

It's probably not wise to deal with the situation any more today.
But call her in tomorrow and discuss the situation with her. Make it
clear that you expect this job to come first. If you need her to work
overtime, you expect her to be available to do it. If she refuses again,
she could subject herself to disciplinary action.

Having said that, here's a strong qualification on it: Many people, particularly unskilled workers and/or heads of single-parent fami-

lies, have to work two or more jobs to make ends meet. Even though this is Bonnie's primary job, she may need the other one to survive. This doesn't give her the right to turn down overtime based on the other job. It does mean that you and she need to look at the situation closely and work out an accommodation if possible.

If she's simply not a flexible person:

If she's a good, well-motivated worker who simply doesn't have the emotional flexibility to make last-minute changes, your options are almost as limited as in the first "cure" above.

If you can arrange the job so that she doesn't get last-minute overtime, fine. Perhaps she can work the overtime if given a day or two advanced notice; can you accommodate that? Can someone else learn her job and take the necessary overtime? Can you take the duties that require the overtime out of her job and give them to someone else who can work the overtime?

If it's not possible to prevent last-minute overtime for her job, you may want to look into reassigning her to another job. If all else fails, deal with it as a performance problem.

Problem 6-9 may give you some additional ideas for this situation.

Things to Think About

Everything above assumed that Bonnie would be honest with you. Suppose you asked when you hired her and she assured you that she'd work overtime? Suppose she checked "yes" when you circulated a questionnaire to your employees last month? That probably means that you need to have serious conversation with her about why, and about her responsibilities as an employee.

There are two "deep" and somewhat contradictory issues here. On the one hand, most families are now two-worker families. This means that each spouse has more before- and after-work responsibilities—and less flexibility about working extra hours. On the other hand, the organization has to get its job done; this often means last-minute changes in schedule. There's no easy solution for this, but planning ahead and being clear with employees what your expectations are will help. So will planning work so that last-minute overtime is absolutely minimized.

And If This Doesn't Quite Fit Your Situation . . .

Look at Problem 8-1 if Bonnie publicly refused to follow an order. Problems 8-3 and 8-5 have useful suggestions if she goes over your head or uses her friendship with your boss as a reason for not doing what you tell her to.

Use Checklists 1 and 2 to develop a cure of your own.

9

Troubleshooting
Ethical Problems
Caused by Your Boss

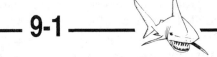

—— 9-1 ——

The Problem: He tells you to "fudge" the figures on a report you prepare.

The Scene

It's just not fair! You've been preparing production reports for as long as you've had this job, and every month things keep looking better and better—until now. One little downward "blip" in the charts—entirely explainable with the change in machinery and two new leaders in the group. But Walter, your boss, isn't satisfied. "Be creative," he said. Creative, ha! He wants you to cheat, no question about it. But he is the boss, and he's the one who has to give this report to the vice president, so maybe it would be OK to be a little "creative"—just this once.

Possible Causes

Your boss may believe that the figures themselves don't accurately reflect the true situation. He may be concerned that *his* boss will react more to the negative figures than she should—ignoring the long range improvements that will come from the new machinery and the replacement of mediocre leaders with some better talent.

Your boss may want to look good with his superiors. He may be willing to sacrifice honesty for the sake of a good report.

Hint: Whether this is an "ethical dilemma" or not for you depends on the situation. If Walter wants you to change the figure in your production report to make it better reflect what's going on in your unit, his motives are essentially good and you may be able to find a way to accommodate him. If he just wants to make himself look better (or avoid looking bad), you'll need to make some hard decisions about how far you're willing to go to help him.

These aren't decisions we can help you with. They're based on your own internal code—about what your responsibilities are to your employer, about your responsibilities to maintain truth and honesty, about how far you can compromise without violating an essential part of yourself. You know what you're comfortable with and what you're not. You know when you have a "gut feeling" that you're about to cross the line. Pay attention to those feelings. They're usually right on target!

Cures

If Walter wants you to change the figures to make the report better reflect reality:

You can probably accommodate him without violating any of your principles, even if you don't agree that this is the best way to present the information.

Wherever you have to change figures to meet Walter's requests, just put a footnote in the margin to show that "These figures have been adjusted for . . ." That should satisfy Walter, but clearly indicate that you haven't done anything to disguise the truth.

If Walter isn't satisfied with the figures/footnotes approach, you can be sure that what he really wants is to look better with his boss. See below.

If Walter wants you to change the figures to make him look better:

This is much like the situation described in Problem 9-2, although the potential for harm to other employees is considerably less. See the discussion there for specific actions to take to protect yourself and the company.

Things to Think About

There are many times just in the course of day-to-day supervision when you're caught in ethical dilemmas. Often these are minor problems where it doesn't make a lot of difference either to the company or to you which way you go. But the decisions you make in these little things will influence how you respond when the tough questions arise—like cheating on some figures or destroying a safety report.

If you're not sure how you'd react, or how you'd decide how to react, there is help available. Training organizations are beginning to develop courses to help you make ethical decisions. Find a course that seems to agree with the way you look at the world, and see what they can offer you.

And If This Doesn't Quite Fit Your Situation . . .

Look at the next problem (9-2) if the situation is more serious than "doctoring up" a routine report.

Use Checklist 5 to develop a cure of your own.

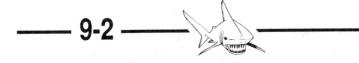

9-2

The Problem: He tells you to destroy a report that identifies serious safety hazards in the work area.

The Scene

"You wanted to see me, sir?" you ask as you walk into Mr. Maxey's office.

"You know that shredder down in the mailroom? I want you to run this through it."

You look down in amazement at the papers he hands you. It's the report on safety hazards that the firm commissioned—and which identified several dangerous conditions out on the floor.

Mr. Maxey looks at you intently. "I have to have your complete trust in this. We need to get rid of it permanently. If I can count on you for this, I think you can count on me to be quite helpful to you later on."

Possible Causes

The causes aren't significant here. Mr. Maxey may be scared because the report points out deficiencies he shouldn't have permitted. Or he may believe that it would be too expensive to fix them. Or if people found out about them, the firm would be liable for large damages.

None of this makes a great deal of difference. He wants you to destroy a report that identifies dangerous hazards—hazards that people working in the area don't know about. They're in danger. Just as important, he's put you on the spot. How long until the next time he does that to you?

What matters isn't why he wants the report destroyed. It's what will happen if you try to go over his head with it. That dictates your actions.

Hint: Brace yourself—this is going to be *tough* no matter what you do.

Cures

If Maxey caused the problems or has another personal reason to hide the situation—and his superiors won't back what he did:

First, make sure this is really the case. It's unfortunate, but some organizations say all the right words—until a decision has to be made. Then they expect lower-level managers to "take care of things" without involving them. If that's the case here, you could find yourself without a job in a hurry.

The other side is that there are concerned firms, who find what Maxey is doing completely reprehensible. The key is to find out what the real-world situation is in your organization. If you have contacts in other parts of the company, you can check with them.

Let's say that the company really does care, and you see that the report gets to Maxey's superiors. They'll be profusely grateful.

Maxey will hate you for it, but they'll probably fire him so that won't matter too much.

You may begin to find, though, that things aren't like they used to be. If you had good chances for promotion, you may find that they've faded away. If you used to get good assignments, you may find that they've dried up. Even if everyone knows that you were right and Maxey was wrong, they may not forgive you for going around him and exposing him. It'll never be anything you can put your finger on, but . . .

In other words, you won't be able to expose Maxey without risk, no matter how careful you are. If you happen to have a friend higher up in the organization—particularly if exposing Maxey makes him look good—he may be able to protect you. If you don't, you'll be taking your chances.

If Maxey will be supported by his superiors:

They may be expecting him to do just what he's doing, even though they'll never say so officially. Not only will telling them be occupational suicide, they'll probably see that the report gets buried at their level.

In short, there's nothing to be gained by trying to move the report further up in the organization. It may make you feel better, but it won't do much good.

If you have a good connection higher in the organization:

We mentioned above how helpful a connection higher in management might be. If you can trust him, and know that he intends to do the right thing, he may be your best avenue. Take the report to him—preferably at home or some other place than his office. If he really does intend to act ethically, he'll see that the situation is corrected—even though you may never hear about it again.

If you're caught, with no good avenue:

Of course, you can simply destroy the report. That's the worst possible thing. If nothing else, put it in a good safe place and lie to

Maxey (we're playing *hard*ball here!). You may need it to protect yourself against him later—in case he decides to get rid of you to protect himself.

You must evaluate the danger to other workers if the hazards aren't fixed. If they're serious, can you live with yourself knowing that you could have prevented serious injury or illness—but didn't? We have to leave that question to you and your conscience.

If you agree to destroy the report, what will Maxey want you to do the next time? If this was a tough choice, how much tougher will that one be? And what happens to your self-respect if you accept this kind of behavior?

Finally, no matter what happens you may want to find yourself another place of employment. You might get away from the situation somewhere else in the company. More probably, you'll have to go to work for another organization. (We warned you that this was a tough one!)

Something to Think About

The only good solution for this kind of dilemma is to not be there when it happens. If you have reason to think that your boss is dishonest and might pull something like this—find another boss. Don't panic, but work on it earnestly. Life is too short to let yourself be seduced into this kind of immorality. There are hundreds of companies and thousands of bosses who'll play straight with you. Find one of them.

And If This Doesn't Quite Fit Your Situation . . .

Look at the other problems in this chapter for other situations in which your boss causes you ethical problems. If you caused the problem by your failure to perform, see Problems 10-1 and 10-3. If the problem is caused partially or fully by your inability to handle your job or office politics, see Problems 10-6 or 10-9. For problems without ethical implications which your boss causes, see Chapters 13 and 14.

Use Checklist 5 to develop a cure of your own.

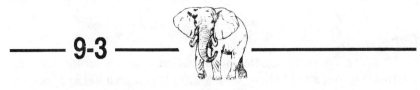

9-3

The Problem: She asks you to loan her a large amount of money.

The Scene

"I have a real favor to ask," Maria pleaded at lunch today. "I have some doctor bills for the kids that have mounted up—badly. If I don't pay, they're threatening to take me to court. It's a thousand dollars, and I just don't know where I'm going to come up with the money. Could you help me out? Just this once?"

Maria's always been a good boss. She expects a lot and gives a lot. You'd really like to help her out. But you can't really afford the money either. Still, she is the boss, so how can you say no?

Possible Causes

It really doesn't matter what the cause is—why Maria needs the money or why she's asked you for it. This is a bad position for her to place you in. Even if you want to help her out, the fact that she owes money to you can create some real conflicts of interest.

The need to reciprocate is almost irresistible. Once you've done a special favor for Maria, she's going to feel obliged to do one for you. If she can find a way of reciprocating outside the organization, that's great. But unless and until she does, she's going to be in your debt—literally and figuratively. So she's going to have a strong tendency to favor you over the other members of her unit, fairly or unfairly.

On the surface, that may be a tempting position to place yourself in. But in the long run, you know that's not the way to win. If Maria can't find a suitable way to reciprocate (one that doesn't violate her own ideas about being a fair and objective supervisor) she may begin to resent the debt she owes—and the person she owes it to (namely, you). Then your position may not be so enviable after all!

Cures

The best way to handle this situation depends on the kind of relationship you already have with Maria. If you trust her and believe that she's not going to hold your refusal against you, you can be honest in your response. If you don't really trust her, and aren't sure that your refusal won't come back to haunt you when it's time for your appraisal or the next promotion, you'll need to use a little more finesse.

If you have an open, trusting relationship with Maria:

Regardless of how good your relationship is with Maria—even if you're personal friends—loaning her the money is a bad idea. The fact that you're now in a supervisory-subordinate relationship changes things. And you can't ignore that completely, even outside the office.

Make your refusal as direct, but sympathetic, as you can. Let her know that you appreciate the bind she's in, but that your loaning her money is not the best way to get out of it.

Offer her other assistance in getting the funds she needs. Maybe you know of somewhere she can borrow the money at a lower interest rate than is usually available or someplace that loans money to people who've been turned down at other institutions. You might know, or be able to find out, programs that are available for people who have special medical problems and free support or counseling services they provide. Whatever you can do for her that doesn't compromise the supervisor-subordinate relationship, do it.

If you don't completely trust Maria:

It's even *more* important in this situation that you not put yourself in a compromising position by loaning her the money. But it's equally important that you protect yourself as you refuse to do what Maria's asking.

Find out what your company's rules are about standards of conduct for supervisors. If there is a prohibition against supervisors soliciting employees for money, tactfully point that out to Maria.

You can suggest to her that, much as you'd like to help her out financially, you're concerned that violating a company rule will hurt her more than the money will help. That's a refusal she can't get too upset about.

If your company has no specific prohibition, you can probably still get out of this situation gracefully. One way is to work around the issue. Talk about your own finances and all the bills that are facing you without actually addressing Maria's request. Or talk about the difficulties in loaning money and still maintaining an objective supervisor-subordinate relationship—again without actually refusing the loan.

If Maria presses, tell her you're not in a position to loan money—again as tactfully as possible, and basing your refusal on reasons that have nothing to do with her personally. Depending on how likely you think it is that Maria will get upset and retaliate (overtly or covertly), it might be a good idea to talk to someone you trust at or above Maria's level. By getting the incident on record with an objective observer, you may be able to protect yourself against later reprisal.

If the chances are great enough that Maria will get nasty if you refuse, and if you don't expect managers above her to support your refusal (and to protect you), and if you can afford it, it may be best to loan Maria the money. The only realistic alternative may be to start looking for another job. It's not necessary to take the first offer that comes along; chances are Maria won't do anything too drastic just because you refused to loan her some money. But in the long run, your chances for success here may be limited. If Maria takes the refusal well, you won't be out anything except a little time and effort. And if she takes the refusal badly, you'll have a head start toward a better situation.

And If This Doesn't Quite Fit Your Situation . . .

Other problems in this chapter and in Chapter 13 discuss dilemmas that occur when your boss' ideas and yours are in conflict.

Use Checklist 5 to develop a cure of your own.

9-4

The Problem: He refuses to accept work from a senior worker because she's female.

The Scene

"But, Mr. Weyant, Denise is *good*. If I give her this project, you'll get a real quality product.

"Now, now, I know she appreciates your loyalty to her—and so do I. But you know she just doesn't have the background she needs for the tough stuff. Give it to one of the men who came up through the ranks and really understands the in's and out's. Anything else?"

You shake your head and leave. Your boss just won't accept that a woman can do the really difficult work. It's always the same— "Give it to one of the men." He supported you when you selected Denise, but now it looks like that was just to make the EEO figures look better. Denise would probably never file a discrimination complaint—but you'd hardly blame her if she did. What can you do to help things?

Possible Causes

Mr. Weyant doesn't believe someone without the same background he and the other men have can successfully do the work.

Mr. Weyant has never seen that a woman can be good at this kind of work. His ideas prevent him from ever being in a situation where he can see that he's wrong.

He is simply prejudiced against women. Once you'd hired a woman into a senior position to meet a "quota," he had no interest in how well she could perform.

Hint: This is one of many situations in which you're trying to change your boss' attitude. Bosses can be effectively supervised, but it takes tact, skill and a great deal of patience. It is, in short, one of those "character-building" experiences your mother used to tell you about.

Cures

If Mr. Weyant doesn't believe someone without his background can do the difficult work:

This mindset is fairly widespread. In many occupations, virtually everyone who enters them comes through one or a very limited number of routes. (For instance, a firm may hire all of its production planners from the shop floor.) Because everyone has the background, everyone assumes it's a necessity to get the job done. Weyant's feelings about Denise may reflect this more than the fact that she's a woman.

Again, this is circular reasoning. Since he doesn't think someone without his background can do the work, he won't let them—so he never finds out whether in fact they can. To be successful, you need to break the circle.

Any of the tactics in the next "cure" could be used for this one, too. You might also concentrate on the process a worker goes through to make the product. If Denise can show Weyant that she can perform the process successfully, he may loosen up some. It may help show him that she knows what she's doing even though she doesn't have his background (for instance, if one of the difficult products requires intricate planning and she shows Weyant she can do it).

Your basic strategy for this "cure" and the one below is to give Denise all of the exposure you can to Weyant. If she's really good, and his mind isn't completely closed, she'll eventually get through to him.

If he's never seen that a woman can be good at this kind of work:

There's a risky way to change this. Give the project to Denise without telling Weyant. When you turn the project in, don't tell him who did it. Do this several more times. Then collect copies of all the work, give them to Weyant, and tell him what happened. When he sees the evidence before him, he may realize that he's been wrong. (On the other hand, he may just get madder than hell!)

A safer course is to give Denise the most difficult projects you can that won't antagonize Weyant. Assuming she does good work, point this out to him at strategic points. Soon, he may relent to let her work on something really difficult. Then she'll have the chance to prove what she can really do.

You might also try using a team made up of Denise and a male employee who works well with her. Weyant may agree to let them do the project jointly, confident that the male employee will keep them out of trouble. Then, after several successes, he may be willing to let Denise do one by herself.

If he's simply prejudiced against women, at least in this line of work:

It's unfortunate, but there's still a lot of feeling that women (like other minorities) belong in their "place." Weyant might have no problem at all with Denise in other occupations, even a profession like accounting. But he believes that women just aren't cut out for this line of work.

In Chapter 2, we looked at several problems in which employees were accused of discrimination against other employees. These were hard—but dealing with discrimination when the guilty party is your boss becomes truly challenging.

It's imperative that as little of your boss's attitude as possible spills over into your group. Support Denise in every way you can (you may find some ideas in Problem 1-4). Make it clear to your employees that you support her, and that you won't tolerate any discrimination against her.

Don't push too hard, but keep promoting Denise and her abilities to your boss. You might also want to suggest at times that "bringing her along" presents a good EEO image. You might even suggest that not letting her handle the toughest jobs might look like discrimination to some people. Even if he doesn't believe in women in the occupation—and wishes you'd never hired Denise—he may go along with you just to keep out of trouble.

Something to Think About

It's often difficult to sort out a situation like this and decide just what the "cause" is. (Of course, there may be a combination of causes.) Remember what we've mentioned before: overt discrimination is largely dead, but more subtle forms of discrimination are all around.

And If This Doesn't Quite Fit Your Situation . . .

Look at Problem 1-4 if part of the problem is that Denise is a newer worker you've promoted and the other employees are resentful of her. If she's a good worker but they're resentful because she's a member of a minority group, see Problem 2-4. If other workers may be discriminating against her, see Problems 2-8 and 2-9.

Use Checklist 5 to develop a cure of your own.

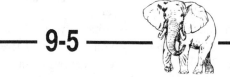

—— 9-5 ——

The Problem: He tells you to fire a good employee whom he doesn't like.

The Scene

Jimmy Csaki is a good, solid worker—not your best, but not your worst. Unfortunately, Norm, your boss, thinks he's a loudmouth—basically because he questioned a remark Norm made in a staff meeting a few months ago about parking assignments. It was, admittedly, a dumb thing to do. (Norm doesn't take questioning well.) Jimmy apologized, though, and things seemed to be going okay. But now every time Norm sees Jimmy in the cafeteria, he gets all worked up again. Finally, this afternoon, Norm decided he'd had enough.

"Get that troublemaker out of here," he stormed. "Two weeks—max. Then I never want to see his smirking face again. Got it?"

You got it all right. But it's not fair to Jimmy or to you. He *is* a good worker. One question two months ago (and not a big deal at that) shouldn't get him fired!

Possible Causes

Norm may have observed things about Jimmy's conduct or performance that aren't apparent to you. There may have been other incidents where Jimmy was indiscreet in his dealings with Norm—incidents that you're not aware of. If these are serious or frequent enough, Norm may have defensible reasons for wanting to fire Jimmy.

Norm may have just taken a dislike to Jimmy. There may be no objective justification for his dislike, and no real reason to fire Jimmy—other than that Norm told you to.

Cures

If Norm knows things about Jimmy's conduct or performance you're not aware of:

Talk to Norm to find out what he's observed. Try to get specifics—times, dates, places, details of the incidents.

Given the information Norm's provided, what is *your* objective assessment of Jimmy now? Is this something you'd normally fire an employee for? If so, take the information you've received from Norm and talk to your Personnel Department about the procedures your company requires in terminating employees.

If the incidents Norm has observed aren't things you'd normally fire an employee for, talk to him about your concerns. Find out why Norm considers Jimmy's behavior so unacceptable. If you feel strongly that Jimmy shouldn't be fired, make your case to Norm. You might even suggest that Norm himself notify Jimmy that he's being fired. But as long as Norm has objective reasons for the termination, he *is* the boss, and this is one time when your appropriate response is "Yes, sir." You can register your objections, but in the end, it's Norm's decision.

After Jimmy's gone and things are back to normal, you should take the opportunity to talk to Norm about his reasons for wanting Jimmy fired. If you and he disagreed about the seriousness of what Jimmy did, you need to find out where the two of you disconnected. There will be other "Jimmys," and it's important for you to understand Norm's philosophy on acceptable and unacceptable behavior.

If Norm's dislike of Jimmy is irrational or unjustified:

Your first step should be to find out as much as you can from Norm about why he wants Jimmy fired. Depending on how reasonable a boss Norm usually is, you may be able to register your objections.

But if Norm is likely to bear a grudge for your less than enthusiastic response, it's better to keep your objections to yourself.

Regardless of how unreasonable Norm's instructions are, he *is* the boss, and you're expected to follow his orders. Just as you expect your workers to obey your instructions and question them later, Norm will expect you to do as he tells you.

Depending on how unreasonable you think Norm's instructions are, it might be a good idea to document your objections in a memorandum or other similar document. Particularly if Jimmy fights his dismissal, in a grievance or court of law, you'll be able to show that you were just following orders.

If the reasons for firing Jimmy aren't just bad judgment but instead are illegal, no amount of documentation will save you. Particularly if you believe that Norm's real motives for dismissing Jimmy are discriminatory, you're better off to refuse—keeping in mind the personal consequences. Let Norm's superiors know in advance that he wants you to fire Jimmy, and why. Then tell them how you intend to handle the situation. Keep in mind that you're taking a risk; they may not support you. In that case you need to weigh the risks of being fired yourself against the risks of civil penalties against you for engaging in discriminatory conduct. It's not a pleasant choice, but by checking with Norm's superiors first, you'll know better where you stand.

And If This Doesn't Quite Fit Your Situation . . .

Look at Problem 14-3 if you have the reverse problem—your boss won't let you fire a nonperformer.

Use Checklist 5 to develop a cure of your own.

9-6

The Problem: He asks you for a date, even though he's married.

The Scene

Well, it happened. Thad asked you for a date—even though he's your boss and even though he's married. In fact, he didn't just ask—he

was insistent. You stalled him for the moment, but you know you'll
have to deal with it again soon.

But how? You genuinely like him. Besides, if you turn him
down he may take it out on you on the job. But he's married, and
you've never gotten involved with married men. And you've never
gotten involved with anyone at work—particularly your boss.

Possible Causes

*Thad genuinely likes you and is letting his emotions overrule
his head.*

*You've established a very friendly but honest relationship with
Thad—and he's misunderstood your signals.* He thinks you really
want a "closer" relationship.

*You've "come on" to Thad without realizing it or admitting it
to yourself.* He's responding to you.

*He thinks that since you work for him he can force his attentions
on you.*

Hint: Before you make any decisions, find someone you can
talk with frankly, preferably someone who's at or above Thad's level
in the organization. Tell them just what's happened. Talk it over
with them, and make sure they know what you plan to do. Then, if
the situation turns nasty, you'll have someone who can vouch for
your side of the story.

Cures

*If Thad genuinely likes you and is letting his emotions run
away with him:*

This is probably the easiest cause to deal with. If he cares for
you as a person, he'll listen to your reasons for not wanting to date
him (though this may take a day or two). Point out the value of the
relationship the two of you have, and the dangers of getting emotionally involved in this way.

An effective and close working relationship is a very different
one from an emotionally charged one. Even if Thad weren't married,
developing this kind of relationship would strain your work relation-

ship. Then, if you ended the personal relationship, the strain at work could prove to be even worse.

If Thad values the relationship as much as you do, he'll see the merit in these arguments. He may not want to, but he will.

If Thad has misunderstood your friendliness as something else:

The situation is much like the one just above, but you have a bit more explaining to do. If he continues to mistake your friendliness, you may have to pull back from the relationship—and this could make it more difficult for the two of you to work together. It could also make your job less satisfying and enjoyable.

This requires some subtlety and tact. Simply telling him that he's wrong and you aren't attracted to him *that* way will probably damage the relationship. Be sure he knows that you do like him and enjoy his friendship—but that you want to keep the relationship on a business level. All of the reasons in the "cure" above are relevant here, too.

Even if you agree to keep the relationship as it is, things may be strained between the two of you for a while (as they may in the "cure" above). Accept this as normal. If you've had a strong relationship, things will improve in a few days or weeks.

One word of caution. Emotions are tricky. Countless times, two people have worked through their feelings, decided to keep everything on a friendly, open level—and then found themselves sabotaged later by feelings they had hidden. You both need to keep this possibility in mind.

If you've "come on" to Thad without realizing or admitting it:

Sure, we know you don't want to face this—but you have to. Emotions run by their own logic. In our heads, we may know the limits on our relationships. Our emotions may run in a different direction—but since we've "decided" not to do that, we hide them from ourselves. It's possible that you decided an emotional relationship with Thad was wrong, so that you ignored your own feelings in this direction. But in one way or another, they slipped out. Thad is responding to them. Oops!

Obviously, you begin by being very honest with yourself. You need to understand what's happening inside yourself before you can deal with Thad. If you have someone you trust deeply who can help you explore this, it will help immensely.

Then you need to be equally honest with Thad. It may be hard on both of you emotionally, but if your relationship is strong you'll both come through it. It may even help you develop a stronger, but still business-like relationship.

If Thad intends to force his attentions on you because you work for him:

This, of course, is a dramatically different situation. You evidently can't count on a strong, honest relationship with Thad to pull both of you past this situation. In fact, whatever relationship you have has now been corrupted.

Did your mother ever tell you to say no "tactfully but firmly"? Well, this is where you put that to use. You don't want to ruin whatever is left of a real relationship with Thad, and you certainly don't want him angry at you. But the cost of giving in to him would certainly be high.

Here's where it would be very helpful to talk with someone who's been in the same situation and (hopefully) handled it successfully. She may be able to give you some ideas on dealing with Thad.

If Thad remains insistent and begins to promise you job advantages or make job-related threats if you don't "cooperate," you have real, serious sexual harassment. This is where it's so important to have kept at least one disinterested outsider aware of the situation; you may have no alternative but to file a complaint of discrimination based on the harassment. If that becomes necessary, you'll need all of the support you can get.

Things to Think About

We plainly haven't dealt with one aspect of the situation: Thad's relationship with his wife. That's really no concern of yours, no matter how strong your beliefs about the marital relationship. It's important to remember this, because Thad (honestly or otherwise) may talk about how unsatisfactory his marriage is and how much he needs your affection. As much as you may genuinely care for him, he needs to solve that problem in some other way.

Through all of this, you've probably been assuming that this is a situation between a female supervisor and her male boss. In this case, it is—but it needn't be. The female could be the boss, or they could both be the same sex. While this might add a certain "kinkiness" to the situation in your eyes, it doesn't change the basic dynamics.

And If This Doesn't Quite Fit Your Situation . . .

If you think Thad may begin to treat you differently because you turn him down, you might want to read over the situations in Chapters 13 and 14 to be prepared.

Use Checklist 5 to develop a cure of your own.

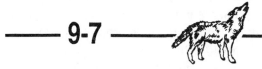

9-7

The Problem: She tells you to give a high rating to an employee who isn't very good.

The Scene

"I'm afraid I can't sign this appraisal," Joan tells you after staff meeting. "Cecilia has done some special things for me and I can't just ignore them. She needs to know that she's appreciated."

Sure, Cecilia needs to know she's appreciated—for running Joan's laundry to the cleaners, and calling the florist on her husband's birthday, and even typing Joan's speech to the school board. But that has nothing to do with her work—which isn't all that great. You have to send a lot of her stuff back to be re-worked, and she tends to be surly with the staff. It just goes against your grain to give a good rating for performance like that.

Possible Causes

Joan may know something about Cecilia's performance that you aren't aware of—aside from the personal things she's done for her. She may also have done some special assignments for Joan that *are* work related and are performed better than when she's done work for you. That additional effort should be recognized.

Joan may be using the company's performance appraisal system inappropriately to reward Cecilia for personal business. Her only motive for wanting Cecilia's rating raised may be these nonwork-related favors Cecilia has done for her.

Hint: The seriousness of this particular problem depends to some extent on the nature of your company's performance appraisal system. In some companies, employees are appraised just because someone along the line decided it was a nice idea—but the appraisal doesn't really mean much because it's not used for anything. In other companies, the appraisal forms the basis for other actions. Pay raises and bonuses may be based on employees' ratings; promotion decisions and retention during layoffs may be affected by appraisal results.

If your company's appraisal system doesn't have any real "teeth," then this battle is probably not worth fighting. If appraisal *does* count for something, though, you have some decisions to make about how far you're willing to bend.

Cures

If Joan has information about Cecilia's work performance that you're not aware of:

Talk to Joan to find out what Cecilia has done that she believes justifies a higher rating. Discuss the incidents with her to try to come to some agreement on how much higher a rating Cecilia deserves. Once you've heard what Joan has to say, you may agree right away that the higher rating is justified.

If you still don't agree that Cecilia should be rated as highly as Joan wants, even after you know what work Cecilia has performed directly for Joan, you have some more discussing to do. Find out what Joan's basic philosophy is about rating employees—what kind of performance, in general, equates to what rating level. You and Joan apparently have a difference in basic approaches to rating, and your life will be a lot easier if you know what Joan is looking for in appraisals.

You should also take this opportunity to discuss with Joan the difficulties that arise when she assigns work to your people without your knowledge. Cecilia's work for you may have suffered simply because she had too much to do—and thought it was more important in the long run to do well for Joan. If your boss bypasses you to your work group more often than you'd like, look at Problem 14-11 for some suggested solutions.

If Joan wants to reward Cecilia for personal favors she's done for her:

Talk to Joan about your perceptions of Cecilia's performance. If you have specific examples of her work, show Joan a few to illustrate why you think the lower rating is justified.

Depending on the level of trust and openness that exists in your relationship with Joan, you may be able to discuss freely your objections to rewarding Cecilia for her personal favors through the company's performance appraisal process. But when (and if) you do question Joan's motives openly, it's a good idea to have some alternatives to offer to her. Maybe Joan could treat Cecilia to dinner, give her a gift certificate or some token present, or send her flowers at home.

If you have contacts with someone at or above Joan's level in the organization, you might consider discussing your dilemma with that person. They should be able to give you some idea of whether you're likely to get support if you go head on against Joan. And if you are likely to be supported, and the high rating for Cecilia will hurt other employees, it may be worth elevating your disagreement with Joan through channels.

In most organizations, though, you're not likely to arouse much management interest over one performance rating—unless management is looking for some excuse to "get at" Joan already. If you're not going to get higher level support, you can document your objections to Cecilia's higher rating in a memorandum for your own files, or you can ask Joan to sign the rating herself since you're uncomfortable with it. But in the end, Joan is the boss, and it's in the interests of your continued employment to do as she asks.

Things to Think About

In all the problems we've discussed in this chapter, you're faced with a choice: you can do what your boss asks (often at the expense of your own principles), or you can take a stand against him or her (often at the risk of your continued employment). These aren't easy decisions to make. Only you know how much you can bend without breaking. Only you can weigh the risks of compliance against the risks of challenging your boss's demands.

We've tried to outline some actions you can take to preserve your integrity and protect yourself at the same time, but sometimes there's not much you can do to protect yourself. It's useful to remember, though, that unethical actions seldom occur in isolation. Environments foster ethical or unethical behavior, and you can usually tell fairly easily which kind of environment you're in. If things are going on around you that you're not comfortable with, it probably won't be long before you'll be caught personally in a difficult situation. The time to get ready is now—before you have to leave or do something you'll regret later.

And If This Doesn't Quite Fit Your Situation . . .

Look at Problem 14-3 if the employee is poor enough that you want to fire him, but your boss won't let you.

Use Checklist 5 to develop a cure of your own

10

Troubleshooting Your Own Personal Problems

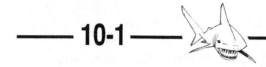

——— 10-1 ———

The Problem: You let your boss get caught with a problem you should have warned him about.

The Scene

"You knew that Sam Jonas was going to complain to the old man about my trip to Rochester?!"

"Well . . . he did say something about taking it higher in the organization."

"And you didn't say anything to me?!"

"Uh . . . no."

"Why in the world didn't you—oh, forget it. I don't want to hear anything more about it. Get back to work, and I'll talk to you later."

Possible Causes

You didn't think you needed to say anything to him. After all, Sam didn't say for sure that he was going to talk to "the old man."

You meant to say something, but it slipped your mind.

Your boss can look out for himself. You have problems of your own—you can't look out for him all the time.

Hint: Regardless of the cause, you are in hot water up to at least your eyebrows.

Cures

If you didn't think you needed to say anything to him:

Did you think that Sam was just "blowing smoke," that he would cool down? Or did you not think it was that serious?

It doesn't matter. In case you haven't learned it, here is one of the fundamental commandments of organizational life:

No matter what else you do, **always** *see that your boss knows about any matter that may affect him. Period. No exceptions. And doubly true if the "matter" is negative. Letting your boss be "blind-sided" by a problem you knew about is close to the top of employee mortal sins.*

There's a simple way to handle this. When your boss calms down, go see him. Tell him you goofed, that you should have picked up on Sam's comment and warned him. *Don't make excuses;* just apologize. Then promise him that it will never, ever happen again.

What if he's angry and yells at you? Let him. You deserve it. Again, don't make excuses. Do your best to direct his attention to the future—the future in which you won't ever let it happen again. With luck, he'll give you one more chance.

If you meant to say something, but it slipped your mind:

This is a first-class "oops"! There's no excuse for it, and you should offer none.

Follow the suggestions in the "cure" above. Are you skilled at being abject? Good—you'll need to be good at it.

But you have an additional problem. How do you make sure that you don't forget to warn him again? There are dozens of ways you can do this. One of us makes lists; the other has an electronic scheduler and memo pad—complete with alarms. You can use a pocket planner. If you're not sure what to do, find someone who does it right and copy him or her. But *do* it. Set up a system so that you will never forget to warn your boss again. In this game, two strikes are out.

If you think your boss can look out for himself:

Bad misunderstanding! Apparently no one has taught you the first law of effective subordinateship:

You have no responsibility greater than that of helping your boss be successful. None. Nada. Zip. Period.

Does this sound harsh and manipulative and scheming and otherwise unsavory? Stop and think a moment about what you expect from your employees. Don't you want them to help make you successful? Is there something wrong with that?

It really doesn't matter whether or not you think there's something wrong with it—your boss probably doesn't. Sam just provided you with a useful learning experience. You should take advantage of it.

When you talk with your boss, admit to him that you just weren't thinking. Tell him how much you have learned since then. Assure him that this failure was the "old" you, one which he won't ever see again. Then make sure that you become and remain the "new" you.

Things to Think About

In many problems in this book, finding and using the right cure is difficult. However, in this situation, this is not the case. It's as simple as realizing you fouled up, admitting it—and then making absolutely, lead-pipe-cinch sure it never happens again. There, that was easy, wasn't it? (And, with luck, your boss will still speak to you.)

And If This Doesn't Quite Fit Your Situation . . .

See the other problems in this chapter. You might also look at the problems in Chapters 4, 5, and 6; if your mistake was like one of those, it might give you some idea of what your boss will do—and want you to do.

Use Checklist 6 to develop a cure of your own.

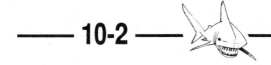

10-2

The Problem: An employee accuses you of sexual harass-
ment.

The Scene

You answer what seems to be a routine telephone call from an employee. But instead you hear:

"Mrs. Pierce, this is Bert Essmann from the EEO Office. I'd like to come over and talk to you tomorrow afternoon, if possible. Don Segali has filed a sexual harassment complaint against you."

Shocked and stunned, you replace the handset. What happens now?

Possible Causes

The specific cause of the sexual harassment charge isn't important here. There are only two possible conditions: either you harassed Don Segali or you didn't.

A charge of sexual harassment is justified if you made unwanted overtures, either physical or verbal, to the employee making the complaint. It does not matter whether the actions or words were intended to have sexual overtones. What matters is that a reasonable person, objectively viewing the facts, would construe the actions or remarks as sexual in nature.

Likewise, confirmed sexual harassment does not require a superior-subordinate relationship. While the situation is worse if you supervise Don, particularly if he alleges that you threatened to take or withhold actions based on his cooperation with you, the absence of such threats or of a supervisor-subordinate relationship doesn't mean that sexual harassment hasn't occurred. Sexual harassment occurs *whenever* an employee is the object of unwanted overtures, regardless of the employment relationship between the employee and the person alleged to have harassed him.

So the first thing you need to do is find out the specific content of Don's complaint against you.

As the person alleged to have harassed Don, you are entitled to know, specifically and in detail, what Don's alleging. You have a right to know not only what charge Don has made against you, but also what evidence he's offered in support of his charge. If he's cited specific incidents of harassing behavior, you have the right to find out the details of those incidents as he recounted them—names, dates, places, what happened.

Before you respond to any of Don's allegations, think carefully about what he's said. Did the incidents occur as he's described them? If not, in what respects do your recollections differ from his? If your recollections are essentially the same, do you see how Don could have interpreted the incidents as sexual harassment? What did you intend?

Only after you know what you're being accused of and have had some time to think over the situation can you respond appropriately to these *very* serious allegations.

Hint: Specific procedures for dealing with sexual harassment complaints differ somewhat from organization to organization. In general, though, you have the right to be represented in responding to the charges against you. Because sexual harassment charges, justified or unjustified, are so serious and potentially so damaging, you should find out what specific rights to representation you have *before* you answer any questions the investigator may pose.

If you have the right to be represented, by an attorney or other representative, explain to the investigator or EEO counselor that you're very concerned about clearing up these allegations without damage to you or Don. Then defer answering any questions until your representative can be present. You need to protect yourself as much as you can. Even if you're completely innocent, you'll benefit from the assistance of an experienced representative.

Cures

Because the circumstances under which sexual harassment charges arise differ so much, there are only general guidelines we can give you in dealing with them. Most important is that you talk to your representative about the specifics of your case and follow her advice. If you're not comfortable with the advice your representative has given you, get a second opinion. But don't strike out on your own. Sexual harassment charges, justified or not, have much greater potential for ruining you personally than any other category of discrimination charge. Our best advice is "Watch your step!"

Your representative will want you to respond specifically and in detail to each charge and incident the complainant has raised. Any documents you have that were prepared at the time the alleged harassment occurred which would support your recollection of events will be particularly helpful.

Wherever you can, identify other people who may have witnessed the specific incidents that were alleged to have occurred. Even if no one was with you at the times Don claims that you harassed him, you may be able to identify other employees who could make written statements about the general nature of your relationship with Don and with other men in the company that would help refute the charges.

You should not interview any of these witnesses personally. One of them could later claim that he or she was coerced into a particular position. It's much better if you provide the names to your representative or to an EEO investigator or counselor, describe the kind of information you expect the witnesses to provide, and then let someone else do the interviewing.

This is also not a situation in which you should approach Don yourself to try to resolve the complaint. If Don has filed a sexual harassment charge against you, it's clear that the relationship with you is badly strained. You cannot trust that anything you say to him informally about his complaint won't end up as a reprisal charge later on.

Once you've helped your representative assemble your defense against the charges, there's not much you can do except to sit back and wait—as calmly as you can. Sexual harassment charges are difficult to prove if there are no witnesses and no previous history of discriminatory or unethical behavior. In those cases, the final decision depends greatly on the credibility of the people involved. If you've been an open, honest, trustworthy person all along, you have a good chance of refuting the charges—even without witnesses who can contradict Don's statements.

In the meantime, treat your employees as you always have—fairly, impartially, and objectively. You needn't avoid Don, but you should exercise some prudence in how you talk to him (and where you talk to him). If you treat all of your employees fairly, you'll have little chance of a reprisal complaint in the future.

And what if, upon reflection, you decide that you did something that Don could reasonably interpret as sexual harassment? Let your representative know *right away*. Then follow the advice you're given to try to make Don "whole" without ruining your own career.

Things to Think About

If you decide that you did really sexually harass Don, there are two decisions you should make *soon*.

The first is a private decision that you will never engage in that behavior again, and that you'll be on your guard against behavior that, however well intentioned, could be interpreted as sexual harassment.

The second is a career decision: If you've been found to have sexually harassed Don, intentionally or unintentionally, it's going to be difficult for you to function effectively in the future as a manager in your organization. You need to begin to look around for someplace where you can put your past mistakes behind you and start fresh. No one who's worked with you in this situation is likely ever to trust you again—the stigma of sexual harassment is *that* powerful.

And If This Doesn't Quite Fit Your Situation . . .

Look at Problem 10-5 for a discussion of sexual discrimination charges that do not involve harassment. Problem 2-5 addresses sexual harassment by one of your subordinates.

Use Checklist 6 to develop a cure of your own.

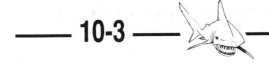

—— 10-3 ——

The Problem: You missed the deadline on a major project.

The Scene

"Millie, would you please see that Mr. Nomura gets this project summary?"

"The one for the general ledger update? Just a little late, aren't you?"

"Actually, it's less than six weeks behind. I think we'll have it up and running for real in another week or so. You know, that's not so bad for a project like this."

"Mr. Nomura isn't so nonchalant about it. When you told him you'd have it by two weeks ago without fail, he promised it to the Comptroller by then. He's already been chewed out once—I'd try not to run into him for a year or so if I were you."

Possible Causes

One of your key programmers left you right in the middle of the project. It took you over six weeks to replace him.

There turned out to be more coding than you expected. The old system was in worse shape than you thought.

Several key managers in the Comptroller's office were late reviewing the preliminary outputs and getting them back to you. They have part of the blame for the system being late.

You did your best, but too many small things went wrong. No one could have anticipated the sheer number of glitches you had to deal with.

Hints: None of the above matters. You promised to deliver a system by such-and-such a date. Your boss relied on you and made a commitment to his peers. Now the date has come and gone and there's no system. You've embarrassed your boss—not to mention fouling up the Comptroller's plans. The excuses don't matter

Now, let's get to what does matter:

- *Your planning was unrealistic.* You counted on everything (or most things) going right, and they didn't.

- *You didn't control the project effectively.* Even if your planning was okay, your execution was faulty.

- *You didn't warn your boss in advance that the project was in trouble.* This might at least have saved your boss the worst of his embarrassment, and let the Comptroller revise her plans.

Cures

If your planning was unrealistic:

You'd better do a detailed postmortem quickly. What happened that you didn't anticipate? Where should you have known better? Where should you have built in some slack just on general principles?

If you don't have clear answers to these questions, you'd better find some first-class training in effective project planning.

If you didn't control the project effectively:

If your planning was realistic (and perhaps even if it wasn't), you let something get away from you. When did the slippage begin? Did anyone realize what was happening? If so, why wasn't it corrected? If not, how long did it slide before someone finally understood there was a problem? You'd better get the answers to these and similar questions—in detail.

Again, it sounds like you need some training in actual project management. It might be a good idea to find it and sign up for it as quickly as possible—preferably before you talk with Mr. Nomura.

If you didn't warn your boss in advance that the project was in trouble:

There's a lot we might say about this. Most of it is said in Problem 10-1. You probably want to look at that problem and the suggested cures again.

No matter what the cause is:

The most serious problem is the impact of this on your relationship with Mr. Nomura. You've let him down *badly*.

If you don't realize how badly, let us help you understand. One of the most valuable assets any individual can have is the absolute confidence of his boss. It doesn't matter whether you're an employee, a supervisor, or a senior manager. If your boss *knows* that he can count on you to produce what you promised, when you promised it—you're halfway home. If he doesn't know this—sorry, but you're not even on the team yet.

What approach should you assume when you approach Mr. Nomura? "Abject remorse" is one phrase which comes to mind. Don't even think of making excuses or offering explanations. You blew it, period.

What you need to do more than anything else is to direct Mr. Nomura's attention away from the past and toward the future—a much improved future. That's why it's important to analyze *why* and *how* the project failed, quickly and in detail. Then plan what you need to do to prevent that kind of failure ever again. (Your steps to prevent it should involve a significant amount of your personal time, not just on-the-clock time.) Get started on these steps right away. If you're lucky, you'll be on your way by the time you talk with Mr. Nomura. Then you can show him concretely what you've learned and how you're going to see that nothing like this ever happens again. Will it be enough? Who knows? We do know that nothing less is apt to help.

Things to Think About

Stop and think. Aren't your really valuable employees the ones to whom you can give a job and then never worry about it again? You assign the project and—unless they warn you in advance—they deliver just what they promised. They're the people who make a manager's life bearable (and occasionally even satisfying).

Do you have something more important to do than to be this kind of person where your boss is concerned?

And If This Doesn't Quite Fit Your Situation . . .

See Problem 4-4 for a description of a worker who has fouled up an important job. It might give you an idea of how your boss will react if you did similarly. If your problem is partially caused by poor organization, see Problem 6-1; if you're generally unable to deliver what you promise, look at Problem 6-3; if you go to pieces under pressure, see Problem 6-4.

Use Checklist 6 to develop a cure of your own.

—— **10-4** ————

The Problem: You've taken over a supposedly well run unit that's actually on the verge of disintegration.

The Scene

This is the third time this week you've found someone *almost* doing something incredibly stupid, but managed to pull back in time! First, John Bolling told the division chief's secretary there was "no way" he could get her the materials she needed for the chief's conference on Wednesday. (Luckily she complained to you first, rather than to Mr. Simpson, so you could fix things up in time.)

Then, Gary Robinson deleted (but did not destroy!) most of his supply orders. So you had to have Data Processing down to "undelete" them.

Finally, yesterday afternoon Paul Chrisman "lost" a shipment of hazardous chemicals on their way to disposal (which, fortunately, someone found in a hallway, just before the trash pickup came).

That's just too many near misses—especially for what was supposed to be a "good" group.

Possible Causes

There may have been a lot of recent turnover in the unit. The workers on whom the unit's good reputation was based may no longer work there—leaving you with a group of new people who don't know their jobs very well yet.

The group may have relied on their previous supervisor to keep things going. Especially if the previous supervisor had a strong directive style and was technically very competent, he may have been the glue holding the whole operation together. The workers themselves may not be accustomed to being held responsible for their own work— they relied on him instead.

The unit's performance may have been deteriorating for quite a while. The last supervisor got out just in time, leaving you to deal with the mess.

Hint: Early on, you need to decide just how bad things are in your group. Are there just a few key players who are doing poorly, but whose performance affects the entire unit's production? Or is almost everyone doing worse than you'd like? Is there likely to be "mission failure" if you don't step in immediately? Is there likely to be some noticeable "mission failure" even if you start working the problem right now?

If things are bad enough that you expect people outside the unit to begin noticing problems, then you need to let your boss know soon what you've found. This is delicate because you don't want to sound as if you're slamming your predecessor—or setting yourself up to look like a hero. But if there are likely to be complaints, he should hear about them from you first!

Cures

If there has been a lot of recent turnover in the unit:

To some extent, time will cure many of the problems you're facing now. But there are some actions you can take to speed the process along.

Review your files and ask other employees in the unit to see if there are standard operating procedures for the jobs that have been filled recently. Read over the procedures yourself and ask experienced employees to look at them also to be sure that they're still current and that they reflect a reasonable way to do business. If the operating procedures are usable, they're a good starting point for your training efforts. You can go over them with the new workers. Make sure they understand what they're supposed to do, and then have them use the operating procedures as job aids when they encounter situations they're not sure about. With any luck, the standard operating procedures you have in place will cover much of the day-to-day work of the unit.

Ask some of your more experienced workers to work with the new people for a while until they're more comfortable in their positions. The more experienced staff shouldn't plan to do the work for the new people, but should be prepared to "look over their shoulders" for a while—to review work and answer questions when unfamiliar situations arise.

If the turnover has been especially heavy, leaving you with few people who know the operation, you may be able to arrange to borrow a few workers from other units. You'll be looking for people who have previously worked in your unit and know the work well enough to be able to get your new group off on the right foot. Ask to keep them for a few weeks—just long enough to get the new people started right, but not so long that they become dependent on the extra help.

If the group relied on its previous supervisor to keep things going:

You have a real challenge here—but one that can reap real rewards if handled well. The key is to teach your staff how to accept delegation. This may not be pleasant at first. You'll be asking them to take responsibility for things they've never been personally accountable for before. But once they've tried it, most of them won't ever want to go back to the old way!

Sit down with your staff and talk to them about how your style differs from that of your predecessor. Without criticizing his style, explain what you see as the advantages to them and the unit of delegated responsibility. Stress the freedom they will have to run their portion of the process pretty much as they see fit—once they've demonstrated to you their competence and willingness to accept responsibility.

Then next step is just to jump in and do it! Begin by assigning specific tasks to individual workers. Agree on what you'll expect to see at the end of the assignment and when it will be due. Make a note on your calendar, and then GO AWAY. Don't initiate a contact with an employee again about the assignment until the day *after* it's due.

When employees come to you with questions about how they ought to do something, unless it clearly requires a policy or precedent-making decision, DO NOT ANSWER THEM. Respond with something like, "I'd have to think about that. How do you want to handle it?" You don't have to prove your technical competence. Your people know you know the work. They need to show you they know it. So resist the temptation to find answers for them. Their job is to come up with answers. Your job is to say "Yes" or "No."

If you've explained your requirements clearly and stayed out of your employees' way as they've carried them out, they should begin very soon to deliver what you want. If not, a few repetitions of this assignment pattern, punctuated with reminders of your basic philosophy of delegation, should get the message across. What if repeated efforts don't result in a turnaround in your employees' willingness to accept responsibility for their own work and improvement in their products? You may need to talk to some of them about a career move—out of your unit.

If the unit's performance has been deteriorating for quite a while:

As we discussed in the problems dealing with individual poor performance, the longer performance problems go unattended, the harder it is to correct them. If performance has been deteriorating over a period of time and is just now reaching the critical point, you cannot afford to delay another day.

Although the situation is not quite as dire—yet—the cures presented in Problem 1-1 outline the basic steps you need to follow in dealing with ongoing organizational performance problems.

And If This Doesn't Quite Fit Your Situation . . .

Look at Problems 1-1, 1-6, 1-7 and 12-2 for discussions of other organizational performance problems. Chapters 4, 5, and 6 discuss individual performance problems, but include some tips that may apply to group performance as well.

Use Checklist 1 to develop a cure of your own.

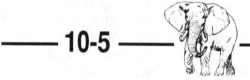

—— 10-5 ——

The Problem: An employee accuses you of discrimination.

The Scene

"He did what?" you shout into the phone.

"You heard me. He filed a discrimination complaint because you didn't pick him for that lead job last week. Why don't you come up right after lunch and we'll talk about it."

You hang up the phone, quite uncomfortable about the tone in your boss's voice. This sounds like trouble.

Henry Macias has always been steady and reliable, but never one of your best workers. Realistically, he shouldn't have expected the job. But he did. What now?

Possible Causes

Henry is discouraged and looking for a reason why he didn't get promoted. He may think he's just as good as the person you picked.

Henry is using the EEO procedures to pressure you. At the least, you may think twice before you pass him over next time.

You may actually have discriminated against him. Perhaps it was in this selection. Perhaps it's been continuing.

Hint: We don't need to tell you, do we? Be careful, and very conscientious, with this one.

Cures

If Henry is discouraged and looking for a reason why he didn't get promoted:

When you're a woman or member of a minority group, and you've felt discrimination in your career, there's always a lingering doubt: Was she or he better than I was, or was it really discrimination this time? And if you've dealt with many discrimination complaints, you know that the answer's seldom clear-cut. As we've said before, blatant discrimination is very rare. Most racism/sexism, though very real, is more subtle and harder to pin down.

If Henry's seen promotions go to others again and again, he may begin to wonder. Even if he's not sure it's discrimination, he may want someone from outside to look at the situation.

No matter how strongly you may feel about the situation, you can't just go talk with Henry. You need to find out your company's policy on EEO complaints first. And you certainly don't want to give even the appearance of trying to pressure Henry to drop his complaint.

The organization probably uses an informal counseling procedure as the first step in an EEO complaint. This provides you the opportunity to listen to Henry. Even though you're confident you didn't discriminate, there may be some steps you can take which are reasonable in the situation. What about a temporary job swap, so Henry can expand his skills and you can see him in a somewhat different situation? Perhaps an assignment somewhat more difficult than he's used to, so you can both see how he handles it? If Henry sees you taking a genuine, positive step to deal with his situation, he may feel that his complaint has accomplished its purpose.

There is an important distinction here. An EEO complaint can be an excellent opportunity to respond to the legitimate concerns of an employee—whether his problem has anything to do with race or not. It is *not* an opportunity to give someone a remedy that's inappropriate, just to get them off your back. It's not difficult to get the reputation for "buying off" anyone who files a complaint against you. That's a sure way to *encourage* complaints.

If Henry is using the EEO procedures to pressure you:

You can see how relevant the paragraph immediately above is to this "cure." If you're willing to give a worker a remedy just to kill the complaint, it becomes a handy way to pressure you. Henry may easily think "Well, I might as well file and see what I can get out of him. After all, look what Isabel got—and I have a lot stronger case than she had."

The moral is clear: deal with all complaints on their merits. Don't try to buy off complainants. If you didn't discriminate, you have nothing to fear from the complaint. (One word of caution here. Many firms have policies or union contracts which require you to follow certain procedures when making selections for promotions. Even if you didn't discriminate against Henry, make sure that you followed the procedures correctly. If you didn't, you may have to take some action to make up for not doing so. That's regrettable, but unavoidable—and much less serious than having discriminated.)

If you actually did discriminate against him:

Hard words, aren't they? But you ought not consider either of the situations above until you're *sure* that there wasn't any discrimination in your treatment of Henry.

After the complaint is filed is a poor time to have to evaluate this situation—especially if your boss is the one doing the evaluating. If you have women and/or members of minority groups working for you, you should constantly evaluate the treatment they get from you and the organization. (Yes, this is just as true if *you* are a woman and/or a minority group member.) If you have any questions about your complete fairness, the time to deal with them is *before* you take an action—not *after* it's done.

If you aren't completely sure you've treated Henry like the rest of your employees, it's better to deal with it now than in a formal proceeding. If you have a good relationship with your boss or the individual who runs the EEO program, discuss the situation with him. If not, try to find someone else to talk with who can listen and give you honest feedback.

If you did discriminate, even unintentionally and unknowingly, make the appropriate offer to Henry now. Make it in good grace, not grudgingly. After all, Henry's not the one who fouled up.

Things to Think About

Perhaps you didn't discriminate against Henry at all—but that may not be the end of the matter. Members of minority groups (and many women) often need more than just "an equal opportunity" to compete effectively. There may be a problem with language, or education—or just with self-confidence.

It's not "reverse discrimination" to respond realistically to their situation. Is Henry able to compete with the others, or does he have problems that need an extra bit of concern from you? Would training, or a special assignment, or just some counseling help him be more competitive? After all, it's to your and the firm's benefit to help *everyone* become as competitive as possible.

And If This Doesn't Quite Fit Your Situation . . .

Look at Problem 10-2 if the charge is sexual harassment. If an employee accuses you of letting other employees discriminate against him, see Problem 2-8.

Use Checklist 6 to develop a cure of your own.

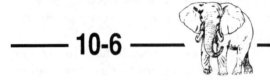

—— 10-6 ——

The Problem: Your job is getting to you.

The Scene

Things just aren't much fun anymore. You get to work early in the morning; you stay late in the evenings; you often take work home on the weekends. Your performance doesn't seem to be suffering— yet. But you just don't get the kick out of it all that you used to. Is it time to move on?

Possible Causes

Your job has grown to the point where it's overwhelming. What started out as a manageable assignment just keeps growing and growing. And while you aren't in quite over your head yet, it's close.

Your personal life is interfering with your work. This could be either because so much is happening at home that you can't concentrate (and work is getting in the way of other problems you have to solve) or because the rest of your life is so stagnant that it's affecting your attitude toward the job too. Either way, the real problem isn't the job so much as it's everything else.

The challenge has gone out of the job. You've solved most of the problems there are to solve—at least once. You've seen most of the situations that are likely to arise—at least once. There's nothing left to conquer, and you're bored.

Hint: Everybody goes through stale periods in whatever they're doing—on the job or off. Marriages go through dull periods, friendships wax and wane, outside interests lose their luster, and jobs get boring. Most of the time the ennui is transient. You just "tough it out" and things get better in time. But sometimes they don't. If your dissatisfaction doesn't go away in a few weeks, then it's time for some real soul-searching. It's particularly important to find out *why* you're dissatisfied, since these feelings can arise from a variety of causes but slip over into all different parts of your life. You don't want to give up a perfectly good job, when what's really bothering you is your boyfriend!

Cures

If your job has grown to the point where it's overwhelming:

Think about what the job is now, as opposed to what it was when you first came on board. What are you doing now that you didn't do then? Are these things that you picked up on your own, or did your boss assign them to you? Are they things that came into your organization and you picked them up personally, or are they things that were meant to be your personal assignments?

Decide what you're doing now that you could delegate to someone else in your unit. The initial effort to delegate will be greater than the time and effort it takes you to do the work yourself. In time, though, your delegation will pay off by getting some of the pressure off you.

Decide what functions your organization has picked up that don't properly belong there (and that aren't buying you any glory for doing them). Talk to your peers about realigning some functions and, once you've gotten agreement, approach your boss with your recommendations.

If your people are already loaded to the limit and you've picked up additional assignments just because there was no one else to give them to, take a look at your organization again. Are there things you're doing that you could do less often (or cut out altogether) without any significant damage to the mission? Most units have at least some work that they continue to do (especially reports and statistics) even after the real need for them has passed. By cutting out some of this unproductive work, you'll free your workers to do tasks with greater payback—and maybe even be recognized for your increased efficiency.

Look at the technology available to your unit. While introduction of automated systems rarely results in saved workyears, better use of existing technology frequently does. Maybe there are additional products or reports you could get from the systems you're already using that would substitute for work you're doing manually. Even if the automated system can't produce an entire product for you, maybe you can gather some of the information automatically to produce a customized product.

Even after you've introduced all these more efficient operating methods and reduced some of your own work load and stress, take a little time to reflect again on how you feel about the job. The reduced work load, combined with the excitement of trying some new and innovative things, may have restored your energy and interest in the job. If not, think again about *why* you're dissatisfied. Maybe what you thought was the cause was really just a symptom.

If your personal life is interfering with your work:

Whatever the problem is, deal with it. If it's a problem that time won't cure, but one that requires some decisions and action on your part, get the help you need to work through it. Talk to a trusted friend or a professional counselor to define the issues, identify your options, and help you make a decision.

If the problem is something you can't "cure" but just need to wait out (like a sick relative, or a child with behavior problems), alert your boss and significant coworkers that things are going on at home that you're having some problems dealing with. Let them know that you're going to do everything you can to see that it doesn't interfere with your job, but that you'd appreciate their understanding and support in the tough times ahead.

Be prepared to arrange with your boss to take the time you need away from the job to work through the personal issues. Your job is important, but it's not your whole life—and it's certainly not worth martyrdom!

All the ideas we discussed in Chapter 3 for dealing with employees who have personal problems apply to you too. But this time, you *know* what the necessary accommodations are. If you ask for them before your boss has to suggest them, you'll demonstrate to her that you really do have the company's interests at heart.

Unlike the first "cure," we don't suggest this time that you reexamine your feelings about the job as soon as you've resolved the personal issues. Emotional trauma, like physical trauma, leaves scars. Even after your personal life is back in equilibrium, you may not get your old zip and pep back right away. Give it some time. Wait a few weeks—maybe even a couple of months—then if your job *still* is getting to you, look at the reasons why.

If the challenge has gone out of the job:

Think about what excited you about the job in the past. The "people problems?" Trying to do things faster, better, cheaper? Introducing new technology? Taking on new assignments?

After you've identified what it is about working that gives you the most satisfaction, think about how much of that you can work into your current assignment. Many jobs are what we make of them. Managers especially, aside from the occasional crunch, have a lot of freedom to develop their own individual styles. Some concentrate on developing their people, on team-building, and fostering harmonious relationships. Others work on peer relationships, looking outward to the mutual benefit of their and other organizations. Still others are intrigued by new work methods and technology that will increase productivity without overburdening the staff. Within some broad parameters, you probably have more freedom to pursue your own inclinations than you realize.

But what if there's nothing that elicits more than a flicker of interest? Maybe you really have stayed too long at the job. If nothing you do makes it any more fun to come to work, then it's time to move on. You may be able to cope now with the lack of stimulation, but time will tell. Eventually, your dissatisfaction will infect the unit. Your performance will suffer, and so will the organization's. Your attitude sets the tone for the whole group, and if you're not happy, chances are they won't be either. So without animosity or hard feelings—and without burning any bridges—it's time to look around for greener pastures.

Things to Think About

All the "cures" we've talked about presume that you've been able, with some accuracy, to identify why your job is getting to you.

But that's not always the way it works. Sometimes you have feelings of vague dissatisfaction whose cause you really can't isolate. It may be that you're suffering from depression—or it may just be that you're so close to the situation that you can't analyze it objectively.

It's not an admission of failure to get some help. Many people, essentially well-adjusted, "normal" people, have times in their lives when they can benefit from some outside professional assistance. Don't let false pride get in your way of using a valuable resource now to save you some real unhappiness later.

And If This Doesn't Quite Fit Your Situation . . .

If your job is getting to you but you're not quite sure why, look at the different problems in this book, particularly those in Chapters 9, 13, and 14. (If you have to deal with many of these problems, it's no wonder you're having difficulty on your job.) If you pick the most serious problems and use our suggestions to cure them, you may cut the stress down to more manageable levels.

Use Checklist 6 to develop a cure of your own.

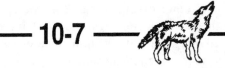

10-7

The Problem: You have to make an important decision, and you just don't have enough information.

The Scene

". . . and let me know by the end of the day, Maury, whether you want to test Super Account at your branch."

"I'm not sure I can tell you by then. Couldn't you at least give me until next week?"

"Sorry. It starts next week, and my folks have to know today whether to set it up for you or for Marilyn's branch. Let me hear from you."

You hang up, frowning. This new Super Account that corporate wants to test has a lot of potential, but it's different from anything the bank has ever done before. If you try it and it's successful, it's a feather in your cap. If you try it and it flops, you'll never live it down. It's too important to make a snap decision on—but that's what they're forcing you to do.

Possible Causes

What's the cause of the short time you have to make the decision? That's really not important. What matters is the cause—and cure—for your concern that you don't have enough information to make the decision. Here are the most likely causes:

The situation is important , and you want to make the right decision. But how can you do this if you don't know the critical information?

You don't like to make decisions in a hurry. You can't be sure that you've considered everything if you have to hurry.

You don't want to make a wrong decision. The only way you can prevent this is to get *all* the facts and study them carefully.

Hint: This is a question about your decision-making style.

Cures

If you want to make the right decision because it's an important one:

This is a very valid concern. It takes good information to make good decisions.

Now that we've said that, the fact still remains: right or wrong, smart or dumb, you have to make the decision today. What can you do between now and the time you have to call your boss to help make the decision? Here are some ideas:

- Do you have tellers or other people who've worked in the branch for some time? Tell them about the Super Account and ask them what they think your customers will think of it.

- During the course of the day, some of your major customers will probably come in. Tell a few of them about the service and get their reaction.

- What about calling several of your customers and asking for their reactions? This lets you be systematic and not dependent solely on the customers who come in today.

- Have other banks in the area tried the same kind of account? If so, how can you find out how successful they are?

- Do you have friends in the bank's corporate headquarters, or in other branches? Why not ask them what they think of the account?

The point of all this is simple: get to work right now to get the information you need. You may still not have enough by the end of the day, but you'll certainly have a lot more than you do now.

Here's a final thought. If you get enough information to make a "yes" or "no" decision, that's fine. Suppose, though, that you get a mixed reaction; customers like the idea in general but don't like a certain feature. Suppose you were to call your boss back and tell him that you like the idea but that some of your key customers wouldn't buy it because of this feature? Don't you think he'd be impressed by what you accomplished during the course of the day? Don't you think the company might consider delaying implementation to work out the problem feature?

If you don't like to make decisions in a hurry:

On the surface, this may look like the situation above. But it isn't, really. This is more a question of style and pace. Here, you want to be careful; you want to make sure you consider every aspect and don't overlook some important factor. You might say that you want to make your decisions methodically.

This is an excellent trait—as long as there's time to be careful and methodical. If there's not the time—and there isn't in this case— you need to develop flexibility. If you do no more than insist that there wasn't enough time, you'll make your boss unhappy. You may also lose a good opportunity for yourself and your branch.

What do you do? First, follow the steps in the "cure" above, and any others you can think of. But what if you're uncomfortable, if you feel that no matter what you find you're still rushing things?

One answer is to say "no"—but to say it only *after* you've done all of your information-gathering. There's a great difference between saying "I don't have enough time, so I can't do it," and saying "I spent the whole day gathering information and I still don't have enough to make the decision, because . . . ." Your boss may still not be happy with the second answer, but he'll understand that you put a lot of effort into the problem.

You might guess that the other answer is to say "yes." You don't know enough, that's true. It may fail, that's true also. But what are the risks of saying "yes"? The Super Account may fail, but if you promote it intelligently and listen to your customers' reactions to it, you may be able to provide corporate valuable information on why it failed. In short, if you continue to make intelligent responses, you may well come out a winner.

If you don't want to make a mistake:

It's normal and human not to want to make mistakes—but it's a poor guiding principle for a manager. Effective managers take risks. They're carefully calculated risks, ones which offer solid rewards. But they're risks nonetheless. In fact, one of the real skills of a manager is knowing when to take a risk and when to make a safe decision.

In this situation, there are real dangers from a wrong decision. There are also real rewards from a right one. How do you tell which outweighs the other?

Here's one way: Take the risk when you can exert a great deal of influence over the success or failure of the outcome. Don't be as anxious to take the risk if you don't have much control over the result.

What do you do in the current situation? You begin by following the steps in the first "cure"; you get all the relevant information that you can in the time that's available. Then you ask two sets of questions:

- Does it appear that the Super Account may be a winner with your customers? Does it have immediate appeal for them? Can you explain the benefits quickly and easily? If you can answer these questions with a solid "yes," your choice is easy—go with it. If the answers are mostly "no," forget it.

• But what if it's not clear, if it's not obviously a winner or loser? That's where the second question comes in. To what extent can you make it a success? Will you be able to control the marketing of it to your customers? Can you tailor any of it to them? Will you be able to reward your employees if they do a good job of selling it to customers? These and similar questions will help you focus on the amount of control you can exert.

Now you can make the best possible decision. If you can really affect the success of the Super Account, it's probably worth the gamble. If not, let someone else be first.

Notice what you have done. You've reduced the risk as much as possible. This isn't the same thing as not wanting to make a wrong choice; you're concentrating on making the best choice. However, you're doing it in the way that has the smallest chance of being wrong.

Things to Think About

We've dealt with this as a problem in your decision-making style. But there are two other issues here. First, can you influence the bank's operations so that you don't have to make last-minute decisions on important matters in the future? Second, does your decision-making style fit the kind of style the bank needs?

When you try to change the way your organization does business, you're setting a rocky road for yourself. Trying to change the ideas of people above you in the organization is a difficult challenge. It may get you known as a rebel and a troublemaker. On the other hand, if your ideas are good and the organization starts to use them, it can move your career ahead rapidly.

What if you're not willing to try to change the bank? Then you need to evaluate the fit between the decision-making style it wants and your own style. Does the bank expect you to make decisions constantly in less time than you're comfortable making them in? Then it may be time to find another bank (or another organization) which is looking for someone with a more deliberate style. One of the keys to success is finding a spot where what the organization wants most is what you're most comfortable giving it.

And If This Doesn't Quite Fit Your Situation . . .

See Problem 6-4 if you tend to go to pieces under the pressure of decisions like this. If you tend to resist changing with the times, see Problem 6-9. (Both of these deal with employees, but you can get some ideas from them that might apply to you.)

Use the General Checklist to develop a cure of your own.

10-8

The Problem: You're not accepted among your peers or employees because you're a woman or minority.

The Scene

"Hey, Mike," called Jerry, "Let's call a break and go over to the Ramblin' Inn for some lunch."

"Sounds good to me," replied Mike. "Let's ask Art Peterson over in Accounting. I haven't seen him for a while."

When you emerged from your office a few minutes later, most of the other branch 'offices along the row were empty. Once again you're left behind. OK, so you're the first, and only, woman at branch level. But why don't you ever get invitations? You already know the answer, even before you ask: You're just not accepted as one of "them"—so you sit alone, eat alone, leave alone.

Possible Causes

Prejudice can stem from many different causes, but the roots are almost always ignorance and fear. People are prejudiced against groups they don't know or don't understand. As we've said before, the days of overt discrimination seem to be largely gone. But covert discrimination, often unconscious discrimination, still exists. Managers can do a lot to eradicate it in their own units. But the object of discrimination—in this case, you—can also do a lot to overcome the ignorance and fear.

There are two things that could be happening here to make you think you're not being accepted because you're a woman or a minority:

You may be misinterpreting the other managers' disinterest as discrimination. You need to consider the possibility that they may not be that friendly to *anyone* at first. This may just be a tight little group, possibly made up of essentially reserved people, who just aren't comfortable making social overtures to someone new.

The other managers may really be excluding you because you're a woman or minority. Whether it's intentional or unintentional, the effect is the same. By separating you from the rest of the group, they cut you off from the valuable information sharing that goes on in informal groups. You need to do what you can to see that this doesn't go on any longer.

Cures

If you've misinterpreted the others' disinterest as discrimination:

It's safest to begin by assuming that this is the case. At worst, you'll have confirmed that you're being discriminated against, and will be able to show that you did what you could to overcome the discrimination informally. At best, you *will* solve the problem so that you don't have to elevate it.

Of the other managers who aren't accepting you into the group, identify the one or two who seem to be *least* resistant. Approach them one-on-one—maybe for a short discussion, an invitation for a lift to a meeting (or a request for a ride), a cup of coffee in the cafeteria to discuss a problem you've both been having or to ask for an opinion on how to handle a sticky situation.

Keep your interactions with these one or two people within the office at first. Don't be too quick to rush into an invitation for lunch or for a drink after work. Let them get comfortable with you in an office setting first. Then, when one or both of them begin to come to *you* once in a while, instead of your making all the moves, you'll know the time is right to extend a social offer.

After you've begun to form relationships with one or two of the other managers, you may be able to invite yourself along with the whole group occasionally. It's even better if the managers you've gotten to know invite you, but fear of their peers' disapproval may keep that from happening for a while. Once you've gone out with the group a few times, they'll probably take your presence for granted and treat you as if you'd been "one of the gang" all along.

Even if these overtures don't produce results, you shouldn't assume that the reason you're not being accepted is your sex or minority group. There's another possibility. Are you doing something that puts off the other managers? Are you so conscious of being the only woman or minority in the group that you're on the defensive? or overly aggressive? or stiff and formal?

This is a good time to have a chat with your boss, presuming that, since he selected you, he'll support you. Tell him, as objectively and non-threateningly as you can, your perceptions of your reception by the other managers. Ask him if you're doing anything that might contribute to your not being accepted. Chances are he'll tell you. And if you're not part of the problem, you will have alerted your boss to the fact that he has a situation that requires his attention.

If the other managers are discriminating against you:

In the first set of cures, we've eliminated most of the other possibilities. You've tried all the things we talked about above, including asking your boss what you may be doing to contribute to the problem. Now it's apparent that the fact that you're a woman or minority *is* at the root of the other managers' failure to accept you.

You've already taken the first steps. You've done what you could to mix in with the rest of the group, and you've alerted your boss to the fact that there's a problem. As the next step, you should do nothing for a little while (not a long while—just a couple of weeks). Give your boss a chance to observe the situation and talk to some of the key players.

If nothing has improved after your boss has had a chance to make some informal adjustments, it's time for you to have a more formal meeting with him. Let him know that you are very concerned about the situation, that it hasn't improved, and that you are prepared to file a formal complaint as soon as an incident occurs in which your nonacceptance impacts your ability to perform on the job. That should get his attention.

Now you have to make a decision. You can stay and fight it out if your boss is still unwilling or unable to change his subordinates' behavior. Or you can begin to look around now for another job where you'll be better accepted.

Something to Think About

Management can be a lonely place to be. In spite of the rise of minorities and women into management over the past couple of decades, there are still a lot of places where you may be the *only* woman or minority at your level in the company. But being alone doesn't *have* to mean being lonely. As you prove your competence and judgment, you'll very likely earn even greater respect from your peers and superiors because they'll come to recognize how much harder you've had to work to get where you are. That may take some time, but there is a potential payoff for you—and for the others who follow in your footsteps without having to blaze the trail themselves.

And If This Doesn't Quite Fit Your Situation . . .

Look at Problems 2-4, 2-8, and 2-9 for incidents of discrimination against your subordinates. Some of the tips for the supervisor may be useful for you in your own situation.

Use Checklist 3 to develop a cure of your own.

— 10-9 —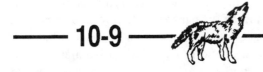

The Problem: You have trouble dealing with office politics.

The Scene

"May, I'm sorry but they picked Adrienne Barth from Marketing to head the new district office. I did everything I could, but it just wasn't enough.

"Yeah . . . well . . . . I know you did your best . . ." May tries to look composed, but you can tell how disappointed she is. And she ought to be. She was far and away the best person they could have picked. But George Stefan in Marketing is always down in the front office, always buddying up to the big brass. And it works.

Possible Causes

You're not comfortable with office politics.
You don't have the skills for it.
Your personality or performance gets in the way of your being effective at it.

Hints: When a company has low trust between managers, unclear goals and objectives, and poor systems for making decisions, office politics becomes the way that it gets things done. This is often harmful for the company.

Even in well-run companies, though, a manager needs to be effective at office politics. If you don't understand why, the information in the "cures" below will help you.

This is the most important point to understand about office politics: It's a way of exerting *influence*. Being good at politics means that you can influence others to do what you want done. Keep that in mind as you read the "cures" below.

Cures

If you're not comfortable with office politics:

You don't ever have to become comfortable with politicking. But you do have to do it.

What does "politicking" involve? It's the effective use of influence, which is based on personal connections between individuals. Here is what those connections involve:

- *Exposure.* You can't have the right connections if you don't go where the other people are. You can call this "glad-handing," "networking," "schmoozing," or whatever you want. It's where everything starts.

- *Competence.* There's the mistaken idea that just being around "the people who count" is enough. Not in any well-run organization! If you're not competent, it just gives others a chance to see that you're not. "Competence," by the way, means both being competent at the work you do and being competent at dealing with others.

- *Reliability.* No matter how much people see you and your competence, it won't work unless you are someone they can depend on. This means both that they can trust the truth of what you say and that they can trust that you'll *do* what you say.

This is the basic prescription for influence. Managers often make decisions on the basis of information from other managers they know, they know are competent, and they know they can trust. These are the people who have influence. If you want to be one of them, you need to make sure that you are known and that you're known to be competent and reliable.

Is it really that simple? Often it is, sometimes it's not. But that's the place to start.

If you don't have the skills for it:

The "cure" just outlined what you need to do to be successful at office politics. Now all you need to do is develop the skills to do it.

How do you get exposure. The first requirement isn't a skill at all: you simply go where the people are you want to talk with. This may mean lunching together, going for a drink after work, playing golf on the weekend, whatever. A lot of it can be done during work itself; you can chat with others before meetings or visit them in their offices.

Just being there isn't enough. You need to have the interpersonal skills to carry on an effective conversation. You need to be friendly, relaxed, a good listener, and so on. If you don't think you have these skills, there are good books, videos, and courses on them.

There is one very specific conversational skill you need: the ability to steer a conversation in a specific direction. When you mingle with other managers, you may not want to talk just about things in general. You may want to make sure, for instance, that Edna McDonald knows that you're interested in the vacancy that's opening up in her branch. When you're talking with her, you want to be able to guide the conversation there smoothly, not just interrupt with it. You need practice to get good at this, but there are books and other sources which will help.

What about the other two elements, competence and reliability? Competence comes from experience, and from learning from books like this one. Reliability comes from self-discipline and organization; many of the other problems in this chapter deal with how you become reliable.

If your personality or your performance make you ineffective:

If people aren't comfortable around you, don't believe you do a good job or don't believe they can depend on you, you'll be ineffective at office politics. By constantly exposing yourself to other managers, you'll simply be reinforcing their low opinion of you.

The answer to this is straightforward, isn't it? Don't complain about others' success at office politics—work on your own abilities. Develop a reputation as a good manager with good interpersonal skills, and you'll develop influence with others.

Things to Think About

We haven't dealt with one obvious question: politicking with the boss or with other managers at his level. To some extent, you have to play this one by ear—but we can give you several suggestions:

- By far the best way to develop influence with your boss is to do a good job for him. That's where you always start.

- Then make sure he knows he can depend on you.

- After that, stay in touch enough to accomplish two goals. First, you want to make sure he sees your competence and dependability. Second, you want to be the first to know if something negative is coming your way.

- The same basic strategy goes for other managers at or above your boss's level. It's great if they know you and think you're competent.

- The other side of this is that once you establish the relationship you want, be very careful about the amount of time
  you spend with your boss or other senior managers. They
  have work to do (just as you do).

And If This Doesn't Quite Fit Your Situation . . .

Look at the other problems in this chapter if your own performance failures might be making it harder to be effective at office
politics. You might also want to look at the problems in Chapter
11—especially Problems 11-2, 11-5, 11-6, and 11-7—if your relationships with other managers are handicapping you.

Use the General Checklist to develop a cure of your own.

11

Troubleshooting Problems with Another Manager

— 11-1 —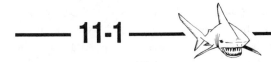

The Problem: A manager is trying to take over one of your functions.

The Scene

"Mark, have you seen what Kim Heiss is doing now?" asked one of your team leaders. "She's offering something called a 'Customer/Client Mixmaster' that sounds an awful lot like our customer relations program."

You knew this would happen sooner or later. Kim and her group have been making inroads into your territory for the past few months. But this is pretty blatant. Customer relations is clearly your function—one of your bread-and-butter areas.

Possible Causes

There may not be a clear line between where your function stops and Kim's begins. While Kim could have been more of a team player and discussed her plans with you ahead of time, what she's doing may not be clearly out of her area.

Kim may have been asked by someone higher than both of you in the organization to take on the project. Again, she could have coordinated her work with you (unless she was asked not to), but she's basically just following orders.

Kim may be trying to strip you of your function. This could be something she's doing entirely on her own (perhaps with the support of her superiors, but not yours) which is intended to increase her influence and power at the expense of yours.

Cures

If there's not a clear line between your function and Kim's:

This is not at all uncommon, especially in large, complex organizations. It's often not very efficient for two or more groups to do the same things, but sometimes it really is the better way—particularly if your customer bases are different. You may do customer satisfaction consulting with service industries, while Kim does the same kind of work with retail companies. There may be enough differences in your approaches, and the skills and knowledge required, to justify your separate involvement.

Whether this seems to be a reasonable division of labor or just a glitch in the design of the organization, if you think that fuzzy functional distinctions are at the root of Kim's incursion into your territory, your first step should be to talk to her. Describe what you see as the overlap and try to find out from her why she's performing the work and what she hopes to accomplish in this function.

She may not even have known that this was supposed to be your territory and began the work to fill what she perceived as a gap. She may not have thought you were doing the work as well as it needed to be done (although she may not put it quite so bluntly). Or she may believe that there's a legitimate role for both of you.

Try to work out the apparent duplication between your two units. Even if you'll need approval from your superiors for any accommodations you make, you'll be able to go forward with concrete proposals and with all the players in agreement. Of course, if this is a real baseline issue in your unit, you'll need to confer with your boss first to find out how she wants you to handle the negotiations.

Record your agreements in writing so there's less chance of another problem in the future. If your company has a formal organization and functions manual, make a change to that document too—so managers all up and down the line know who's responsible for what.

If Kim was asked to take on the function by higher managers in the company:

This is another good reason to check with your boss before you begin negotiating with Kim. If someone at a higher level has already decided that Kim should be performing the work, you're certainly not going to be able to negotiate it back.

There are two reasons why Kim may have been asked to do the work instead of you: your superiors may believe that the work more properly belongs in Kim's area or they may have been displeased with the way you've done work in the past. In the first case, Kim may have been looking at you for some time the way you're looking at her now—as if you've been trying to steal one of her functions. In the second case, you've lost the confidence of the people above you—and you've got a lot of fence-mending to do.

In either case, Problem 13-5 addresses this situation in more detail and can give you ideas on how to work it out.

If Kim is trying to strip you of your function:

In this case, your basic line of defense is through your customers. Kim will only be able to take away a function that is rightly yours if others allow her to. If you can keep your current customers satisfied, and continue to market your products, Kim won't have a chance to replace you.

That's true whether your customers are external to the organization or internal. Every function you perform has a customer. Unless top management decides otherwise (as in the second "cause"), your ability to maintain the mission and functions you have depends on how well you keep those customers satisfied. Do a good job, and they won't look elsewhere to have their needs filled. Do a poor job, and Kim will have your whole organization before you know what's happened.

At the same time that you're increasing your customers' satisfaction with the way you do the work (as opposed to the way Kim does it), you should subtly let Kim know that you're aware of her attempts to take over your function. It's probably better not to do this directly, since that kind of conversation can become a confrontation that would be difficult to work around later. It's much better if you can let the word get around the organization more informally—no threats, no confrontations, just for her information.

Depending on how far apart you and Kim are organizationally, it might also be a good idea to enlist your superiors' support in thwarting Kim's ambitions. Of course, the best way to get that support is customer-related. If it's apparent from the reports coming back from others that you're doing a good job, those above you will be less likely to consider letting someone else take the function over.

Things to Think About

While we've described this scenario as a takeover of one of your bread-and-butter issues, sometimes other managers may try to take on things that are legitimately yours but that you don't really want anyway. In that case, you may be tempted to say, "Fine, let it go. It's more of a headache than it's worth." And maybe it is. But even in that situation, you can't foster the perception that you're a sitting duck for every ambitious manager who comes along. Regardless of how secretly thrilled you may be to get this monkey off your back, at the very least you need to let the other manager know that you're aware of what she's doing and that you will permit it to happen because you agree it's best for the overall organization. If it's not clear to the rest of the organization that you are in control of your functions, soon others will be raiding your group in more vital areas.

The best way to ensure the security of your own job and the maintenance of your function is to earn the confidence of your boss—and those above him. If your boss is convinced that no one can do the job as well as you, then others' attempts to take over things you're assigned won't get anywhere. The other managers' will just look like fools for trying something so obviously futile.

And If This Doesn't Quite Fit Your Situation . . .

Look at other problems in this chapter, particularly Problem 11-2, for ideas on how to handle other situations in which a peer is threatening you or your organization.

Use Checklist 4 to develop a cure of your own.

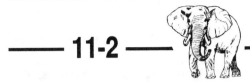

— 11-2 —

The Problem: A manager keeps criticizing you to your boss.

The Scene

"Max, I'm not sure what you're doing, but you certainly have Don Flores unhappy with you. He's complained about your unit and how you manage it twice this week already."

You finish the conversation and get out of your boss's office as quickly as you can. As if there weren't enough to worry about, now you have to find how to get Don Flores off your back.

Possible Causes

You and your unit are doing a poor job on work that matters to Don. He's decided that talking to your boss is the only chance he has of getting you to improve.

Don doesn't like you and/or the way you run your unit. He hopes that by pressuring your boss he can get her to make you change.

You've done something to make Don look bad, and this is his way of getting even with you.

Don wants your job. He believes that if he complains enough about you, your boss will move you or get rid of you.

Hint: The most important factor here isn't what Don's motives are but what your boss's opinion is of you. If she has confidence in you and your abilities, she'll support you and perhaps even help you resolve the situation. What if she doesn't? Don may provide her the excuse she's been looking for to do something about you.

Cures

If you and your unit are doing a poor job on work that matters to Don:

Sometimes when a manager complains to your boss it's because he's concluded it's his only chance of getting you to produce the quality or quantity of work he needs. Perhaps this is Don's situation:

he depends on your unit for work that he needs, and you don't provide what he needs when he needs it.

If this is the case, then the nature of the problem changes. The problem isn't that Don is complaining to your boss, but that your unit is producing work that doesn't satisfy him. There are three different responses you can make in this situation:

- You can change what your work unit produces so that it satisfies him. This means that you accept that you have a performance problem, and you solve it. Chapter 1 deals with work unit performance problems; Chapters 4, 5, and 6 deal with individual failures to produce. You should find the answer to your current problem in one of these chapters.

- You can negotiate with Don (or any customer) for him to be satisfied with a different product. Perhaps you're providing Don with data his unit needs to develop production plans. He wants the data by the fifth of the month, but you physically can't produce it before the tenth. Since you can't change your production, you negotiate with him to settle for the tenth. If you're successful, he's satisfied and the problem is solved.

- Suppose you explain the situation but he won't change; it's the fifth or nothing. In this case, you may want to evaluate the third option: get out of the game. If there's no way you can satisfy a customer, you may want to let someone else furnish him what he needs.

If Don doesn't like you or the way you manage your unit:

This is a very different situation, one that probably can't be cured by your unit doing a better job. So what do you do?

If the way you manage your unit is causing the problem, you may be able to change it, or persuade Don that he can accept it. For instance, you may be lenient about accepting tardiness of a few minutes, while Don is very strict about it—and he feels that you're making it harder for him to maintain discipline. This is something the two of you can negotiate and perhaps find a solution to.

What if he just doesn't like you. You start by trying to find out why. If it's because you're a woman or an Hispanic or a reserved person who won't respond to his "glad-hand" approach, there may be no real solution to it. But if you do things in a way that offends him, you may be able to change—or to persuade him not to be offended. At least there's something to talk about.

Whatever the situation is, don't ever accept as final the fact that another manager doesn't like you. Both people and conditions change. If you keep an open mind to Don, he may begin to change his mind about you.

If you've done something to make Don look bad, and he's getting back at you:

The solution here is clear: do what you have to do to make up for what you did. Perhaps you don't think it was so bad, or even that what you did was justified. This doesn't matter if Don doesn't see things the same way.

Get with him and deal with the problem openly and open-mindedly. You don't need to sacrifice your pride or integrity, but you can try to understand why he was offended and deal with that. You really didn't mean to offend him, did you?

If Don wants your job:

This is the most serious of the various causes—but at least potentially the easiest to deal with. In this case, it probably doesn't matter why he wants your job. What does matter is how your boss sees the situation.

Here's where there's no substitute for being an effective manager. If you've done a good job of supervising your work unit and doing what your boss needs done, you've probably got her support. If you can lead her to see what Don's motivation is, she'll probably side with you. (This may sound trivial, or even Pollyanna-ish. Take our word for it: it's not. Your best protection against a wide variety of organizational problems is doing an effective job for your boss.)

Things to Think About

We've already discussed the importance of your relationship with your boss, but it deserves one last mention. Every manager—you included—has people he can depend on and people he can't depend on quite so much. He's ready to go to bat for the ones he depends on; he needs them and doesn't want anything to happen to them. The ones he can't depend on quite so fully? Draw your own conclusions.

If you have any doubts about what you need to do so that your boss can really depend on you, look at Problems 10-1 and 10-3, and at Chapters 13 and 14.

And If This Doesn't Quite Fit Your Situation . . .

Look at Problem 13-8 if your boss encourages other managers to criticize you by chewing you out in public or Problem 14-4 if he complains about you to your peers. See Problems 11-5 and 11-7 if the situation is that the other manager won't cooperate with you.

Use Checklist 4 to develop a cure of your own.

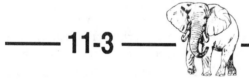

—— 11-3 ——

The Problem: A manager lets his unit keep giving you substandard work.

The Scene

"Look here," pointed Emil. "There's no way I can make a good assembly if the parts Jorge Ramirez' people machine aren't any good. And they usually aren't. Sometimes we catch them, but my people aren't technical experts in this. Sometimes we don't know they're bad until we get a complaint from a buyer. But Jorge's unit's poor quality work is making all of us here look bad too!"

Possible Causes

Jorge may not know that his unit is producing substandard work. Since the blame falls on your unit, he may believe that what he's producing is perfectly acceptable.

Jorge may be producing substandard work for everyone. He may not have good quality production systems in place to ensure that what goes out of his unit is good.

Jorge may have decided that your unit is lower on his priority list than some of his other customers. Even if his work is generally good, he may not have sent a message to his people that everything should be a quality product. In that case, if you're not high on his list, your unit is one more likely to suffer.

Cures

If Jorge isn't aware of his unit's poor work:

Get together some samples of poor products that Jorge's unit has passed on to yours. Look them over to see if there is a pattern of errors or if they seem to occur randomly. When do the errors occur? Are there certain times of the week or month, or certain parts of the production cycle, when errors are more frequent? Get as much information as you can from your people about the kind, frequency, and timing of the poor products you're getting from Jorge's unit.

Then go to see Jorge. Straightforwardly, but not accusingly, lay out the situation for him. Supply him all the information you have about the substandard work you're getting, and explain to him exactly how his poor products affect your unit's ability to do its work.

Enlist his support in developing a quality production mechanism that would be helpful for both of your units. Outline the benefits to him of not having to rework products—either before they leave your area or after they've left the company.

As much as possible, try to set up systems that make the workers themselves responsible for the quality of their own work. Not only will you have fewer errors leaving the unit uncorrected, but you will, in time, reduce the base error rate.

If all else fails and Jorge fails to get his unit under control, you can set up your own inspection system for all products entering the unit. Anything that you find to be substandard, send back! It won't take very long for Jorge to get the message.

If Jorge is producing substandard work for everyone:

The cure here is much like that described above. Only your approach to Jorge need differ. In the first "cause" you were attempting to enlist Jorge's help in solving a problem of mutual concern. In this case, Jorge already knows he has a problem, and probably wants desperately to fix it. But appeals to him aren't going to do any good because he doesn't know how to solve his problem.

Your job now is either to find out as much as you can personally about quality production techniques so that you can make some useful suggestions to Jorge about how to improve his unit's work or to find someone else in the company or outside with whom he can consult to solve his problems. Instead of enlisting Jorge's support, your approach here should be to offer him yours.

If your unit's work has a low priority with Jorge:

Again, talk to Jorge about your concerns and the impact his poor production has on your ability to perform. Even if his regular work for you seems to be less important than the work he does for some other units, think of something you can do for Jorge or with him that would be of benefit to him or his unit.

When you talk to Jorge, discuss with him those areas in which you can benefit him and where you can work a "trade"—he'll produce better work for your unit if you will . . . .

If the priority of your work is a real problem (which you'll know because several units are paying less attention to your needs), you may need to talk to your own boss about the problem. Is it necessary for anyone to do the function? Are there other ways the work can be performed without placing additional demands on other units? Could your unit be resourced to take on more of the work itself, cutting down on your reliance on other parts of the company? You may be able to get some support, particularly if this part of your work is something no one seems to get too excited about.

Whatever arrangements you are able to make with Jorge, be sure to follow through on your part of the bargain. While this function may be low priority, chances are that there's other work you do that's not. If you want cooperation in the big things when you need it, you have to prove that you can be counted on in the lesser things too.

Things to Think About

This is not just a problem between you and Jorge. Since it has to do with a quality issue, it affects the products and services of the company itself—and the company's reputation with its customers. You can't do quality work if what Jorge gives you it substandard. While it's always best to try to solve problems at your level, this is one situation where you shouldn't hesitate to elevate. If all your attempts to get the quality of Jorge's work to improve fail, you can't just put up with the problem. Let your boss know what the problem is and what you've done to try to solve it. He'll want quality work from Jorge's unit at least as much as you do—maybe even more!

And If This Doesn't Quite Fit Your Situation . . .

If you're getting substandard work but none of the reasons above seem to fit, check out the other problems in this chapter. Jorge could be giving you substandard work as a way of setting you up to take over your function (Problem 11-1), to get you to give him special priority (Problem 11-7), or for a number of other reasons.

Use Checklist 4 to develop a cure of your own.

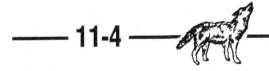

11-4

The Problem: A manager is trying to recruit your best employees.

The Scene

You've always been suspicious of Tamara's "friendly visits" to your unit. The last time that happened, one of your best workers decided to transfer to Tamara's unit.

Sure enough, it's happening again. Ken Estes just told you that she's offered him a job with the promise of a promotion in three months. You need to put a stop to this—but how?

Possible Causes

There are really two sets of causes in this situation, and you need to take account of both of them. The first concerns you and your employees; the second concerns Tamara.

Where your unit is concerned, it may be that

- *You have the reputation for hiring and training excellent workers.* They have such a good reputation that other managers would really like to have them.

- *Your employees are unhappy, so it's easy for other managers to recruit them.*

Where Tamara is concerned, it may be that

- *No one has ever said anything to her about not recruiting other managers' employees.* She thinks it's okay, so she does it.

- *She's knows she shouldn't do it, but she's always been able to get away with it.*

Hint: You need to solve both problems.

Cures

If everyone wants to recruit your employees because you select and train them well:

This is a real bind. On the one hand, it's flattering that you and your employees have such a reputation. On the other, it makes you a hunting ground for everyone else. On the one hand, you should be happy that your people get ahead so rapidly. On the other, you *do* have to get your work done.

You need to deal with Tamara and anyone else who blatantly tries to recruit your employees. You also need to accept that if your people are that good others are going to want them—and you don't want to block their advancement. You may find some ideas to help you hold on to them a little longer in the next "cure."

If your employees are unhappy and easy to recruit:

Even if your workers don't have a tremendous reputation, other managers may try to recruit them if they're known to be unhappy.

Are they unhappy because of the way you manage? This may be a hard fact to accept, but it may be true. In one way, though, it's good news: You can change the way you manage. Talk to other managers, people you trust, perhaps even your employees themselves. Find out what you're doing that they don't like. Then find a way to change the situation—either by changing yourself or by persuading them that your management style isn't so bad after all.

What if you supervise them effectively but the work itself makes them unhappy? This is more difficult, but there may still be solutions. Can you reorganize the jobs so that individual workers perform more of a process or get to take more responsibility for the process (job enrichment)? Can you delegate more responsibility, so that employees have more freedom in how they do the work? You can find some additional suggestions that might help in Problems 12-3 and 12-4.

Are they unhappy because there aren't many promotion opportunities in your unit? If so, can you reorganize the work so that a few jobs can support a higher rate of pay? If your unit has a good reputation, can you get some additional work that's worth a higher rate? If neither of these is possible, resign yourself to a high turnover. You can also take some pride in the fact that you're doing a good job of getting effective workers into the organization.

If Tamara doesn't know that directly recruiting other manager's employees is poor practice:

No matter which situation you believe is the case with Tamara, you begin by talking with her (*not* with her boss). Tell her that you're not happy that she's recruiting your people without coming through you. See what her response is.

If she seems genuinely surprised, you should be able to resolve the situation then and there. Tell her what your expectations are (see the next "cure"), and then negotiate what she'll do in the future.

If she knows she shouldn't do it, but has always been able to get away with it:

This is the time to put an end to it. Does this mean that she's never to talk to your employees or encourage them to consider a job with her? No.

The important point is this: if she wants to recruit your people, she should work *with* you, not *around* you. You're responsible for the production of your unit, so you have the right to know when someone else wants to hire your workers away. Insist on this right.

If Tamara won't cooperate, this is one of the times when it's appropriate to take the situation to your boss. It's reasonable to expect him to talk to Tamara's manager and get the situation straightened out.

Does this mean you prevent Tamara and others from offering jobs to your employees. No. You have to find what you believe is the correct balance, but you don't want to stand in the way of your people getting ahead. Certainly the turnover causes you extra work in hiring and training and disrupts production. There is a silver lining, though. If individuals know that by coming to work for you they enhance their chances for promotion, your recruiting will be that much easier and that much more effective.

Something to Think About

All managers (both of the authors included) want to hold on to their best workers. As long as you can do this by offering them challenging work and a satisfying work environment, you and they both benefit. If you have to hold them by keeping other opportunities away from them, it's not so beneficial. Don't do it. If your employees know that you'll help them get ahead, they'll work much harder and more effectively for you. That's worth the extra time and trouble caused by higher turnover.

And If This Doesn't Quite Fit Your Situation . . .

Tamara may also be trying to take over some of your functions; if so, see Problem 11-1. If her recruiting is made even worse because you can't get effective new employees or ones that are skilled, see Problems 12-2 and 12-3.

Use Checklist 4 to develop a cure of your own.

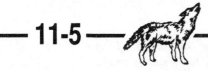

— 11-5 —

The Problem: A manager won't cooperate with you on a joint project.

The Scene

"When do you think we can get together to decide who's going to do what on this staffing proposal?" you ask Crystal. "How about Monday afternoon?"

"Oh, I don't know about that," she replies. "I have meetings most of Monday, and Tuesday too."

"But it's due Friday morning," you counter. "If we don't get started soon, our deadline will have come and gone, and we'll have nothing to show."

Possible Causes

Crystal may really not have any time or resources to devote to the project. It may be an area in which she'd really like to be involved, and she may be the sort of person who usually comes through, but she's just been caught at a bad time.

Crystal may want to make you look bad by failing to produce on this joint project. She may think that she has a good enough reputation in the organization that you'll be blamed for any deficiencies in the final product (rather than to her). Then she'll have "proof" that you're not doing your job.

Hint: The causes and cures in this problem really come down to one issue: Do you want to help Crystal look good or not? If she's the sort of manager who usually produces well, who may even have helped you out of a bind before, and whom you don't want to see fail, you'll do what you can to make the project come out well for both of you. If, on the other hand, Crystal is the sort of manager who consistently doesn't produce, whom you may have gotten out of binds before (only too often), or whom you suspect is out to discredit you, then you'll do as much as you need to cover yourself and hang her out to dry.

Cures

If Crystal doesn't have the time to devote to the project (but you want it to turn out well for both of you):

Talk to Crystal about what she is able to do. If she can't come to meetings or devote her personal time to the project, does she have someone on her staff who could carry information back and forth (or even do part of the work she was responsible for)? Can she feed you information that you can put together in the final product? Can she give you some ideas on how to approach the problem, which you can then feed to your own people to work on? Define clearly at the beginning what Crystal can contribute and what she'll have to leave up to you.

Since Crystal is someone whom you can trust to do what she says she'll do, we'll assume that she follows through on the things she's promised—or at least has someone else in her unit do the work. Take what she's given you and put together the best final product you can. If there are areas you just can't finish without additional input from her (because they're things only she knows about), get back with her with *specific* questions.

Allow Crystal an opportunity to see the final project before you submit it to your superiors. Give her a "drop dead" date after which you'll not be able to accept any changes and still get the product finished by your deadline. Let her know in advance also that this is a technical review only. If the material is correct and she simply disagrees with your approach or your methodology, this is not the time to raise those issues. She had an opportunity to be more involved in the first planning sessions and declined. By depending on you to put together the final project report, she implicitly agreed to defer to your judgement.

If Crystal is as good a person as you think she is (and you must think she's one of the "good guys" or you wouldn't have pitched in like this for her), she'll give you top billing and lots of credit for the success of the project. She'll also have the grace to assume her half of the blame for any failings in the final product. If not, you'll know the next time around how unreliable she is—and treat her accordingly (see below).

If Crystal consistently takes advantage or wants to discredit you:

Keep track of the attempts you've made to collaborate with Crystal on the project. Identify the parts of the project you believe you should be responsible for and the parts that only Crystal has the information to produce. Give the list to Crystal and try to get her agreement. Chances are you won't get disagreement—just no response at all. In that case, keep a copy of your memo to her, and start working.

Once you've completed as much as you can without Crystal's input, go back to her one more time to get the information you need. If she still refuses to cooperate, put together a mock report. Make it as complete as you can, but identify clearly the information that's missing and its possible impact on the validity of the report's conclusions and recommendations.

Give Crystal a copy of your "mock" report with fair warning that, if she doesn't do her share, this is exactly what will go forward as the final report. Chances are pretty good that Crystal will finally come through.

If not, be as good as your word. You can, with a little finesse, make the report look quite professional and technically acceptable on the surface, while making it clear to anyone knowledgeable about the subject (like your boss) the source of any deficiencies.

Even if Crystal does come through, you needn't have suffered all that aggravation in vain. A well-placed word to your peers (maybe even a discreet word to your boss in the right context) will get the message across. Keep in mind too that Crystal's failure to help you is probably not an isolated incident. If she hasn't performed for you, there have probably been times when she hasn't performed for her superiors either.

Something to Think About

There are only so many things you can do to get your peers to cooperate with you. While good peer relations are critical to your

own success as a manager, you'll inevitably run into managers who
don't want to play fair. When that happens, try your best to work
things out with them. But if your attempts fail, do whatever you
must to protect yourself. Don't let an unsuccessful manager take
you down with her.

And If This Doesn't Quite Fit Your Situation . . .

Look at other problems in this chapter, particularly Problems
11-3 and 11-7, for more discussion of situations in which other managers won't cooperate with you in getting work accomplished.
Use Checklist 4 to develop a cure of your own.

11-6

The Problem: A manager refuses to deal with anyone in your work unit but you.

The Scene

You sigh as John Wolensky closes the door behind him. You've
just taken 20 minutes to clear up a problem for him. That's 10 minutes
longer than it should have taken. You had to call Ahmal, the technician
who services John's organization, and get the details from him. Then
you made the same decision Ahmal would have made. If John had
dealt directly with Ahmal, he'd have gotten his answer in 10 minutes
and not taken up your time. But John won't bring his problems to
Ahmal. How do you get him to change?

Possible Causes

John hasn't learned to have confidence in your people.

*He believes it's beneath him to have to deal with anyone but
you.* He's a manager and, as he sees it, he should only have to deal
with other managers.

You give him higher priority than your people do. He knows
that if he comes to you, he'll get his problem taken care of more
quickly.

Hint: None of the suggested cures will work unless you continually support Ahmal—and make it clear to John that you're supporting him.

Cures

No matter what the situation is:

Have an informal talk with John. Find out why he'd rather deal with you. This may take some tact; John may or may not be willing to level with you. And you certainly don't want to seem unresponsive to him.

Hopefully, you can get an idea what his reasons are. If so, use the proper "cure" below. If not, make your best guess—but be prepared to switch to another "cure" if the first one isn't working.

If John hasn't learned to have confidence in your people:

Do you know why? If not, ask him. If he's willing to tell you, don't argue or get defensive. Listen. If you believe he's wrong, don't tell him so. Ask him to give you a chance to show him that your people can provide what he needs. Then do it.

Suppose your unit really has let him down. Find out in as much detail as you can how and why it happened. Then deal with the cause. You may find helpful ideas in Chapter 1—which deals with performance problems that the entire unit has—and in Chapters 4, 5, and 6—which deal with individual performance problems.

Be very careful here. If you ask why he lacks confidence and he tells you, you *must* deal with the problem. You may not think it's a problem; you may think that he's wrong. It doesn't matter. If he's honest with you and then nothing changes, you've had it.

If he believes it's beneath him to have to deal with anyone below your level:

Some managers have strong beliefs about protocol. It appears demeaning if they have to deal with someone below their level. Whatever their reason, and no matter how inconvenient, this is an honestly held belief.

If this is why John insists on dealing with you, respect his reason. Sure, it takes a little more time and doesn't give your people a chance to show what they can do. It also provides John the service he expects.

When you deal with him, try including the technician who should be working with him. Don't just call Ahmal to find out the situation or get an answer; ask him to come to your office. Make sure that John knows him. Let him give John the answer. In time, John may decide that he'll be just as satisfied dealing with Ahmal as with you.

Be sensitive to John's reactions, though. He may feel offended if you seem to be pushing Ahmal at him. Your first job is to see that your customers are satisfied—and John is your customer. You want to lead John to work with someone other than you, but you may have to be patient and tactful to accomplish this. Keep at it (and see the next "cure").

If you give John a higher priority than your people do:

There are two dangers here.

- The first one is that you may begin distorting your unit's priorities. You should have established priorities, and everyone in the unit should share these same priorities. If you violate the priorities, your employees will begin to wonder how serious you are about them. Then they may begin to give priority to the people who complain the loudest. Oops, there goes any rational priority system.

- The second danger is an even worse one: other managers may start to believe that the only way to get their work done is to deal with you; then you'll be overloaded, while your people wait around to find out who's going to be the next priority. In this circumstance, your unit's work is almost guaranteed to drop sharply.

The cure is simple and straightforward: make sensible priorities and see that everyone—yourself included—abides by them. Make it clear to John that you'll give him the best service possible, but that you want to give this same level of service to everyone. Then stick by both statements; give him the best service you can, and give the same service to everyone else.

Something to Think About

It's extremely important for your people to be able to deal directly with their customers. If you become an intermediary, their job commitment will start fading—as will their productivity. The ideal situation is one in which you deal only with the most unusual and complex situations. Let your employees handle all the others.

And If This Doesn't Quite Fit Your Situation . . .

Look at the next problem (11-7), which describes a manager who won't cooperate unless you give him special treatment. Also see Problem 11-2 if he tries to put pressure on you by criticizing you to your boss or Problem 11-3 if he pressures you by letting his people give you substandard work.

Use Checklist 4 to develop a cure of your own.

— 11-7 —

The Problem: A manager won't cooperate with you unless you give his projects special priority.

The Scene

"You know, Gene, I'd love to help you balance those expense statements for your department," explained Eric, "but it would be nice to get a little support from your folks too. I've had requests in to hire three accountants for the last two and half months, and from what I can tell, no one's done much of anything to recruit them for me."

Well, that's fine for Eric to say. His boss didn't just tell him to hire 50 new people for the Shipping and Receiving Divisions by the first of next month. But that's the way Eric is: to get one little

thing out of him, you have to make him think he's Number One on
your list.

Possible Causes

The cause isn't particularly important here. What is important
is that Eric obviously isn't satisfied with the service you normally
give him. Maybe his expectations are realistic—and maybe they
aren't. But you really have only one question to ask yourself: Is Eric
important enough to your success to warrant making special efforts
for him? Your answer to that will affect everything else you do.

Hint: Just because Eric wants to be treated as if his projects
have special priority doesn't mean that you have to give them that
treatment. All you have to do is convince Eric that he's getting
special treatment. There are many techniques for doing that and still
accomplishing your work in the priority order most advantageous to
you (and your boss).

Cures

If Eric is worth special effort:

Talk to him about the other demands that have been laid on
your unit. If this is one of a *very* few times you haven't come through
for him, he may be understanding enough to let his work slip—and
still help you with yours.

If Eric isn't willing to compromise, assure him you'll get right
to his requirements—and do it. This doesn't contradict what we said
in Problem 11-6 about the dangers of your distorting your unit's
priorities. You've already asked yourself whether good peer relations
with Eric were important enough to the success of your unit to warrant
some accommodation for him. If they are, then satisfying Eric becomes one of your unit's regular, established priorities.

Make sure your workers know that Eric's work should come
near the top of their lists—and what that means in terms of day-to-day
operations. Do they drop everything when he calls? When one of his
subordinates calls? Do they let other work go to get his jobs filled?
Or only the ones that are particularly difficult to fill? You'll probably
need to specify in some detail how much special treatment Eric gets

(or be prepared to work it out with your staff as individual situations arise).

Make a point of talking to Eric every once in a while to see how things are going with him. Check to see if there are projects or requirements he's particularly concerned about; then have your staff concentrate on satisfying those concerns. Check also to see if Eric's more satisfied with the general level of service he's getting from your unit. And if there are still areas where he doesn't believe he's getting the treatment he deserves, address them.

If being in Eric's good graces isn't that important to the success of your organization:

While you don't want to make enemies of any of your peers, there are some of them who just aren't that important to you or your unit. Their cooperation is nice, but it's not essential. The trick is to make them think you're concerned about them—without letting their requests get in the way of your "real" work.

Think about what happens when someone asks you or your unit to do something. How do you respond? "I'll get to is as soon as I can"? (as you place the request on top of a stack of other papers)? Or "I'll get on that right away"? You can almost always do *something* that takes just a few minutes to get the ball rolling—so the requester feels somebody's paying attention to him.

Think too about your feedback mechanisms. Often when someone wants "special treatment," they already know there's not much extra you can do for them—but they *would* like to know what's happening along the way. If requesters know their work is being acted on (and isn't just sitting in a drawer somewhere), they'll have more confidence in you.

While you don't need to take time you don't really have, it wouldn't hurt to visit with Eric every once in a while to see how things are going with him. Without making any promises beyond those you'd make to any other manager, you'll still convey your interest and concern. Those cordial relations may stand you in good stead some other time.

Remember that your decision not to give Eric special treatment isn't final. Situations change. There may be a time when it's worth

your while to do something special for him in return for help for
your unit. On the other hand, bouncing him around in your priorities
is probably worse than keeping him with the general run of work.
He may come to expect favors when they aren't forthcoming—and
will be disappointed when nothing happens. Better that he knows
what to expect—and then gets it consistently.

Things to Think About

Eric obviously isn't satisfied with the level of service you normally give him—otherwise he wouldn't be pressuring you to give
his work special treatment. Regardless of how well *you* think you're
doing, you have a problem with the perception at least one of your
peers has about your unit. Are there others? Does it seem that *everyone*
uses your requests for assistance as an opportunity to demand more
of you? You may have more of a problem than you realize.

Consider making regular visits to the managers you deal with
most to see how you're doing with them. You don't need a specific
agenda item—not special problem to work out or request to ask or
service to offer. Just stop by for a friendly chat to let them know
that you're interested in what they think. Once they find out that
you're sincere in wanting to know, they'll tell you *exactly* how things
are going.

And If This Doesn't Quite Fit Your Situation . . .

Look at Problems 11-3, 11-5, and 11-6 for more instances of
strained peer relationships.

Use Checklist 4 to develop a cure of your own.

12

Troubleshooting Internal Management Problems

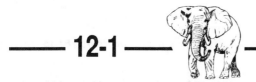

— 12-1 —

The Problem: An employee tells you that if a planned production increase goes through the employees will deluge you with grievances.

The Scene

"Now, look, Mrs. Chang—we don't have anything against you. You're a decent person and you're fair to us. But we just can't let this ridiculous 10% production increase go through. If the company goes ahead and puts it in a week from Monday, I promise you you'll have a dozen grievances on your desk Tuesday morning—and that's just a start. If you've got any pull with management, you'd better use it now. We're not kidding!"

When she finished, Sandy walked out of your office without even waiting for you to answer. It's clear she means it. Now what do you do about it?

Possible Causes

Your unit's productivity is much less than it ought to be. The 10% increase is a reasonable one.

Their productivity is high, and they're being penalized for the low productivity of the branch as a whole.

Their current productivity is acceptable, but they could easily increase it by 10% if they wanted to.

Productivity has nothing to do with it. They're unhappy with you and/or the company, and this is their way of showing it.

Hint: This is a classic example of the situation that a first-line supervisor gets caught in. On the one hand, you owe loyalty to management to support the production increase. On the other, your people think it's unfair and are up in arms against it. You're right in the middle.

Cures

If your unit's productivity is much less than it ought to be:

No matter how strongly they may feel about the increase, you can't defend their reaction to higher management. Your job is to get them to accept the increased production. If you don't, both you and they will suffer.

Your most important job is to persuade your employees that they need to increase their productivity—whether the company imposes a new rate or not. Problems 1-1, 1-6, 1-7, and 1-9 deal with low productivity in the work unit as a whole. Problems 1-2 and 1-5 deal with related issues. You can probably find some helpful ideas in one or more of these.

Chapters 4, 5, and 6 deal with individual productivity problems. You may find ideas in them that you can use in this situation.

If their productivity is high, and they're being penalized for the low productivity of the branch as a whole:

This is the reverse problem: your people are productive, but they get stuck with the same increase as the rest of the organization—which isn't as productive. If you don't do something, they're are going to be punished for doing so well. You can figure what that will do to their productivity and motivation in the future.

How you deal with this one depends on how your company deals with productivity. If there are established goals which your people have been exceeding, it should be easy to show higher management that the 10% increase isn't fair. It should also be easy to show them if your employees have a higher rate of production than other similar units.

What if there aren't records that will show how productive your unit is? Here's where your boss's confidence in you comes in. If he believes that you've been getting production from your unit, he may go to bat for you.

Your other alternatives aren't very good ones. Do what you can to talk management out of the increase and to talk your employees into being patient. Then find a way to demonstrate how high their productivity already is.

If their current productivity is acceptable, but they could easily increase it by 10% if they wanted to:

This is another challenging situation. You wouldn't be embarrassed if you sided with your employees and tried to persuade higher management to drop the increase. On the other hand, you wouldn't be out of line to try to get your people to accept the increase.

The basic question for your employees is this: Why should they increase their output if it's already acceptable? That's the question you'll have to answer for them if you want them to change. Perhaps the company is in trouble and increasing production would make their jobs more secure. Or upping their productivity might qualify them for a greater year-end bonus.

What if you can't find a reason for them to increase production? As you might suspect, you'll be in a difficult situation. Higher management will be expecting the increase, but your employees won't be willing to produce it. This is a true impasse, and one that's not easy to resolve.

While you need to explain the situation to higher management, you need even more to find a reason for your employees to increase their production. The easy and obvious reasons have already been covered above; finding a good one will probably be difficult. Still, you need to find it. Here's where credibility with your boss and your employees will stand you in good stead. If you have credibility, both of them may be willing to give you some time to find a solution. If you don't have credibility? Sorry—wish we could help, but . . .

If your employees are unhappy with you or the company and the productivity increase is just an excuse:

This isn't so unusual a situation, but it's a difficult one. If the real cause of their anger isn't the increase, nothing you do about the increase is apt to help.

If you suspect that your workers are unhappy with you, try to get more details from an employee with whom you have a good relationship. If she's willing to level with you, don't argue with her or get defensive. Take what she says, think about it, and find a way to respond to it. Then remedy the problem, if you can.

Suppose the unit is unhappy with higher management. Once again, you need to find out the cause of the unit's unhappiness, in as much detail as you can. If the cause is related to something that higher management might be willing to change, have a talk with your boss about it. If you're sure it can't or won't be changed, see if you can talk with your people and defuse the issue. Perhaps your employees have misinterpreted some management statement or action, and talking with them can straighten out the situation. Perhaps management had to do something distasteful to your unit, but you can show them why it had to be done.

Things to Think About

When a company tries to boost productivity just by setting a higher rate, it often runs into trouble. Employees can fight back by filing grievances, "working to rule," refusing to cooperate with other units, and in a dozen other ways. They can also work faster and turn out more products with a higher rework and rejection rate.

How do you prevent this? Here are two solutions that come to mind:

- One alternative is to get greater productivity by training employees more effectively. They may not know the best ways to perform their tasks—even if they've been doing them for some time. High-quality training in the best procedures might enable them to produce more with no more effort or strain. (Don't discard this idea out of hand. It's surprising how often employees don't know the best way to accomplish their tasks.)

- Relate the productivity increase to a pay increase. You might be able to do this yourself, if you have the authority to pay bonuses on your own. If not, can you put in a form of piecework or at least extra pay for high performance? (Don't forget, an increase in productivity only earns a bonus or higher pay if quality is maintained.)

And If This Doesn't Quite Fit Your Situation . . .

If the problem is mainly a performance problem, see Chapter 1 (if it's a group problem) or Chapters 4, 5, and 6 (if it's an individual problem). If the group is being egged on by an informal leader who's not a really good performer, see Problem 6-8.

Use Checklist 1 to develop a cure of your own.

—— 12-2 ——

The Problem: The new employees you're getting aren't doing well.

The Scene

"You know, Barb," reported Kit, "Marta just isn't working out the way I hoped she would. Somehow she's managed to scramble up mail Zena's already sorted—and lost an order from one of our best customers in the process. I don't know *how* many times I've gone over the steps with her—one, two, three. But the next time I look, she's screwed something else up. It's not *that* tough a job. I guess I shouldn't complain about Marta especially, though. She's no worse than the rest of the employees we've hired lately."

Possible Causes

Marta may not have the basic skills she needs to do the job. She may lack such essential skills as basic literacy, or ability to alphabetize, or basic math skills. More and more of our entry-level work force does.

Marta may not like the work. She may have interests or aspirations in another direction and not be interested in the assignments you've given her.

Marta may be poorly motivated. She may just be filling in the time until something better comes along, or she may not see any value in the work she's doing. But for whatever reason, she's really not motivated to do a good job.

Hint: If you're not sure whether the problems you're having with your employees are due to lack of skills or lack of interest, you can answer that question by asking yourself another. "If this employee's life depended on performing this job adequately, could she do it?" If the answer is "yes," then you have a motivation problem. But if the answer is "no"—if the employee couldn't perform, even if her life depended on it—then you have a problem with her skills or abilities.

Cures

If Marta lacks basic skills to do the job:

Talk with Marta and review her application and the other items in her personnel file to find out as much as you can about what skills Marta does have and the kind of work she's done in the past. Your Training Department may also be qualified to give basic literacy and computational literacy tests to find out what skills Marta has. If they can't help, you might try the testing services of your state's Employment Services Department.

Check with your Personnel Department to see if there are any formal classes available that will teach the skills Marta needs. If there aren't, and if the skills deficiencies Marta has seem to be shared by a lot of your new workers, talk to the Personnel Department about developing courses or contracting with local schools or training vendors.

Try to identify a mentor for Marta to whom she can go when she has questions and who can check her work and help her correct her errors. She's more likely to consult another employee, since she won't feel her job's being threatened when she admits problems.

If there are several parts of the job Marta needs to learn or isn't doing well in, parcel out some of the work to other employees. Then start teaching Marta the parts that are essential to the job. As she masters those, you can add in the rest later.

Encourage Marta whenever you can. By dealing with a skills problem early, you give the employee a much better chance of improving before she develops negative attitudes about the work—or about working for you.

If Marta isn't interested in the job:

Talk to Marta to find out what kind of work she'd rather be doing. Then point out to her those parts of the job that are most similar to the kind of work she likes.

Let Marta know that, if she does well in the job she's on now, you'll try to arrange for more of the work she finds interesting or help her find a job that's closer to what she's looking for.

At the same time, make it clear that Marta can't expect you to help her if she doesn't help herself. She's got to show you that she can do good work before you give her something more responsible to do or recommend her to another manager.

Make sure also that Marta is aware of the consequences of continuing to do poorly in this job. Regardless of how uninteresting she may find the work, she needs either to do it well, find herself a new job, or face termination from this one for failure to perform.

If Marta is poorly motivated:

Different people are motivated by different things, but if Marta's level of motivation is typical of the new employees you're getting, you need to ask yourself some questions: Is the job set up to reward employees for doing the right things? Or are there rewards to employees for doing the wrong things (or for not doing the right things)? For instance, does your company reward quantity production exclusively—without consideration of the quality of work? Do your employees understand how their jobs fit into the "big picture" of work that's done in the unit or in your company? Do they see the unit or company's work as worthwhile? Are there obstacles to doing good work here that discourage employees from even trying (like insufficient work space or materials)? The answers to these questions won't benefit just Marta—they'll benefit the whole work group.

If employees don't see any benefit in doing a better job, consider setting up an informal system of recognition for each job that's done well. This can be a public "pat on the back" or a more tangible form of recognition such as a certificate, a bonus, or a gift certificate. Set up systems also that make the employees themselves the ones who suffer the consequences of their poor work. Give your employees regular feedback on what they're doing well and not so well. When the work's not done well, make sure they do it over again until it's right. When new employees like Marta come on board, talk over with them your reward systems, so it's clear from the first why they should do good work.

If workers don't see the "big picture," put together an orientation program for your new employees that describes what each kind of job does, who the customer is (internal or external), and what impact the job has on other people or operations. Describe the company itself in some detail, identifying the services it provides or the products it makes. If it's not obvious, explain what value these products or services have. Then make sure everyone, including Marta, receives the orientation as soon as possible after joining your unit.

You might also consider revising your recruiting literature or your interviewing techniques to emphasize the contributions the company and your unit make. If employees are excited about the kind of work you do before they even start work, they'll be much more likely to perform enthusiastically (and well).

Review your work situation to see just what's getting in the way of doing a good job. Talk to your current staff. Examine the work flow and your organizational structure. Make any changes you need to see that tasks are done in a logical sequence and that segments once completed don't require rework farther down the line. Make sure someone is ultimately responsible for the quality of every product and that she sees the final result before passing it on. Do whatever you need to do to get your local supply department on your side. Workers who don't have the necessary equipment or supplies can't do a good job, no matter how well motivated they are.

Things to Think About

When we've talked about some of the basic skills Marta may need to acquire to do her job, it's been in terms of skills that make up the content of the work (like reading, writing, and similar skills). But there are another whole class of skills that Marta may not have—basic work discipline skills. These include things like knowing that you have to come to work each morning—on time, knowing that you don't spend your day on personal telephone calls or out in the hall chatting with friends, or knowing that when you make a commitment to do something you're expected to follow through.

Many of our newest entrants to the work force lack even these basic skills. They weren't taught them in school, and they haven't picked them up anywhere else. Appalling as that may seem, it's a situation we're going to encounter more frequently in the years ahead. So we'd better start now thinking about how we're going to train those *very* essential areas.

And If This Doesn't Quite Fit Your Situation . . .

Look at Problems 4-2, 4-5, and 4-6 for discussions of performance problems with individual employees. Also see Problem 1-7 for an examination of the fit between the job and the reward structure.

Use Checklists 1 and 2 to develop a cure of your own.

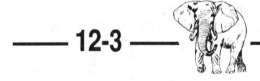

—— 12-3 ——

The Problem: You have to hire a trainee when you desperately need someone who's fully trained.

The Scene

"I'm sorry, Sam, but we just don't have the budget for a fully trained adjuster. If you want anyone, you're going to have to get a two-year college graduate or someone like that and train them to do the job. It's that or nothing."

Dejectedly, you leave your boss's office. It was bad enough that the number of claims your unit has handled is up 25% so far this year. Then you lost one of your best adjusters. Now you have to fill the vacancy behind her with a raw trainee.

Possible Causes

This is one of those situations where the cause is clear: your boss has made a decision and you need to live with it. The only question is how you're going to do it, with the least possible loss of productivity.

Hint: Don't pick just one of the "cures" below. Use every one of them you can.

Cures

Don't overlook good sources of qualified people for the job:

Does this sounds a little silly? Of course you don't want to overlook good sources of candidates! If you're not careful, though, you may put unnecessary limitations on yourself. Don't just assume you'll get a so-so candidate. Stop and think: Where might you get someone who could learn quickly but would be willing to come to work for what you can pay?

- A good place to begin is with your employees and their friends. It's important to your people that the job gets filled with someone who can learn quickly and do a good job. Ask them for suggestions—and follow up on any leads they give you.

- Is there a group or even an employment agency that specializes in placing workers who are in their fifties or above? Look into that source. You may find someone with good work experience who'd like the job and could learn it rapidly.

- What would happen if you hired a fully qualified person part time? Perhaps a young mother with experience would be willing to work the 5 to 6 hours a day that her children are in school. Or maybe a well-qualified retiree would be willing to work two or three days a week.

- Could you get a better quality "worker" if you hired two people part time for the job? Lots of companies do it, and they have success at it. For instance, you might fill half the job with a mother willing to work in the mornings and the other half with a college student who has his afternoons free.

You get the idea. Use your imagination. Let your employees, and your personnel office, help you. Don't start off with the idea that you're defeated. You may be surprised how well you'll be able to do.

Provide intensive training to the individual:

Many offices don't have established training programs. New employees learn from watching and working with experienced workers. Or the firm hires nothing but trained workers, so it never sees there might be a problem.

If your company doesn't have an established training program, find out quickly if there are some training sources you can tap. A local college or junior college? Courses in the area given by a professional association or an organization which specializes in training? Perhaps even a video course that you can rent or buy?

Whether or not you can get formal training, develop a structured on-the-job training plan. Let the new employee work with an experienced worker who is good at the job as well as good at helping others. Make sure he knows he has relief from his work load and that training the new employee is important. Then follow up often enough to be sure that the training is progressing on schedule.

Don't forget books on the subject. There are dozens and often hundreds of books on almost every occupation. Can you find one or two that deal with your kind of work and see that the new employee reads them? Perhaps you and he could meet once or twice a week to discuss them.

Separate out the simpler work and give it to him:

When everyone in an organization is well qualified and well trained, the most difficult work is often assigned among all of the jobs. That means that each employee also does some of the simpler work. If this is the case in your unit, a little job redesign will let the trainee become productive very quickly.

Get together with your best workers—or perhaps even all your workers—and find the simplest and least challenging work they have to do. You can count on their help, since most of them will be happy to get rid of this work. Identify enough of the routine work to make a separate job and assign the trainee to that job.

You still want to hire the most qualified individual you can and see that he's trained. Now, though, he can begin making a useful contribution to the unit much more quickly.

There's a decision you get to make after a few weeks or months: Do you leave the individual doing just the simpler work, or do you bring him along to become a full performer? That depends on many factors, one of which is the individual's progress in the job. Keep that decision in mind as you evaluate his performance from the beginning.

Things to Think About

Every manager likes to have the best qualified employees possible. It generally makes life much easier. There's a down side to it, though. What happens if your people are highly qualified and motivated, but much of the work is boring? They may lose their motivation and look for more challenging jobs elsewhere.

In other words, it often makes sense to concentrate the simpler work in one or a few jobs. Then you can hire less qualified, less expensive individuals for these jobs. If they have the ability and the motivation, they can move up into the more skilled jobs. If they don't, they can still make a contribution doing the less demanding work.

And If This Doesn't Quite Fit Your Situation . . .

Look at Problems 1-1, 1-2, 1-5, 1-6, and 1-7 if you need a fully qualified worker because your unit is performing inadequately. If part of the cause is individuals with personal or performance problems see Chapters 3, 4, 5, and 6.

Use Checklist 1 to develop a cure of your own.

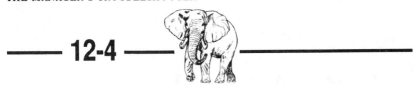

——— 12-4 ———

The Problem: You can't promote a talented, ambitious employee who is already looking for jobs outside the company.

The Scene

"Don, I know there's nothing you can do about this," began Tony, "but I think I owe it to you to let you know that I'm looking around. I think I've taken this job about as far as I can go. There don't seem to be any new challenges to meet, and it's all getting pretty routine. But it doesn't look like there's anywhere for me to go as long as I stay with Smart Systems. I know it's not your fault—there just aren't any openings higher up right now. But it doesn't look like there are going to be any soon either. And I think it's time for me to move on."

You're not surprised. Tony's right. He's gone about as far as he can with the job he has, and it doesn't look like anything's going to open up you could promote him into. But he's such a good worker! Isn't there something you can think of to get him to stay?

Possible Causes

Tony may not feel appreciated in this job. He knows he's done well for the company, but he believes the company hasn't done well by him. He believes that the contributions he's made ought to buy him some recognition—preferably a better job with more money.

Tony may not feel challenged in this job. He's mentioned that he thinks he's taken this job as far as he can go. If there are no new worlds to conquer, doing the same old work day after day can get pretty boring. Tony's looking for something where he can regain the excitement and challenge.

Hint: The best way to find out the cause of Tony's dissatisfaction is to ask him. He's been honest with you about wanting to leave. He'll probably also be willing to tell you specifically why.

Cures

If Tony doesn't feel appreciated in this job:

Even if you can't promote Tony, chances are there are forms of recognition you can offer him—a bonus, a gift certificate, mention in the company newsletter, recognition as "Employee of the Month" or "Employee of the Quarter." Identify those things you can do, and choose one that you think Tony will like and that's appropriate for his contributions.

You may be able to change Tony's title or stature in the office without giving him a real promotion. Maybe he could be a lead worker or a "special assistant." This "no-cost" promotion, accomplished with a significant amount of fanfare and accompanied by a more tangible bonus or reward, may let Tony know that his employers do appreciate him.

Finally, make sure Tony understands the way promotions work in your company and what you are able (and willing) to do to help Tony get promoted—either within your section or elsewhere in the organization.

If Tony doesn't feel challenged:

Identify special projects or assignments you could give Tony that aren't a regular part of his job, but that would give him a chance to expand his skills. Be careful in what you assign Tony. Don't give him anything too much higher than what he's doing now. If he gets mad at you later, he could sue you for giving him work he's not being paid to do!

Talk to Tony about his long term career goals. Would he like to continue to expand his technical expertise, completing progressively more demanding assignments? Or would he prefer to complement his technical skills with managerial assignments? Try to structure additional responsibilities around the things that he's most interested in.

At the same time that you're enhancing Tony's assignments to give him greater challenges, look into taking away from his job some of the more routine work (or work he's mastered so that it's become routine). Assign those duties to someone else in the organization who you believe will be able to perform them creditably. It's not fair to Tony to keep piling work on him without relief. While a good employee consistently looks for greater challenges, he also resents being overburdened because of the attitude "you can always count on Tony."

What if there is no more challenging work in the organization you can offer Tony? In that case, you need to have a straightforward discussion with him and explain that he's already doing the most interesting work the unit has to offer. Then do what you can to help Tony find the kind of work that will satisfy him—preferably retaining his skills within the company, but going elsewhere if that's what he needs.

Things to Think About

There are some things you can do to encourage Tony to stay, at least for a while—and we've talked about them in the "cures" above. But you also need to ask yourself at some point if the effort's worth it. If you can't give Tony what he thinks he wants—a promotion, the things you can give him may not satisfy him for long. Or he may be becoming so resentful of the company's failure to recognize him that he's not going to do as good a job for you as he has in the past.

In either case, his dissatisfactions will surface again—possibly before very long—and he'll resume his job hunting. If that's likely to happen, then your best course of action is simply to express your understanding of the difficult situation Tony is in, acknowledge your inability to satisfy him, and offer your help in finding him something better elsewhere. You can't be all things to all people.

And If This Doesn't Quite Fit Your Situation . . .

Look at the problems in Chapter 4 for hints on handling the situation if Tony's failure to be promoted results in his losing his motivation.

Use the General Checklist to develop a cure of your own.

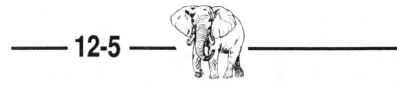

—— 12-5 ——

The Problem: One of your best workers has asked to go part time so she can attend college—just as an important project is starting.

The Scene

Why did Maria have to do this to you now? A year ago you'd have been happy to give her a leave of absence for college. Eighteen months from now, you'd be happy to give it to her. But six weeks from now, the week after you start reviewing every company operation to see whether it could be contracted out? Ow!

If it were anyone but Maria, the answer would be simple: No. Maria, though, has been with you for five years, and she's an excellent worker. If ever anyone deserved help getting through college, it's her. How in the world can you tell her "no"—but how can you tell her "yes"?

Possible Causes

The causes aren't the critical elements. Whatever Maria's reasons are for wanting to go to college, you support them. Your real concerns are (1) how you can help her get college courses without totally disrupting your operations and (2) how useful those courses will be to the company.

Cures

If Maria's education will make her more valuable to the company and you expect her to stay with you:

In this case, both you and Maria benefit. You want to do everything you can to help her get her college courses. No matter what arrangements the two of you make, though, you need to keep these two points in mind:

- If possible, the company should provide financial assistance. This shows your support for Maria's ambitions and will probably help her concentrate on her studies. If the company has a program for this, use it. If not, talk with your boss and anyone else who can help arrange it.

- Make all your commitments contingent upon successful performance at work and college. Both you and Maria should make your agreements on a quarter-by-quarter (or semester-by-semester) basis. At the end of the quarter, look together at how she's doing and make a decision about the next quarter.

Here are some of the options the two of you can consider:

Maria converts to part time.

- For instance, could Maria take off only a few hours each week for the college courses themselves and do all her homework at night and on weekends? This would keep her on the job, and if she's really that good she may accomplish more on part time than a replacement could working full time.

- You have a strong motivator working here. If Maria sees that you've really made an effort to support her college goals, she'll probably work even harder during the time that she's on the job.

She does some work at home.

- If you really need Maria full time, would it help if she did some of her work at home? Perhaps she could take off time during the day for college and then make it up by doing work at home at night or on the weekend.

- This solution doesn't give Maria the additional time for college. It does give her more control over her schedule, and that may be enough to make it practical.

She attends college at night.

- If you just can't spare her, can she attend college at night? This may put quite a strain on her, particularly if she's a single parent or has to care for her own parents. Look at it carefully, though—because there are steps you can take to make it easier for her.

- For instance, you might work out a flexible work schedule for her. If she has a late class, she might start work an hour or two later than normal the next day. If she needs a class that starts in late afternoon, perhaps she can start work that day earlier than usual.

- Working at home can also help, for the same reasons that we mentioned earlier. If she has a job that permits this, using it liberally could be a major help to her.

- If you can agree that she'll go to school at night, at least while the project is "hot," you should provide her as much financial assistance as possible. If she's really that good and your company will allow it, could you pay even for babysitters and parking—if that's what it takes?

She puts off attending college.

- This is a last resort. If none of the alternatives we've just looked at work, would she be willing to wait a year or 18 months to start?

- Don't make the effort one-sided. If you're going to ask her to wait on something as important as this, there needs to be some commitment on your side, too. For instance, you might make a firm commitment that she can start part time in a year, no matter what. Does that make you nervous? You've given yourself a year to plan to handle it; isn't that enough?

If Maria's education won't make her more valuable to the company:

Suppose she wants to become a nurse, but you're an accounting firm? Or she wants to prepare herself for a job where you already have plenty of well-qualified applicants. In other words, the education she wants may pay off for her but it doesn't pay off for you.

The list of alternatives here isn't as long. One of the first is to talk with her about taking courses that *will* help the company. If you're an accounting firm and she doesn't want to become an accountant, could she study human resources management? The company might be able to use that skill.

What about reducing the number of hours Maria works over several years? During the first semester or two, she can work full time and attend college at night. Then she can shift to half time for a few semesters, as she trains a replacement for her job. When she finishes her education and moves to a new career, she will leave a fully trained replacement behind her.

These aren't realistic? Is there another way that you could support her desire for education and still act responsibly for the company? Do your best to find it.

Things to Think About

Education is a very precious possession in America in the 1990s. We need every college-trained person we can get. It benefits us all to support Maria and everyone else as fully as we can. Even if there's no immediate payback to the firm, it's probably worthwhile to help Maria get to college.

There's also a very practical reason for helping. If your company won't let Maria shift to part time (or otherwise help her), she has another option available to her. She can leave you and go to work for a company that will help her get a college education. If she's good, that probably won't be too hard. Most firms are delighted to have employees who are putting themselves through college. It may be a hardship to shift her to part time—but is it more of a hardship than losing her?

And If This Doesn't Quite Fit Your Situation . . .

If Maria needs to be absent because of personal problems, look at Chapter 3, particularly Problems 3-1 and 3-4.

Use the General Checklist to develop a cure of your own.

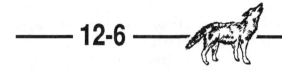

12-6

The Problem: One of your best workers has asked you to make an exception to a rule for her.

The Scene

"I know this is a little irregular, Ben, and I know I was off on the day after Thanksgiving last year, but I really need to be off again this year," Fran asked. "It's important to be consistent, I know, and this policy of "one year on, one year off" is a good one, but my parents are coming in this year. The kids and I haven't seen them for three years, and I'd really appreciate being able to spend some time with them. Couldn't you make an exception, just this once?"

Fran's always been somebody you could count on—to stay late, to work over, to cover for somebody else who got in a crunch. You can sympathize with her wanting to spend some time with her family. But if you make an exception for her, what about the rest of the group? Are they all going to come in wanting off the day after Christmas? And if you make an exception for Fran, how can you deny anybody else?

Possible Causes

If we assume that Fran's reasons for wanting you to make an exception are legitimate, then it doesn't really matter much beyond that what they are. The real questions here have to do with the rule itself and the importance of applying it consistently. To decide what to do when an employee requests an exception to a work rule, ask yourself the following questions:

How important is the rule? In this case, Fran's asking you to make an exception to a rule that's clearly discretionary (determining who gets to take off the day after a major holiday). But if the rule were something affecting workers' safety (like a requirement to wear a hardhat in certain areas) or if it affected the quality of your unit's products or services (like a request to skip a checking step to meet a customer's production requirements), your flexibility in granting exceptions would be more limited.

How much discretion do you have in granting exceptions? Is this a rule you made, or is it a part of your labor agreement? Is it something your superiors require, that they consider "sacred" even if you don't? What are the bounds of your authority to make exceptions?

What message do you want to send to your employees about this rule, or your application of it? It doesn't matter *what* kind of exception Fran is asking for, or how discreet you and she are about granting the request. You can almost guarantee that *someone* else in the unit is going to find out that you've made an exception. Is it important that you be as consistent as possible in how you treat this rule, or this particular group of workers? Will granting the exception make you look like a humane and concerned manager? Or will it make you look like a wimp? Will granting this exception make it harder to enforce the rule next time?

Cures

If the rule isn't critical to the success of your unit and if allowing Fran the exception won't set a precedent for the rest of the group:

Allow Fran to take the time off she's asked for. Explain to her what prompted your decision so she (and other workers who may ask the same favor) will know under what circumstances you consider the exception appropriate. If possible, arrange for Fran to reciprocate (perhaps by working another day that she would normally be permitted to have off).

If the rule itself is important, but some flexibility in your application of it is appropriate:

Ask Fran for her suggestions of ways you can meet the spirit of the rule, while still granting her the exception she wants. Maybe she could trade days off with another worker. Or maybe she could work part of the day after Thanksgiving—the hours when her presence is most critical, then take the rest of the day off. Between the two of you, you should be able to come up with some accommodation that will preserve the integrity of the rule itself, but without being rigid in applying it.

If you can't come up with a way even to meet the spirit of the rule, then you'll need to rethink how important it is. If it's really important to conform in some measure to the requirements, then you'll have to deny Fran's request.

If the rule itself isn't that important, but it's critical that you be consistent in its application:

Consider Fran's request in light of other requests for exception you may have received. Can you make a policy decision that would permit these exceptions for all workers who meet specified criteria? Maybe employees who have seniority could be permitted to select the days they'll work or request exceptions? Maybe employees could be allowed to switch with coworkers as long both people agree?

As above, if you can't come up with a set of criteria that you could apply across the board, then think again about how important it is to be consistent? Will it really do that much damage to your ability to enforce the rules if you grant an exception to a good employee? Are there extenuating circumstances you could cite to make it clear that you won't grant exceptions just to suit each employee's whim? If consistency is that critical, and if you can't think of a way to grant Fran's request without undermining that consistency, then you have no alternative but to deny Fran the time off she wants.

If the rule is one over which you exercise little or no control:

Explain to Fran that you don't have the authority to grant her request. Let her know who in the supervisory chain she should see about her request and the kind of backup information or arguments she'll need to have it approved.

Something to Think About

Consistency isn't as great as it sounds. While you may think that granting a request for one employee means you have to do the same thing for others, that really isn't so. Nor is it practical in many cases to come up with a policy that will cover all the possible situations and reasons for exception that may arise. Most employees will understand why you've given someone a special exception (as long as you don't favor certain employees consistently over others) and won't try to take advantage. They'll be much more impressed with your humane, reasoned approach to requests for exception than a mechanically consistent application of every rule.

And If This Doesn't Quite Fit Your Situation . . .

Look at Problems 3-1, 3-4, and 3-7 for descriptions of situations where special handling is clearly warranted. Problem 12-5 also discusses an employee's request for an exception to normal policy.

Use the General Checklist to develop a cure of your own.

12-7

The Problem: Your unit's supplies are being pilfered but you don't know who's doing it.

The Scene

Tina just brought you the third loss report on a missing calculator this month. Then there's the power stapler that no one can find. And the boxes of disks and printer ribbons that can't be accounted for. Nothing big is missing—yet—but you're getting concerned. How can you stop all this before it gets really bad?

Possible Causes

Your employees think it's okay to take small equipment and supplies to use at home. Over the years, this has become an informal "fringe benefit" for them, one that they count on.

Someone in the unit has a substance abuse problem. Most theft in this country is committed to support drug habits. That may be happening in your unit.

You simply have a thief in your unit.

Security in your office is too lax. Someone who doesn't work for you is stealing from you, because you don't have control of visitors in the work area.

Hint: This is a good time to be careful, systematic and rational. Don't jump to conclusions or take rash steps without getting the facts. See if there's any office gossip about the thefts, but don't act on it until you've verified it for yourself.

Cures

If your employees think it's okay to take small equipment and supplies for personal use:

This may seem strange, particularly if you're used to an office where supplies are strictly controlled. It does happen. It may be a practice of long standing. It may simply have grown up without anyone authorizing it; employees have been taking small items simply because no one told them they shouldn't.

You might start by talking with other managers and see what they believe the firm's practices are. One or two of your senior workers might be willing to talk with you about it. You'll also need to find out what the formal company policy is.

If the company doesn't intend for employees to take equipment and supplies, you need to stop your employees from doing it. *Don't* start by being judgmental and demanding. Explain how the situation developed, and that you expect it to stop. If you know what the cost is to your unit and/or the company, tell them that. Most employees will understand. If one or two of them don't, and you've made what you expect clear, treat them as thieves. The next three "cures" will help you with this.

If someone in the unit has a drug abuse problem:

If the supplies and equipment are being stolen by one person, and if they're items that could be resold—there's a very good chance that that person (or someone close to him or her) has a drug abuse problem. This doesn't make the theft permissible; it just gives you a specific place to start.

Talk to some of the employees you trust the most. Have they noticed that someone is behaving differently or showing other symptoms of an abuse problem? Combine this with your own observations. Someone who's abusing drugs enough to start stealing to support the habit is probably showing his habit in other ways, too (late for work, increased errors, etc.)

If it appears that an employee is abusing drugs, deal with the problem promptly. You can find suggestions on how to do this in Problems 2-6, 3-3; and 4-3.

If you have a thief in your unit:

If one of your employees is simply a thief, catching him may be very difficult. First of all, he's probably had experience at it. Second, he can pick his times and places; if necessary, he can hold off for a few weeks until you and everyone else relax. Finally, he knows that you have to be very careful about accusing anyone, to keep from offending innocent employees.

If there are several employees in whom you have complete confidence, solicit their help. If two or three people are watching constantly, it's much harder to pilfer. Remember the paragraph just above, though; don't let up just because a week or so goes by without a theft.

If your situation permits, you may simply want to lock up the items that could be stolen. Then they can be checked out to employees when they're needed and checked back in at the end of the workday.

If security is too lax:

Perhaps the problem isn't with your unit at all. It may be easy for someone from another work area, or even from outside the company, to slip in and walk off with small items.

This is often the easiest situation to deal with successfully. There's almost always something you can do to improve security. At the very least, you can have your people keep their eyes open and notice anyone from outside the unit immediately.

This need not be negative in any way. It's courteous to greet individuals from outside the work unit and ask if you can help them with something. If they have business with your unit, they'll appreciate the attention. If they don't belong there, this will help them decide to leave.

Even if one of the other causes seems to be the right one, you should check out the security of your work area. Is it easy for outsiders to get in without being noticed? If it is, change your security. You don't need to keep people out, just to make sure that you know when and why they're there.

Something to Think About

If your employees aren't taking small equipment and supplies because they think it's okay, look carefully at the possibility that drug abuse may be behind the thefts. Many people who develop a drug habit can't afford to pay for it with their salary. They have to "augment" their pay by stealing.

And If This Doesn't Quite Fit Your Situation . . .

Chapter 1 describes a number of situations in which employees might be angry or demoralized enough to engage in theft or other aggressive behavior against management.

Use Checklist 2 to develop a cure of your own.

—— **12-8** ——

The Problem: An employee won't tell you when something's bothering him, then disrupts the group.

The Scene

There goes Darrell again! You *knew* he wasn't happy about your sending Glenda on the trip to Phoenix with him. He wanted to spend time visiting relatives, and now he'll feel obligated to socialize with Glenda at least part of the time they're out there. But did he say anything to you about it? No, of course not. He said something to Ken, and Tricia, and Curt—trying to get sympathy. You can deal with problems head on. But when people just whine behind your back, it's a lot harder.

Possible Causes

Darrell may believe that complaining to you won't do any good. Have you established a relationship with your employees in which they trust you to listen to their concerns and act on them? If not, then they won't come to you when they're unhappy. They'll try other tactics.

Darrell may recognize the wisdom of your decision, but want some understanding and sympathy from his peers. Whether your decision was objectively reasonable or not, he may just want someone to empathize with his tough break.

Hint: While this kind of situation is rarely a serious problem, it is the sort of thing that can sneak up on you and grow to more serious proportions. All you may see is that there's some grumbling in the ranks. Or you may notice slightly less cooperation among the group, but not know why. Little problems can grow—or they can be symptomatic of greater concerns. It's best to find out what the trouble is and deal with it now.

Cures

If Darrell believes that complaining to you won't help:

Look first in your own backyard. Is there anything you've been doing in your relationship with Darrell that would make him believe you won't listen? Or that you'll listen, and make empty promises to fix things? If so, fix your own problem first before you approach Darrell. Unless you change what you're doing so that employees believe that coming to you will make a difference, it won't matter how much you *say* you have an open door. Your door may be open, but is anybody really home?

If you've decided that you're not doing anything to discourage Darrell from coming to you when something's bothering him, then approach him about the problem directly. Let him know that you're aware of his dissatisfaction. Then tell him what you're willing (and able) to do to make things better.

At least for the first time you challenge Darrell about his mode of expressing his concerns, you should be prepared to do something to resolve the problem. You might offer to let him out of this trip entirely, since it's not working out the way he'd like. Maybe you could send Glenda for just part of the time. Or perhaps you could let Darrell take some extra vacation time once the work is completed so he can mix business and pleasure. But somehow, you *must* demonstrate that you hear his concerns and that you're prepared to do what you can to help him. If you don't send that message, you'll simply have confirmed Darrell's belief that coming to you won't do any good.

Make sure Darrell knows that you're aware of how he's been dealing with his dissatisfactions and that you don't think he's using the most productive methods to resolve them. Encourage him to come to you directly in the future, and explain that you can only fix problems you know about—that there's not much you can do in response to vague grumblings.

It may take a few attempts before Darrell gets the message. But once he sees that coming to you really does yield results—maybe not *every* time, but often enough—he'll change. He may even encourage others who complain to him to come to you instead.

If Darrell just wants sympathy:

It's inevitable that you, as a manager, will make some decisions your employees don't like—even if they agree that they're reasonable decisions. But if a good decision inconveniences an employee or spoils other plans he's made, he's not going to be happy. And there's not much you can do to change that. When Darrell's grumbling is just a bid for sympathy and doesn't disrupt the group much, it's better to let him express his feelings, work through them with his peers, and get back to work. So you can ignore most of this kind of minor disruption.

Make sure you give Darrell an opportunity to express his feelings to you too. Even if the decision is one you can't change, he needs to know that you, as well as his co-workers, empathize with him.

You might consider allowing the unit to make as many of its own operating decisions as possible—to give your employees a sense of "ownership" of the decisions that are made. That might cut down on the grumbling.

And If This Doesn't Quite Fit Your Situation . . .

Look at Problems 6-8 and 8-6 for descriptions of more serious problems with workers who disturb the rest of the unit.

Use Checklist 2 to develop a cure of your own.

13

Troubleshooting Problems That Your Boss Causes

——— 13-1 ———

The Problem: He forces you to hire a poorly qualified minority group member so the organization's statistics will look good.

The Scene

"I know how much you wanted to hire that Boynton fellow," Mr. Tretsker told you this morning, "but we need some more minorities in the organization, and you've got one on your applicant list. He may not be the best person you've talked to, but he's going to have to do. Personnel will never let us by with another selection that's not a minority. You'll just have to make the best of it."

"Not the best person" is a real understatement! George Jones was very nearly the worst candidate you interviewed. He doesn't know anything about production control, he just worked on an assembly line one summer when he was in high school. How are you going to be able to do anything with him?

Possible Causes

There could be a number of reasons why the minority representation in your organization is so low that Mr. Tretsker must force a selection of a poorly qualified applicant. We'll assume in this scenario that you and the other supervisors in your organization haven't been

339

discriminating against the minority candidates who apply for your jobs. In that case, the most likely reasons for the low minority representation in your unit are the following

Not many minority candidates apply for your jobs. They may not know that the jobs exist, or they may believe that they don't qualify for them. They may also believe (based on your current EEO profile) that they wouldn't be selected even if they did apply.

Not many minority candidates are qualified for your jobs. Your positions may require knowledge or skills that members of certain minority groups traditionally have no opportunity to acquire.

These are both situations that you have some power to change. It may not help you much in your current dilemma, but solving these problems will reduce the chances that you'll be put in this situation again.

Cures

For the immediate situation:

Be careful here not to confuse lack of knowledge with lack of ability. Just because the minority candidates you've talked to aren't currently qualified for your jobs doesn't mean they can't learn them. It will take longer than if you hired someone who already knew the work, but you may still wind up with a very productive employee.

If there was more than one minority candidate considered for the job, ask Mr. Tretsker for his approval to hire whichever minority seems most likely to be able to learn the job well (as opposed to the specific candidate he designated). Then rework your selection criteria to focus on *aptitude* rather than actual job experience or knowledge. Talk to your Personnel Department, State Employment Agency, or other testing services about using aptitude tests that would identify those people with the best likelihood of success in the job. Make arrangements for your minority candidates to take the test (at the company's expense) and use the results to help you make a selection decision.

If there are company restrictions on formal aptitude testing for job applicants, you can still assess aptitude. Reinterview the minority candidates, focusing your questions on school or work experiences that would point to an aptitude for work that's similar to yours.

After you've made your selection decision, but before your new employee reports for duty, work with your Training Department to design a training program to teach the skills most new entrants bring to the job with them. These could be formal training courses or on-the-job assignments that will bring your new employee up to the level where your regular training or orientation program begins. With an aptitude for the job, and an extra boost in "makeup" training, your new employee has a good chance of becoming a very valuable addition to your staff.

And what if the new person *doesn't* work out, even with extra help? Try first to place him or her elsewhere in the company, in a position more compatible with his or her skills and background. If that doesn't work, you may end up terminating the new worker—for deficiencies that aren't entirely his fault. So it's best for both of you to do all you can to work for his success in this new field.

For the future, your goal should be to increase the number of qualified minority candidates who apply for your positions, so you're not stuck in this spot again. Then, even if you have some new employees who don't work out, your minority representation statistics won't necessarily suffer—and you'll be making positive steps toward an integrated work force.

If not many minority candidates apply for your jobs:

Expand your advertising and recruitment efforts. Particularly if you rely on word-of-mouth to spread information about your vacancies, you're likely to end up with candidates who are friends of friends. Those candidates are most likely going to be of the same minority (or nonminority) group as the people who referred them. So your minority profile will continue to look just like it does now.

Post vacancy announcements in local newspapers, trade journals, state employment services, union halls, social service agencies, schools, community centers. Many of those places won't charge a fee for your announcements; they'll welcome your jobs as an opportunity to obtain work placements for their members or clientele.

Sign up with your local speakers bureaus to explain the kind of work your company does and opportunities for minority applicants to succeed and progress within the organization. Make sure you send your best speakers—even if they're not supervisors. Sometimes a committed worker can "sell" the organization better than the boss.

When your company does something good, or when you have special recognition ceremonies for your employees, arrange for some press coverage. Maybe no one in the minority community even knows you're out there, and that's why they're not applying for your jobs. Spotlight minority employees already in the company who achieve successes. You're more likely to get candidates if they think they'll be accepted in the organization.

If not many minority candidates are qualified for your jobs:

Expand the training program you set up for your first minority worker to cover different situations where candidates come in without the basic skills they need. This might include basic literacy and math skills or entry-level instruction in production methods or machine operation. This kind of program is distinct from the training you give to *all* new entrants to the jobs. It's not training for your *specific* job; it's training people need for *any* job. Problem 12-2 discusses this basic entry training in more detail.

You might also set up an internal "upward mobility" program that focuses on people who are already within the company, but in dead-end jobs. While the training requirements will be much the same as for the people you bring in from outside, these workers already understand the company, its goals, and its methods of operation. These new employees will only need specific training in the operations you perform in your unit that differ from the work they've done elsewhere in the company.

Something to Think About

There's no evidence to suggest that particular ethnic groups have greater or lesser aptitudes for various kinds of work. There *are* some groups who, because of cultural differences, emphasize various occupations over others. But any employee who has the basic aptitude and a sincere interest in doing the work can learn to do the job—given the right training and a supportive supervisor. Whether your problem has been getting applicants for your positions or getting *qualified* applicants, you can take steps to help integrate your work force—and make points with your boss!

And If This Doesn't Quite Fit Your Situation . . .

Look at Problems 2-3 and 2-4, which describe very good and very poor minority workers after they're on the job.

Use Checklists 1 and 5 to develop a cure of your own.

13-2

The Problem: He assigns you a high priority project that you have no one capable of working on.

The Scene

"But Mr. Paulsen, I don't have anyone who can do this."

"Then train some one to do it, or hire someone—just get it taken care of! Everyone else is overloaded, so yours is the only unit I can give it to. You have three weeks to get it done, and I want it done well. Any more questions?"

You shake your head and turn toward the door. No one in your organization has any experience at this, and you don't have enough time even if someone did. It's going to be a disaster!

Possible Causes

Your boss has tremendous confidence in you and your unit. As difficult as the project seems, it's a show of confidence in you that he gave it to you.

He's looking for an excuse to reassign you or get rid of you. He's not happy with you in the job, so he wants to replace you with someone he has more confidence in.

He simply is desperate. Your unit is the best alternative he has.

Hint: Worry about why your boss did it *second*. Worry about how you're going to get it done successfully first.

Cures

No matter what your boss' reasons were, you need to make sure the job gets completed successfully. Here are some ideas:

Check first with each of your employees. Perhaps one or two of them actually know something about the project you've been given. You may be able to get it done with your own people. If you can, free them to concentrate on it.

Does another manager have someone qualified to do the project that you could borrow? Here's where the time you spend developing good relationships with other managers pays off. Perhaps a manager even owes you a favor she can repay this way. If not, make it clear that if you can borrow one of her workers, you know you'll owe her one.

If no one in the organization can handle the project, can you hire someone temporarily to do it? This may not be as far-fetched as it sounds; a tremendous range of talent is available for temporary work. If the person needs organizational knowledge, can you assign one of your employees to work with him and furnish this knowledge?

None of these will work? What can a team of your employees—perhaps with you as part of it—accomplish? Clearly, it will stretch all of you. You'll probably have to work nights and weekends. Look on it as a challenge; no matter what your boss's motive was, successfully completing the project inhouse will be a real victory. (If you complete it successfully inhouse, reward your people lavishly for their efforts. They'll have earned the reward.)

If he did it because he has tremendous confidence in you and your unit:

No matter how you complete the project, finishing it successfully will justify your boss's confidence in you.

There's another side to this. If you keep completing "impossible" projects, your boss may conclude that you and your unit can do *anything.* That's a great reputation to have—just make sure you and your employees are prepared to live up to it.

If he's looking for an excuse to reassign you or get rid of you:

You certainly don't want him to get away with this. It doesn't matter what you have to do (generally within reason, of course)—get the project done successfully.

The larger question is why he wants to move you out of the job. If it's because you have been managing poorly, this is your opportunity to turn things around. Then you may want to keep referring to this book to help you deal with the other challenges you're going to handle successfully, starting now.

Perhaps the situation has nothing at all to do with your job performance. Maybe your boss needs to place someone else he feels loyalty to; maybe his boss is behind it. Get the project done successfully, and then have a heart-to-heart talk with him. If he really wants you out of the job, see if you can't negotiate a mutually acceptable way to accomplish this. For instance, he might give you a day or two off each week to do job hunting and provide you with good references.

In other words, if nothing you can do will make your boss want you in your current job position, don't try to hang on. Negotiate the best solution you can, and then get a job in a company where they want you.

If he simply is desperate:

Here's your chance to show that you can indeed come through for him. No one warms a manager's heart more than someone he can depend on in a real crisis. Use this occasion to demonstrate that he can always depend on you and your people.

Something to Think About

No matter the reason, this is a real opportunity—if you approach it as one. Certainly it's going to be difficult, perhaps almost impossible. Don't let that defeat you. Make up your mind to succeed, no matter what—and then succeed. If you and your unit have been having problems, this could be the event that turns the situation around.

And If This Doesn't Quite Fit Your Situation . . .

Look at Problem 14-11 if you think he's doing this to get rid of you. Problem 13-5 deals with the opposite situation: he gives a project that should have been yours to another unit.

Use Checklists 1 and 5 to develop a cure of your own.

——— 13-3 ———

The Problem: He makes unreasonable demands for quantity or quality of work.

The Scene

Just who does Brent Townsend think he is? It doesn't seem to matter how much the staff work themselves to death, he's never pleased. It's never fast enough, and it's never good enough. You've *never* worked for a boss who was so unreasonable. Doesn't he have any idea what you're up against?

Possible Causes

Your boss may be getting pressure from those above him. Not every demand is a reflection of your own boss' needs or desires. Just as you may have to push your people to make the boss happy, sometimes he has to push you to make *his* boss happy.

Your unit may not be performing a reasonable quantity or quality of work. Maybe this isn't your boss's problem at all. Maybe it's yours!

Your boss may really not understand what it's reasonable to expect of you and your unit. This is particularly likely if he's been transferred recently from a unit that does different work or is operating in a different environment.

Hint: As with most of the other problems in this chapter, your first concern must be to do whatever it takes to satisfy your boss. In this case, there may be ways to do that (or negotiate what's satisfactory) without stressing out you or your employees.

Cures

If your boss is getting pressure from those above him:

Sit down with Brent and tell him exactly how much you think the unit is capable of producing. Don't overestimate to make yourself look good, but be optimistic enough that the unit will be reasonably challenged.

At the same time, find out from Brent what the priorities are. If you can't do everything, you need to know what it's most important that you do. Are there things your unit is doing now that could slide altogether? Or things that could wait until the pressure eases up?

Negotiate priorities and due dates for each of the assignments Brent's being pressured to produce. Then live up to them. Remember what we said in Problem 10-1 about the importance of making your boss look good? Think about that. If you make your boss look good to his superiors, you'll look pretty good to him too!

If your unit really isn't producing satisfactorily:

This is a major problem. You should approach Brent *immediately* to talk to him about what it is he wants you to do better. What are his production goals? What does he consider "complete staff work" in the assignments he gives you to perform? Maybe you've misunderstood his expectations of you.

If it's still not clear after talking to Brent what quantity or quality of work he expects, you might consider talking to a colleague who also works for him (or who's worked for him in the past). You might get some ideas about how much or what kind of work it takes to satisfy him.

Once you know what Brent's looking for, it's up to you to produce it. Maybe you're not organized as efficiently as you could be. Maybe you've let some of your own people slide, and haven't expected as much of them as you should. Now's the time to tighten up. You can't produce any more than the people in your unit produce for you. Your leverage is through them. You can't do it all yourself. So make sure the people who work for you know what you expect and the consequences of their failure to meet your expectations.

Look at other problems in this book for ideas on how to improve your organization's performance. Problems 1-1, 1-6, and 1-7 discuss organizational poor performance. Individual performance problems are discussed in detail in Chapters 4, 5, and 6.

If your boss' demands really are unrealistic:

Your goal here is still to satisfy your boss, but you may be able to negotiate down his requirements. What kind of relationship do you have with him? Does he seem to respect you and your abilities? Or do you think he may be looking for an excuse to dump you? Will he listen to your ideas?

If you have the kind of relationship that allows you to discuss with him the problems you're having in meeting his demands, then talk to him. If you have previous production charts or performance review results that show other observers' satisfaction with the quantity and quality of work your unit has produced, show him. Try to find out if anything has changed in the company's priorities that changes your own unit's work priorities.

As in the first "cure," work out a mutually acceptable production schedule that meets the demands of the people Brent reports to. If this is a temporary crunch, where Brent really is asking too much of you because he's got a special requirement he has to meet, look at Problem 2 in this chapter for ideas.

What if Brent really is being unreasonable, but isn't willing to change? You've shown him your honors and commendations from previous supervisors or audit teams, but he just won't be persuaded. He's convinced that you can do more and better than you are, and he expects you to improve. If you really can't find any way to meet Brent's demands, then your best bet is to try to get out of the job. This is a no-win situation, where it looks like there's no way to satisfy Brent. Rely on your previous good record, go to other managers, and sell your services elsewhere. In the meantime, do the best you can to satisfy Brent, so he won't sabotage your efforts to find a better situation.

Something to Think About

While the third "cause" and "cure" are the most tempting from your point of view, they're also the least likely. (That's why they're last on the list.) Most second-line managers have worked their way up through first-level supervisory jobs. They have a pretty good idea when they become second-tier managers what is reasonable to expect and what isn't. If there's a disagreement about how much your unit ought to be producing, or what quality of work it's reasonable to expect, chances are it's your problem, not your boss'. In the interests of retaining the position you've worked so hard to achieve, it's best to assume that *you're* the one who's got to change.

And If This Doesn't Quite Fit Your Situation . . .

Look at Problems 13-2 and 13-6 for other situations when your boss is pushing your unit to the limits of its resources. Performance improvement is discussed in Chapter 1 (organizational) and Chapters 4, 5, and 6 (individual). And if you think these unreasonable demands are Brent's attempt to get rid of you, see Problem 14-1.

Use Checklists 1 and 5 to develop a cure of your own.

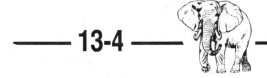

—— 13-4 ——

The Problem: She gives you a poor performance rating.

The Scene

"But, Mrs. Morales, this is the lowest rating I've ever gotten."

"I expected that you wouldn't like it, but it's the rating I'm giving you. If your performance improves, I'll be happy to give you a higher one next year."

There's obviously nothing you can do to change her mind. You pick up the paper and head for the door—wondering what to do now.

Possible Causes

Mrs. Morales has been directed to give lower ratings this year. Organizations often decide that ratings are too high in general, so they direct managers to give lower ratings to everyone.

She can only give a certain percentage of good ratings. Your performance wasn't that bad, but it wasn't as good as that of several others who're getting the higher ratings.

She's setting you up to get rid of you. If you have a poor rating, this will be easier for her.

Your performance really was that bad. There's nothing wrong with the rating. Perhaps it's even a little generous.

Hint: These aren't four equally important causes. The fourth one is probably the right one. You need to look at the other three first, though—to make sure you don't waste effort unnecessarily.

Cures

If she's been directed to give lower ratings this year:

This requires some real sensitivity on your part. She may feel that it would be disloyal to the company to tell you this. She may also feel embarrassed that she had her authority limited. No matter what, she may not tell you what the situation is.

One way to find out whether this is the case is to ask her how you could have gotten a better rating. If she answers the question in great detail, you can be fairly sure that she developed the rating herself. If she's vague or evasive, she may just be following directions from higher management.

If you conclude that this is the reason for the poor rating, let the matter drop. Accept the poor rating and then do the best job you can this time around. (It may help to tell yourself that your performance really was okay, and that this is just a bad break.)

If she can only give a certain percentage of good ratings:

This is a lot like the situation right above. The difference is that she's been told that only a certain *percentage* of her ratings can be high; the others have to be average or even lower. This happens often in organizations which believe that ratings should follow a "normal" distribution.

If this is the situation, there's no point in fighting the rating this year. Just make sure that your performance improves to the point that next year you'll get one of the high ratings. (You can console yourself with the same thought as in the situation just before this one: your performance really was better than your rating.)

If she's setting you up to get rid of you:

You're in a serious predicament, and you need to make a sound decision concerning what to do about it.

In Problem 2 of this chapter, we suggested that if your boss doesn't want you in your job you should start looking for another one. That's one option here. If it sounds like a workable alternative, read that part of Problem 13-2.

What if you don't want to leave, if you think you're being treated unfairly? Probably the first step to take is to have a frank and honest discussion with Mrs. Morales. Why does she want to get rid of you? Is there something you can do to change the situation?

If you decide that you just can't look for another job, and Mrs. Morales sticks by the rating, you need to fight it however your firm permits. It will help if you've not only done a good job but can show that you've done it. This is a risky course, but if you succeed, you may prevent Mrs. Morales from doing anything like it again.

If your performance really was that bad:

As we suggested above, this is the most probable cause. You may not think your performance was that bad, but *she* does. Your job is to perform effectively this year—and make sure that she recognizes how effectively.

The first step is to find out how your performance fell short. This is a perfectly proper question to ask Mrs. Morales, as long as you're honest about it and not defensive. If she tells you, *don't argue with her.* If you believe she's wrong, let it alone for now. Concentrate completely on finding out what she thinks.

Suppose she won't tell you what you need to do to improve? That's certainly not helpful, but it may happen. Accept it, and then see if someone else can give you useful information. Perhaps her secretary or a clerk knows what Mrs. Morales expects from you and can tell you. Another manager who works for her or with her may be able to give you suggestions. If you know her boss, and can't get information any other way, you might very discreetly see if he can find out for you. It doesn't matter whom you talk to, as long as you get accurate information.

Once you've found out what's wrong, correct it. You really were performing well but she didn't realize it? Do whatever you must to see that she realizes it this year. You weren't performing as well as you should? You know what to do about that. (Using this book and others like it throughout the year may help you improve significantly.)

Things to Think About

There's one situation we didn't deal with. Suppose you and your boss disagree on just what you should be doing or how you should be doing it? What then?

Start by asking a question: What's at stake here? If there's a principle or a matter of vital interest to you, it may be worth the disagreement and the low rating. Otherwise, it seems best to do what she wants done the way she wants it done.

Suppose you have a vital interest. Suppose she wants to reduce your authority or limit your freedom to make decisions. This is the time to have an honest discussion with her about your concerns. Perhaps you misunderstand her intent. Perhaps she didn't realize what's troubling you and is willing to change. Perhaps you can work out another alternative together. At the very least, you'll have the matter out in the open, where you may be able to resolve it at some time in the future.

And If This Doesn't Quite Fit Your Situation . . .

Look at Problem 14-1 for a situation in which your boss clearly wants to get rid of you. If you think Mrs. Morales is discriminating against you because of race or sex, you may find some useful information in Problems 2-5, 10-5, and 10-8.

Use Checklists 1 and 5 to develop a cure of your own.

—— 13-5 ——

The Problem: He gives a major new project that should have been yours to another section.

The Scene

You slam down the quarterly status report in disbelief. Joan Jordan is working on the hypertext enhancement that you suggested to your boss six months ago. Who does she think she is, taking over your project? But, then, she didn't do this on her own. Bud Turner, your boss, must have given her the assignment. She's just not the sort of manager who builds her own empire by stealing from others. So why didn't Bud give the project to you? And what can you do about it now?

Possible Causes

Your boss may have had to make a decision between two close functions. There may not have been any intention to keep you out of the project. Your functions and Joan's just happen to overlap in this area, and Bud made a choice to go with Joan.

Your boss may believe that Joan's group will do a better job. In this case there *was* a conscious decision not to give the project to you. You've got a problem.

Hint: Turf battles are seldom productive. You will probably never, by sheer strength of personality, be able to convince another manager (or your mutual superiors) that an assignment properly belongs to you. So fighting it out isn't usually a useful response to your boss' assignment of a project to another section. The way you get functions—and keep them—is by demonstrating that you can do the work, satisfy your customers, and meet your boss' needs better than any one else can.

Cures

If your function and Joan's overlap in this area:

Talk to Joan to let her know you're interested in the project and to offer her your assistance. Make it clear to her that you're not trying to take over. It's an area in which you're interested, and you'd like to do what you can to help her out.

Assuming that Joan trusts you and accepts your offer at face value, give her whatever assistance she needs. In the course of this project, meet with her to work out specifically what the two of you believe are the limits of your respective organizations. Put your agreements in writing so there's less chance in the future that Joan gets a project that should have been yours (or vice versa). If your company has a formal organization and functions manual, draft changes to that too. Then go, with Joan, to your boss to present your proposal for splitting up the work.

If Joan refuses your help and seems pleased to have an assignment that would normally fall in your area, your problem is more like that described in Problem 11-1. Look there for hints on how to handle a manager who's trying to take over your projects.

If your boss believes that Joan's group will do a better job:

Your real problem isn't the project that got away. It's your poor performance record. You'll need to do some soul-searching about the causes for your boss' low opinion of your group. And once you know *why* your boss thinks less of your group than he does of Joan's, fix it.

Chapter 1 deals with organizational performance improvement; particularly Problems 1-1, 1-6, 1-7, and 1-9. Chapters 4, 5, and 6 cover various aspects of individual performance improvement.

Your boss is sending you a clear message here about his lack of confidence in you and your organization. Listen to it. For whatever reason, you've failed to produce as well as he'd like in the past. The only way you'll get the projects you want in the future is to show him *now* that you can perform.

Things to Think About

It's possible that it wasn't your boss who decided that the project should go to Joan's group rather than yours. Maybe someone higher than Bud in the organization decided the question for him. Maybe a customer specifically requested that Joan work on the project (or that you *not* work on it)! While the source of the decision differs, the root causes are the same as those described in the second "cause" and "cure" above.

It's also possible that your boss gave Joan the assignment because it's a high-visibility project and he's grooming her for advancement in the company. That's good for Joan and too bad for you, but the question still remains: Why is he grooming Joan for advancement and not you? Maybe because of the level of confidence he has in you and your unit? Sound familiar? See the second "cause" and "cure" again. There's no substitute for good performance.

One final point, which was mentioned in the first "cure" above. In this problem, we counsel caution. When your boss made the decision in a genuine close call, that's appropriate. But if another manager is trying to take over one of your functions, caution isn't the best response. Look at Problem 11-1 for suggestions on what to do in that situation.

And If This Doesn't Quite Fit Your Situation . . .

Look at Chapters 1, 4, 5, and 6, which all discuss various ways of improving your workers' and unit's performance so that your boss's first choice for any project becomes *you.*

Use Checklists 1 and 5 to develop a cure of your own.

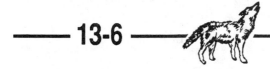

13-6

The Problem: He tells you to reduce your staff, even though the work load hasn't diminished.

The Scene

"We've been directed to cut our staff by 10%, Gina. Since you have two vacancies, I'll have to start there. I'm afraid you can't fill them until at least the first of next year."

"But, Mr. Meredith, my work load is up almost 10% in the last four months. You know I need to fill those vacancies to keep up with it."

"Sorry, but if I don't do this I'll have to start thinking about who to lay off. I'll let you know if anything changes."

Just when you thought you were going to catch up, this happens. Now what?

Possible Causes

Your boss is trying to set you up to get rid of you. He thinks the easiest way to do this is to create a situation where you can't perform successfully—and then get you for not performing.

Your boss is making the right decision from his point of view. Otherwise, he really would have to start letting permanent employees go.

Hint: As with several other problems in this chapter, the cause is generally less important than what you need to do to handle the situation.

Cures

If he's trying to set you up to get rid of you:

This probably isn't the case. If you think it may be, look at Problems 13-2, 13-4, and 14-1 for some suggestions.

If he's making the right decision from his point of view:

The only course you can take is to make the best of it. Here are some ideas:

If your employees understand that the alternative was to let permanent employees go, they may be willing to produce more—at least in the short run. After a few weeks or a month or two, though, this may start to sound a little hollow to them.

Whether your employees can produce more or not, you need to see that the highest-priority work gets done. Be sure you and your employees know what the priorities are. If you have to, talk with your boss to see that the two of you understand them the same way. Then pass this on to your employees—and spend as little time as possible on the low-priority items, as much time as possible on those at the top of the priority list.

Challenge your people to come up with better and quicker ways to get their jobs done. In this circumstance, they certainly won't have to worry about losing their jobs if they become more efficient. When they come up with good ideas, see that they get recognized for them and, if possible, paid handsomely for them.

Spend even more time than usual making sure your people have the equipment and supplies they need. If they've been needing some new equipment, this may be the time to try to get approval for it—as long as it doesn't cost so much that the budget cuts rule it out. If fluctuations in the work you receive from other units make it harder for your people to do their job, work with the other units to smooth the work flow out.

If you start getting seriously behind, explore borrowing employees from another unit. (After all, the cut you took may have saved that unit from taking one.) If your output is the input to another unit, they may be particularly willing to help you.

If your unit really has to stretch to make up for the vacancies, and especially if they come up with real improvements—make sure your boss knows. Nothing could be worse than his believing that you handled the cuts because you were overstaffed to start with.

If part of the problem is poor performance by the group or by individuals, you may find it helpful to review Chapter 1 on group performance problems and/or Chapters 4, 5, and 6 on individual performance problems.

Something to Think About

Like so many of the other problems in this and the following chapter, your boss's action puts you in a bind. Just remember that fighting the situation won't help much, but concentrating the energies of yourself and your people will. If you and your unit can successfully deal with the challenge, you may enhance your reputation significantly.

And If This Doesn't Quite Fit Your Situation . . .

Look at Problem 13-2 if the problem is lack of skills rather than lack of staff or Problem 13-3 if he's making unreasonable production demands on your unit.

Use Checklists 1 and 5 to develop a cure of your own.

13-7

The Problem: He isn't clear about assignments.

The Scene

You walk out of your boss's office shaking your head in puzzlement. After 20 minutes of listening to him expound, you're still not sure what he wants. It could be anything from a marketing strategy to a technical report—all you know for sure is that it's something written and it's something about the new mutual fund accounts. But what? And by when? More and more your assignments come like the plots of a detective novel—a clue at a time, and sometimes too late to prevent another fatality!

Possible Causes

Your boss may not know what he wants. He may be thinking aloud and relying on you to put substance into his ideas. But even if he doesn't know exactly what he wants, he'll know it when he sees it—and he'll know it when he doesn't!

Your boss may have received the assignment from a superior, and maybe he's not sure what she wants. The instructions he received may have been even less clear than the ones he's given you. He's added as much substance as he can, but basically you're both flying blind.

He may not be able to articulate his ideas clearly. He may know *exactly* what he wants. He's just not very good at conveying those ideas to you for execution.

Hint: Sometimes, being a good subordinate means being a good mind reader. That's nothing unique to managers. You may have run across the same problem when you were doing technical work. The difference is that back then, if you misinterpreted your boss' assignments, you were the only one whose labors were wasted. Now, if you misinterpret your boss's assignments, your whole unit may waste its time on unproductive efforts.

Cures

If your boss doesn't know what he wants:

If you can pull it off without making your boss impatient with you, ask him for the details he can provide about what he's looking for. Perhaps he's seen a product similar to the one he wants you to develop, or perhaps he knows of someone in another organization who's worked on something similar. Be careful about pressing for details, though. Your boss has probably told you as much as he knows of what he's looking for. Your pushing for more information than he has available may embarrass him and will certainly irritate him.

Talk to other people whom you trust in the company about how they've handled similar situations. What kinds of things are usually important to him? substance? presentation format or style? orientation to a specific audience? Then try to gear your products to those things you've identified as usually being important.

As soon as you have a concept and approach roughed out, go back to your boss for confirmation of the direction you're taking. Listen carefully to his criticisms. He may still not know exactly what he's looking for, but his initial reactions will tell you something about the things that strike him most forcefully. Then try again, and again, and again—until you get it right.

Don't be discouraged by this lack of specific direction. Things are going to be tough for a while, and you may begin to believe you can't ever please him. But little by little, you'll begin to get a feel for what your boss is looking for.

If your boss received vague instructions from his superiors:

As above, try to work out as many details with your boss as you can. Focus on the objective and goals of the assignment and on its intended audience. If there are people you know and trust in the company who've done work for the manager who's ultimately going to receive your products, consult with them for advice and hints on how to proceed.

Review company reports and formats to see how top management is used to seeing information presented. Look particularly at those portions of annual reports or publications that relate to the subjects you're dealing with. Model your product after the published items you've found.

Try to arrange to accompany your boss when he presents your proposals and drafts to his superiors. That way you can get firsthand feedback on how your product measures up to expectations.

Rely also on your boss' advice as you proceed. *He's* the one higher level management tasked with this assignment. You're the vehicle for getting it done. But if what you produce isn't what they want, he'll look just as bad as you do. So this is one time where it's clearly in your boss' best interest to help you succeed.

If your boss can't articulate his ideas clearly:

This situation is a little trickier than the first two, since in this case your boss *does* know what he wants—and probably thinks you should too, since he's explained it to you. Chances are very good that he doesn't realize that he communicates poorly.

If your boss is someone with whom you have an open and trusting relationship, you can tell him directly that you don't know what he's asking for. Then make pointed inquiries until you get what you need.

If you don't trust your boss enough to be able to admit your confusion, go to trusted coworkers for advice. They'll probably know what kind of things are usually accepted. What you've been asked for may be a routine report or product that you can put together easily—once you know what it is.

For the long term, listen carefully as your boss gives assignments to *other* managers. Then talk to them about what they developed in response to the assignments. In time, you'll have picked up enough clues about what your boss's instructions mean to be able to interpret them accurately.

Something to Think About

Whenever you're having a communication problem with another person, whether it's your boss, a coworker, or someone who works for you, you should at least consider that the problem may be yours—not his. Perhaps you're not asking the right questions. Or maybe you're filtering his answers through your own view of things so that you can't see the other person's point of view. Especially if there seem to be *lots* of people with whom you have communication difficulties, it's a possibility certainly worth considering.

And If This Doesn't Quite Fit Your Situation . . .

Look at Problem 13-3 if you think what your boss is asking for is unreasonable.

Use Checklist 5 to develop a cure of your own.

13-8

The Problem: He chews you out in front of other managers.

The Scene

". . . You screw up like this once more, and you're history!" Your boss banged the desk for emphasis, then turned and stalked out of the room.

The three other managers in the room with you looked at each other and followed him out without a word. Joyce was the last one out, and she looked back at you and shrugged as she left.

This wasn't the first time your boss had chewed you out—but this was the first time he had done it in front of your peers. Joyce and Mike were embarrassed; Bernie kept a straight face, but you know he was delighted at the whole thing.

You drop your head into your hands, wondering how to overcome this.

Possible Causes

Your boss lacks the self-discipline to wait to talk with you alone. He just lets go without considering its impact on you.

He was dissatisfied with others as well as you, and wanted to make an example of you. He expected the others to learn what might happen to them if they failed him.

He was so angry that he paid no attention to the fact you weren't alone. Normally, he'd talk with you alone. This time, things looked so bad to him that he simply exploded.

He thought that chewing you out in public was the only way to communicate how blatant he thought your failure was. This is a step beyond any of the previous cases. He did it because he didn't think anything less would get through to you.

Hint: No matter what his reason was, getting chewed out in public is a tremendous blow to anyone's ego. It may take you a while to work through your hurt and angry feelings. That's okay; give yourself the time you need to recover.

Cures

No matter what the cause is—maybe:

When you've recovered, you can talk with him. That's the best way to find out what the cause was. Then, if it's appropriate, you can tell him how you feel and ask that he not chew you out in public again.

Be careful with this one. It may be days or weeks before he's willing to talk to you about the situation—if he ever is. This is where you have to use your judgment. Talk with him if you can; otherwise, try to work things out on your own.

If he doesn't have the self-discipline to wait until he can talk with you alone:

How you handle this one depends on your relationship with him. Is the relationship basically a strong one? If so, you can probably level with him about how the public chewing out made you feel. You may even influence what he does next time. The relationship isn't so strong? This is probably an excellent time just to take what he did and work quietly to restore his confidence.

If he wanted to make an example of you:

If this was the case, he can probably tell you so. (At least if we did it for this reason, we'd call in the poor victim and let him in on the secret.) This may help salve your feelings a little.

If he was so angry he paid no attention to the fact that you weren't alone:

The two "causes" above weren't necessarily too serious. Your goof might have been a relatively small one. Not so with this and the next one. If he was so angry that it overrode his better judgment, he was angry. And you need to act.

Do you know why he's angry? If so, even if you don't know all the details, start to work fixing it immediately. Then, if you have to ask him for more information, you can show him what you're already doing to fix the situation. (If you have to ask him, it may be best to wait a day or two or even a week or so for him to calm down. Then ask. Don't be defensive, argue with him, or try to justify yourself. Just find out exactly and completely why he was so angry.)

Then, fix it quickly and make sure it never happens again. If the problem was one of those described in this book, use the suggestions provided. If not, or if you need more information, find some other book to help you. Talk to your friends. Attend a training course. Do whatever you have to do—and then make it clear to your boss that you did it.

If he thought that chewing you out in public was the only way to communicate how blatant he thought your failure was:

The problem isn't at the Wolf level any more; this is an Elephant, perhaps even a Shark. He's sending you a strong, strong message. You can't afford to ignore it.

Most of the suggestions in the previous "cure" are applicable here— but more urgently. Take quick, *visible* steps to correct the problem (if you can) and ensure it never happens again.

It's absolutely essential that you transmit a strong, positive message to your boss. He should be able to see that you're capable both of dealing with the situation and preventing it from ever recurring. This may be your last chance to do that.

Things to Think About

You've probably noticed that we don't have as much to say on this one as on many of the others. Unfortunately, there's not a whole lot to say. When your boss chews you out in front of your peers, it hurts—and it's embarrassing. Because of this, you would never even *think* about chewing one of your employees out in public, would you?

A final thought. If this situation starts to happen to you again, try tactfully to prevent it. Perhaps you can stop your boss and the two of you go to a private room. If not, maybe you can signal the others to leave quickly and quietly. You may not succeed, but it's definitely worth the effort.

And If This Doesn't Quite Fit Your Situation . . .

If you think that this is a sign that he wants to get rid of you, look at Problems 13-2, 13-4, and 14-1.

Use Checklists 1 and 5 to develop a cure of your own.

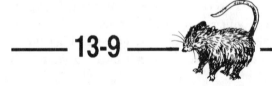

——— 13-9 ———

The Problem: He turns down a bonus your employees really deserve.

The Scene

Well it's just not fair! Your people worked themselves to death trying to meet the deadline for processing those payment vouchers, and now that old miser Shrukta won't let you give them the bonuses they've earned. Why they saved the company thousands of dollars in interest charges alone! Surely that deserves some recognition! If one of his precious "special assistants" had done something worthwhile, he'd fall all over himself giving them bonuses and rewards. So why not your employees who do *real* work?

Possible Causes

He may not have the money to pay for the bonuses you're proposing. Maybe it's more important to him to upgrade your telephone system than to pay bonuses. If money's tight, he's going to look first to those things that have the most tangible productivity impact.

He may not be as convinced as you are that the bonuses are deserved. Maybe he's seen what he considers similar accomplishments in other units that have gone unrewarded. So he doesn't see the need for a bonus for your staff.

He may not think rewards are necessary. There are still a lot of people of the "old school" who think that the best reward for good work is continued employment.

Cures

If your boss doesn't have the money to pay for the bonuses you've proposed:

Find out first whether there's *any* money for bonuses. If so, consider whether you can negotiate a reduced bonus for your unit and whether the reduced amount would still be enough to serve as a motivator for continued high performance. Remember, there's a point where the amount of the reward is *so* low that your employees will be insulted. Then the bonus will have the opposite effect of the one you intended.

If the amount of money available is too little for meaningful money awards to your unit, is there enough to put together some other kind of celebration? a catered lunch for the group? certificates of appreciation? a token gift (like a coffee mug, a team cap, or a lapel pin)? It often isn't the kind of reward that matters, but the fact that it's given at all.

And if there really is *no* money with which to reward your employees, there are still other things you can do to let them know you appreciate their efforts. Incentive leave (time off the job for doing good work) is an option that's growing in popularity.

If your boss isn't convinced that your unit deserves a bonus:

Pull together as much information as you can about the worth of the contribution your employees have made. Concentrate on *tangible* benefits to the company (like increased production, less rework, decreased costs). Then propose to your boss that your employees receive a specific share of the dollars the company has saved (or earned).

To the extent that you can, demonstrate how your employees' contribution differs from what other units have done, again relying heavily on dollar savings or earnings. Try to show the long-term benefits of the work your employees have done—such as permanent, significant quality improvements or cost reductions.

If other units are making similar accomplishments, but don't give bonuses like the one you're proposing, talk to those other managers. Why don't they? Is the work really something that should be expected as just a normal part of employees' jobs? Or do these managers fail to see an opportunity to spur their workers on to even greater achievements? If you can come to some agreements with the other managers in your organization about when it's appropriate to give bonuses, you can then make a proposal to your boss. With an established set of criteria, it will be easier to justify rewards in the future.

If all else fails, and you still can't convince your boss that your employees deserve the bonus, there are still some token gestures you can make to show your employees that you appreciate their efforts. Notice that these are token gestures; it's important that you not appear to be going behind your boss's back in rewarding your employees without his approval. Consider certificates (or letters) of appreciation, recognition of the employees at your next staff meeting, or an office potluck in honor of your staff's accomplishments.

If your boss doesn't think rewards are necessary:

You may not be able to do much for this particular situation beyond the token gestures we discussed above. For the long term, though, take steps to convince your boss that bonuses and other rewards can pay off for him.

If your company doesn't already have a system in place, find out all you can about gain-sharing systems. This is a kind of pay-for-performance plan in which employees receive bonuses that are directly tied to their productivity. Employees who process payments, for example, might get a bonus for processing a certain number of payments above a minimum with no errors (or a very low percentage of errors). The gain-sharing bonuses are given according to an established schedule that everyone in the unit sees.

Sell the gain-sharing plan to your boss on a trial basis as a no-cost reward system. Gain-sharing takes nothing out of the company's basic operating monies, but simply allows employees to share in the *additional* profits they generate for the company. If processing 20 payments above standard without additional errors saves the company interest charges or late payment fees, the employee shares in those gains. But the company still saves more money than it would if employees just worked to standard.

While gain-sharing is an excellent introduction to reward systems for hesitant managers, it's hard to apply in jobs that don't directly affect the company's bottom line (like staff jobs in human resources or finance or planning offices). And your boss may not like the idea, regardless of how well reasoned your arguments may be. In that case, just resign yourself to continuing the token gestures we've already discussed, consider putting on a special treat for your employees occasionally out of your own pocket, and let them know by what you say and do that you appreciate their efforts. It may be enough.

Something to Think About

To serve as effective motivators, rewards must always link employees' *specific achievements* to *specific payoffs* for the company. The detailed information you give employees about why they're being rewarded (so they know exactly what behavior you want them to continue) is exactly the same information your boss needs to justify your investment of money in employee bonuses. A well-argued case, directly linked to the company's bottom line, is always the most effective way to get your boss' support for bonuses and other rewards.

And If This Doesn't Quite Fit Your Situation . . .

Look at Problems 1-1, 1-6, and 1-7 for further discussions of organizational performance enhancement.

Use Checklist 5 to develop a cure of your own.

14

Troubleshooting Problems with Your Boss

 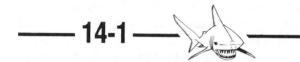

The Problem: He wants one of his people in your job.

The Scene

"Marv, are you absolutely sure that's what you heard?"

"No question about it. He told Phyllis that if she'd keep doing what he told her, he'd have her in your job by April. And, I tell you, he *meant* it."

"Marv, I really appreciate your telling me this. Now I see why he's been leaning on me like he has. All I have to do is figure out what to do . . . ."

Possible Causes

He wants to take care of a friend by giving her your job. It doesn't have anything to do with you or your performance.

He isn't comfortable with you and/or the way you manage. He wants to deal with someone who'll do things the way he wants them done—and he's decided that someone isn't you.

You've been doing a very poor job, and he wants someone who will do a good job for him. He simply believes that Phyllis is a much better manager than you are.

Hint: Do we need to tell you how critical this one is? We didn't think so.

Cures

If he wants to take care of a friend by giving her your job:

Let's assume in this "cure" and the next one that you've been doing at least a satisfactory job. Your performance isn't an issue—so you can't help the situation by performing better.

Essentially, you have three alternatives:

- You can avoid dealing with the situation head on. You can work hard, do nothing that might get you in trouble, and hope that the crisis blows over. This doesn't sound like a very "strong" stance, but it may prove to be the best solution for you. Situations like this do blow over eventually. Even if it doesn't, if you perform well enough your boss may decide that it's not worth the trouble and pick on someone else.

- You can start looking for another job. If you can find another job that pays as well but doesn't have this strain, it may be worth it to take it and leave. Since this makes it easy for your boss to put Phyllis in your job, he'll probably be glad to give you a good reference.

- You can fight the situation. Don't take this road unless you are prepared to follow wherever it takes you. If you decide to go this way, start first by talking with your boss. Be careful to protect Marv—you certainly don't want to get him in trouble. Let your boss know that you know. See what his reaction is. At that point, you have several options. You can threaten to take the issue as far as you necessary—to his boss, to the EEO system, or to the board of directors. Or you can offer to leave if he's willing to help you get another job (either inside or outside the company). Make it clear to him that you're holding all the cards, and that his success in this situation depends on what he is willing to do for you. (We told you not to think of this one unless you were willing to take it all the way—and we were serious.)

If he isn't comfortable with you and/or the way you manage:

Unfortunately, of the three alternatives in the first "cure," two of them won't help here. Doing nothing will get you nowhere but out, and you don't hold any chips to bargain with your boss. You can take the second alternative and start looking for another job.

Probably the best alternative of all, though, is to have an honest talk with your boss. Why isn't he comfortable with you? What does he want from you that you're not giving him? How could you change the way you're managing to make him more comfortable?

The answers to those questions will point the direction in which you need to move. If you can do what he wants you to, and are willing to, simply do it. If you're unwilling to do it, you might try to find a middle ground both of you find acceptable. If you can't? Your best move is probably to see if he'll help you find a job elsewhere—or at least give you acceptable references.

You may resent the way he wants you to manage. That's normal, but not necessarily relevant. If you can reasonably change to manage the way he wants, you may learn something from it. If the way he wants is really uncomfortable, go somewhere that your boss will be comfortable with your style. If he seriously expects you to act immorally or illegally, leave as soon as possible. (See Problems 9-1 and 9-2 for more information on this last situation.)

If you've been doing a very poor job, and he wants someone who will do a good job for him:

This cure makes the alternatives even sharper: shape up or ship out.

Make sure you know what he expects. (See Problem 13-8 for suggestions on this.) If you can, start giving it to him immediately. If you're not sure you can meet his requirements, start looking for a job elsewhere.

It's worth asking for his help in finding another job. At the worst, he'll know you intend to leave, even if he's not willing to help you. At the best, he'll give you decent references and possibly even open a door or two for you.

Things to Think About

Sometimes it's difficult to tell which of three situations you're in:

- You're performing poorly.

- Your performance is okay, but your boss doesn't like your style.

- Your performance and style are fine, but for personal reasons he wants someone else in your job.

Difficult or not, it's important to find out which is the case. Then you can take the proper action.

And If This Doesn't Quite Fit Your Situation . . .

Look at Problem 14-5 if he may think that you're out for his job or Problem 14-9 if he just may not like you.

Use Checklists 1 and 5 to develop a cure of your own.

—— 14-2 ——

The Problem: He's talking about abolishing your job.

The Scene

"Don, could you come in here a minute," called Mr. Elizondo. "I've been looking over all these charts for the proposed reorganization, and the only one that seems to make sense to me is this one right here. But, see, it requires that your unit be split up between these other two sections. Gary would take one, and Georgia would take the other. I might be able to reassign you to a staff position. But when I'm getting so much pressure to flatten the organization, keeping your unit separate is just a lot of wasted overhead."

Possible Causes

Your boss may believe that the work will be accomplished more efficiently elsewhere. He may have decided that the current organizational structure doesn't meet the company's real needs. Your job just doesn't fit in.

The company may be faced with serious cutbacks. Your job may be just one of several that is being abolished. It's called "downsizing," and it's a fact of life in many companies today.

Your boss may not be satisfied with the way you're doing the work. If he doesn't want to confront you about your failure to meet his performance expectations, he can sidestep the issue by abolishing your job. That gets you out of the way, but without unpleasant confrontations.

Hint: This situation looks extremely serious at first glance—and maybe it is. But the fact that your job is being abolished doesn't necessarily mean that you're going with it. Before you panic, take time to find out what's really going on. If your boss considers you a valuable employee, he'll do his best to find you another job.

Cures

If your boss believes that the work will be accomplished more efficiently elsewhere:

Talk to him about how the new organizational structure will work. What kinds of supervisory jobs will be available. Which ones could you be a serious candidate for? Which ones would you like to work in?

Make your bid for the jobs that you'd like under the new structure. Talk to your boss about your qualifications for the work, and point out the strengths in your management style that have made you successful in your current job. (Your boss will know those already, but it doesn't hurt to do a little self-promotion right now.)

Whatever job you're assigned, accept it gracefully. If it's something you don't want, you're still free to look elsewhere. But it's a lot easier to find a job when you have a job. And by doing good work wherever you are, you'll get a better reference from your boss when you find a position you prefer.

What if there is no position for you in the new structure? It may be because there just isn't enough money to support it. If there are five managers in your section and only four supervisory jobs in the new structure, someone's going to be left out. You need to find out why it's you. Do the workers who were placed have greater seniority? Are you not qualified for any of the new managerial openings? If you are qualified and have comparable seniority, what makes you a less desirable selection than your peers?

If there are sound reasons for your not getting one of the available jobs that aren't within your control (like qualifications or seniority), your situation is the same as for any other cutbacks. See the second "cure" below.

If the problem is your performance or your ability to work comfortably with your boss, the problem is much more serious. Not only are you out of a job, but you're not likely to get much help from your boss in finding another one. See the third "cure" below.

If your company is coping with serious cutbacks:

Take comfort in the fact that there isn't anything "personal" about the situation. Lots of managers have been through this before, and many others will go through it in the years ahead. That doesn't find you a new job, but it does relieve you of any guilt you may feel.

Ask about outplacement services your company offers to help displaced workers find new employment. Talk to your Personnel Department about your entitlements upon separation (such as severance pay, pay for unused sick days or vacation time, early retirement buyouts available). Do some financial planning, with a professional consultant perhaps, to figure out how you could get by without your salary for a while.

Make a systematic plan for finding a new job. Identify commercial placement services if your company doesn't have outplacement help available or to increase your chances of finding a job quickly. Rely on friends and business acquaintances to help you find openings for which you can apply. Use the network you established during your employment to help you now in pending unemployment.

Don't panic! If potential employers think you're desperate, they're much less likely to consider you seriously. They'll figure you're going to take *anything* now just to get a job—and jump ship as soon as something better comes along. Stay calm, and plan your strategy. With a little planning, you may come out of this with an even better job than you left (honest!).

If your boss isn't satisfied with your performance:

It may be too late to save yourself, but it's worth one last try.

Talk to your boss about what he wants and expects—and about what he isn't getting. Problem 13-7 has ideas on how to find out what your boss wants when he isn't clear in telling you. Then give it to him. Ask for feedback on how you're doing and what you could do to improve. Let your boss know you're serious about doing better work, and he may hold off on the decision to abolish your job until you've had a chance to prove yourself.

If you don't think you can meet your boss's requirements, or if he's not willing to give you another chance, it's better to quit than to be fired. Use the ideas in the "cure" above to find a new job. Then resolve to perform better in your new organization.

Something to Think About

It's scary to think about being out of work—whether it's your fault or not. Even in these days of two-income households, many families rely on both incomes just to break even. Loss of one income may mean financial disaster. But it's important to realize that no job is absolutely secure. So it's best to plan ahead for financial setbacks. The six-month rule still applies. (Save at least the equivalent of six months' salary for a "rainy day.") And with the help of a financial consultant, there are even more things you can do to make your family more secure. You may not be able to avoid a decline in your standard of living, but with a little prior planning you can avert financial disaster.

And If This Doesn't Quite Fit Your Situation . . .

Problem 1-3 deals with rumors of layoffs and cutbacks. Problem 13-4 has additional ideas for dealing with your boss's assessment that you're performing poorly. If he wants someone else in your job, see Problem 14-1. If he apparently just doesn't like you, see Problem 14-9.

Use Checklists 1 and 5 to develop a cure of your own.

— **14-3** — 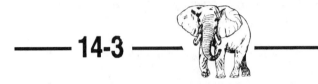 —————

The Problem: She refuses to let you fire nonperformers.

The Scene

"Ms. Jonas, Bev simply isn't working out. She gets sloppier and sloppier every day, she accuses me of picking on her, and she's disrupting the other employees. I've got to get rid of her.

"I understand how you feel, but I'm not at all sure you've given her a fair chance. Work with her some more—I think you can bring her around."

"But . . . "

"No more. I've made my decision. Now you go back and shape her up."

Possible Causes

Ms. Jonas may have organizational reasons for not firing Bev that have nothing to do with your situation. The fact that you don't know about them doesn't keep them from being important.

She may be unwilling to fire employees. She's concluded it just isn't worth it, for one reason or another.

She may be friends with Bev, and unwilling to let you take any action against her. Her friendship is more important to her than any damage that Bev's poor performance can cause.

She believes you really haven't given Bev a fair chance. She thinks that she has to intervene to see that you don't compound the problem you've caused.

Hint: The situation has the potential to undermine your authority in your work unit. You want to prevent or minimize this, no matter what the "cause" and "cure" of the problem are.

Cures

If Ms. Jonas has organizational reasons for not firing Bev that have nothing to do with your situation:

She may be responding to pressures that have nothing to do with you or Bev. Because Bev is female (and perhaps minority), the organization may not want to see her fired. Perhaps Ms. Jonas knows that a "freeze" on hiring is coming and believes that keeping Bev is better than having a vacancy. Any one of another dozen reasons could be the cause—and Ms. Jonas might not feel she could tell you what it was.

There is one consolation in this situation: Bev probably doesn't know that you can't fire her—at least not yet. You still have some leverage with her. Use it. Keep insisting that she perform satisfactorily. If she won't, discipline her to the maximum extent that your boss permits.

Chapter 5 contains dozens of suggestions on dealing with employees who aren't performing. Particularly look at Problems 5-1, 5-2, and 5-3 for suggestions on how to handle Bev.

If she's unwilling to fire employees:

How would you know that this is the case? Either from your prior experiences with Ms. Jonas or from what other managers have told you. In the long run, it makes a difference whether she won't fire employees in general or is just responding to immediate organizational pressures. In this situation, it makes no difference.

So what do you do? You can use the suggestions from the "cure" just above in this circumstance, too. You might also try to persuade Ms. Jonas to let you try it this once—with the understanding that you'll take all the heat from it. If it works out, she may be more willing to let you deal with nonperformers next time. If it doesn't work out, you haven't really lost that much.

If she's friends with Bev and unwilling to let you take action against her:

Refer to the suggestions for handling this situation in Problem 14-10.

If she believes you really haven't given Bev a fair chance:

This is more serious than the other three causes. In them, the problem is Bev and—at least in your eyes—your boss. Here, the problem is your relationship with Ms. Jonas.

First, you need to review the situation. What's happened that might make Ms. Jonas think Bev hasn't gotten a fair chance? Did Ms. Jonas misunderstand—or is she right? Have you been treating Bev differently from other employees?

Let's say you honestly believe you've treated her fairly. Why does Ms. Jonas think you haven't? Has Bev gone around you and complained to her? If so, see the suggestions in Problem 8-3. Does Ms. Jones suspect that you may be prejudiced against Bev because she's female or a minority? See Problems 10-2 and 10-5 for suggestions. Are there other reasons why she thinks you haven't given Bev a reasonable opportunity to succeed? Look through the different problems in the book to see if you can find suggestions on how to deal with this situation.

Suppose you discover you may not have been treating Bev fairly? You also have to make sure that Ms Jonas *sees* that you're treating her fairly. A number of the problems in Chapter 10 have suggestions on making sure that your boss knows you've changed. You may want to look at them.

Things to Think About

Few aspects of your job are more important than making sure that your boss has confidence in you. This confidence is more important than almost any situation that can arise.

Why is it so important? The problems in Chapters 10, 13, and 14 provide several reasons. One of the most important is illustrated in the last "cure" to the present problem: If your boss mistrusts you, your freedom to manage is going to be sharply limited. If she trusts you, she'll probably go along with your actions even if she has misgivings about them.

And If This Doesn't Quite Fit Your Situation . . .

See Problem 4-2 if Bev is new and poorly motivated, Problem 4-5 if she's new and won't accept help, or Problem 4-7 if she's nearing retirement. If you believe Bev's poor performance may be unintentional, see the problems in Chapter 6.

Use Checklists 1 and 5 to develop a cure of your own.

14-4

The Problem: He complains about you to your peers and his boss.

The Scene

"I don't know what you did to upset Bill Grumledge," Jerry remarked, "but he sure was hot this morning. And he's usually such a low-key supervisor. But he complained about the Brigsley report all the way to staff meeting—and about what a terrible job you did getting the team together to work on it. I read the summary and it didn't look that awful to me. There were a couple of areas I would have approached differently—but nothing to get Grumledge all fired up like that. In front of the rest of the staff too. I sure wouldn't want to be in your shoes right now!"

Possible Causes

This is one of those cases where it doesn't make a lot of difference *why* your boss is complaining about you. The fact that he is means that he's not satisfied, and it's up to you to find out why. The question of whether this is appropriate behavior for your boss or not (in general, it's not) is really irrelevant. He's not happy, and other people know it. So your job is to do what you can to redeem yourself.

Cures

Regardless of the specific cause of your boss' complaints:

Talk to your boss about his dissatisfactions. Don't worry that he didn't tell you directly. The fact that he so openly criticized you to your peers probably means that he wanted the story to get around to you. (Maybe he didn't want a messy confrontation.) Find out why he's unhappy—and what you need to do to fix things. If he's not clear about what he wants, look at Problem 13-7 for help.

Then as soon as you find out what it is you're doing wrong, fix it. It doesn't matter whether you believe you're doing that badly or not. Your boss does. (The exception, of course, is if he wants you to do something illegal or immoral. In that case, look at Problems 9-1 and 9-2 for advice.)

Make sure your boss knows that you're making serious efforts to improve. The way to do this is not just by telling him, although a report of the steps you've taken to correct the problem may be a useful early step. However, you also need to demonstrate to him by improved performance that you've fixed whatever he was unhappy about.

How well do you get along with your boss in general? And how much do you trust him? Once you've fixed the immediate problem and he's satisfied with your work again, you might make an opportunity to talk to him about how he treated you. Let him know how embarrassing it was to find out from someone else that he was unhappy. Then reassure him that you won't get defensive if he approaches you directly the next time he's concerned about something.

If he continues to complain about you to your peers and others, particularly if he hasn't been able to identify specific performance problems, you're probably dealing with a conflict of styles. The real problem has little or nothing to do with your performance. Your boss just isn't comfortable with the way you operate. Problem 14-1 has some ideas on how to work this one out.

Something to Think About

One other possibility we haven't discussed yet is that this may just be the kind of person your boss is. Maybe he complains about *everyone* to anyone who'll listen. Regardless of how nice he is to you when you're around, you never know what he's saying about you to someone else. Do you really want to work in that environment? If this is an ingrained habit of your boss's, chances are he's not going to change. Maybe you should look around for a better place to work.

And If This Doesn't Quite Fit Your Situation . . .

Look at Problem 13-8 when your boss does talk to you directly about his dissatisfaction—in front of other managers.

Use Checklists 1 and 5 to develop a cure of your own.

—— **14-5** ——

The Problem: He thinks you're out for his job.

The Scene

". . . and, furthermore, I intend to stay in this job until I retire or someone promotes me. You'll just have to wait until then to get it. If you want a promotion that bad, go find a job with a supervisor who's easier to fool!"

You stumble out of your boss's office, dumfounded. Twenty minutes ago, you made what you thought was an exceptionally good presentation to the corporate staff. You thought your boss would be proud of you; instead, he was furious—because he thinks that you did it as another step to get his job.

Possible Causes

You've been presenting yourself so that it makes you look good and your boss look bad. He's drawn the logical conclusion that you want to get him out of his job and yourself into it.

You're innocent, but you haven't been paying any attention to how you're making him look. This cause is not quite as serious, but still bad.

You keep trying to make him look good, but he distrusts you. No matter how hard you try, it always ends up this way.

Hint: We've mentioned this before, but it bears repeating. One of the fundamental jobs of any employee is to make her boss look good. It doesn't matter what you think of him or how he reacts to it; doing it is extremely important for your long-term success.

Cures

If you've been presenting yourself so that it makes you look good and your boss look bad:

Oh, no—you couldn't be doing this. Before you jump to that conclusion, make an honest review of the matter. Do you talk to other managers so that it sounds like you're succeeding despite your boss? When you make presentations, does the same thought come through? How do you *feel* about your boss? (For instance, scorn and arrogance show through pretty clearly.) Are there other ways you imply that you'd be even more effective if it weren't for him?

If there are, then stop. Stop now!

How you feel about your boss's competence is your own affair—but what you convey about it to others isn't. He may get in your way, veto your best ideas, drive you crazy with nit-picking. That's your burden to bear, and it can be a heavy one. It's not one you can share with the world in general.

Loyalty to one's boss is a fundamental rule of the organizational world. It may seem feudal, even dishonest. No matter, it's still the rule. You don't have to give him phony credit or flatter him—but it won't hurt to let him share the credit you get and to build him up. Who knows, if you start treating him like an effective, supportive boss he may begin to become one.

If you're innocent, but you haven't been paying any attention to how you're making him look:

All of the thoughts on loyalty in the previous "cure" apply here. Presumably, you already knew how important loyalty is. You just forgot for a while.

Now it's time to concentrate on it again. Demonstrate loyalty clearly—but don't overdo it. The last thing you want is for your boss to think you're insincere about it. Make subtle changes in the way you present yourself and your work. Include him quietly but positively in the credit. Start slowly; then build on it until it becomes automatic.

It might also be appropriate to apologize to him for having created the misleading impression. That depends on the relationship between the two of you—but if the relationship is at all strong, an apology is proper.

If you keep trying to make him look good, but he distrusts you:

This is tough, so treat it as a challenge. Be as sensitive as possible. Are there particular times and/or situations which seem to reinforce his distrust? Can you modify what happens so it's less threatening to him? Keep working on the problem; a number of small changes may start to turn him around.

You also need to have another concern: Is he undermining you? If he believes you're after his job, he may try to undercut you in the organization. Loyalty works both ways. If you give it, you have every right to expect it.

Is it possible to have a frank discussion with him? If you can, you might be able to negotiate out what both of you expect as loyalty from the other. That would certainly be desirable from both of your points of view.

Things to Think About

It's sometimes tempting to try to "show up" your boss, even to try to get his job. It may work, but it's dangerous. Even the manager who puts you in your boss's job will distrust you; if you were disloyal once, won't you be disloyal again? Disloyalty is an almost sure way to trade short-term career success for long-run career stagnation.

The other side of that is the danger in working for a boss who doesn't show you loyalty. If he doesn't, you may not have much job security—and what you have may be up for grabs every time he gets mad at you. If this is your situation, you need to evaluate it carefully. A job change may be disruptive—but it might be the best step you could take to achieve your long-run career objectives.

And If This Doesn't Quite Fit Your Situation . . .

Look at Problems 10-1, 10-3, and 10-6 if he thinks you may have caused him major problems on purpose. If you may have irritated him because you handled an internal political situation badly, see Problem 10-9.

Use Checklists 1 and 5 to develop a cure of your own.

—— **14-6** ——  ——

The Problem: He "micro-manages" you and won't delegate.

The Scene

"I just wondered how things were going on that Sylvestri case," Carl said as you walked into his office. "Have you had Lois look into those precedents I told you about? And have you been making Charita record all the time she's spent on the phone for this one? What about those statistics I gave you to review? Oh, and one other thing; let me look at that letter to the PrestoPop people before you send it out. Anything else you wanted to discuss?"

"Not really," you're tempted to reply. "Just what I have to do to get to run my own unit!" But instead, you depart with a smiling, "No, sir" and go off to do Carl's bidding while the things *you* know need to get done sit for another day.

Possible Causes

Carl may have come up through your unit and still identifies with it. This is a common problem. You know by now that supervisors tend to get very attached to the organizations they run. It's hard to give them up—even when the supervisor's promoted to a higher level job.

Carl may think that he's operating the way a manager should. He may be reacting to the abuse of delegation he's seen by going too far in the direction of "hands on" management.

Carl may not think you're doing a very good job managing by yourself. This is another case where he perceives you as a poor performer.

Hint: Although this is a difficult situation and *may* reflect Carl's dissatisfaction with your performance, it's much more likely that this is just the way Carl operates. That doesn't make it any easier for you to manage around him, but it should reassure you that Carl's probably not out to get you. You just have a difference of opinion about management style.

Cures

If Carl came up through your unit and still identifies with it:

You have two tasks facing you: convince Carl that you can do a good job running "his" unit (recognizing, of course, that you'll never match *his* achievements), and wean him away from the substantive work in the organization.

Begin by letting Carl know in advance every move you plan to make—before he has to ask. You're not asking his *permission* to take specific actions; you're letting him know because you are aware of his interest. Gradually begin to let him know about some less important items *after* the decision's been made and the action taken. Continue to discuss many items with Carl in advance, but offer to "take care of the details" so he won't have to be bothered. As time goes on, you should be handling more and more of the "details" without consulting Carl first. Let him know when your efforts are particularly successful—tactfully, since you don't want him to feel that you're outshining his performance in the same job.

To achieve full delegation for running your unit, you will probably need to divert Carl's attention with other matters. (This is known as "managing your boss.") Bring problems to him that properly belong in his sphere—organizational issues, administrative matters, questions of interrelationships among units or with outside organizations. If you can keep him busy with these "big picture" issues (many of which will *never* be solved), he won't have time to meddle in the affairs of your unit.

If he still insists on getting involved to any appreciable degree in the substance of your work, try to limit his participation to specific areas. Maybe there's a cross-functional project team he'd like to head. Maybe there's a pet area he'd like to do some basic research in (research that you may or may not have a need for later). You'll very likely be able to channel his interests into areas that aren't an integral part of your unit's work.

And if he still insists on "micro-managing" your assignments? He's still the boss, and if he has the time and energy to do his job and yours too, there's probably not much you can do about it. You could make a tactful suggestion that he not work so hard, and leave more of the "grunt" work to you. But if he wants to get involved, you really can't stop him. Decide whether you can operate comfortably in that environment, and, if not, start looking around for something better.

If Carl believes that he's operating the way a manager should:

Recognize that Carl's instincts aren't altogether bad. There are a lot of "high flyers" who are more interested in getting ahead and making themselves look good than in producing something of real value. Carl's "hands on" approach shows he has a sincere interest in the good of the organization, and he's to be commended for that. At the same time, he's doing the job you're paid to do, and that makes your job even harder.

Much of what we said in the first "cure" about convincing your boss that you can do a good job with the unit applies here as well. Gradually assume more and more of the details of running the organization at the same time that you direct Carl's attention to issues that are more properly handled at his level.

How well do you and Carl get along? Does he trust you? If you think he won't be threatened by the conversation, talk to Carl about his management style. Point out the extra burdens it places on him to do two managers' jobs and the difficult position you're in by not being allowed to make your own decisions. That little talk, coupled with your demonstration of your competence and willingness to attend to detail, may convince Carl to delegate more.

As above, the final decision about how much to delegate is Carl's. If he's not comfortable giving you greater freedom, it's a situation you'll have to learn to live with—or find another situation elsewhere.

If Carl doesn't think you're doing a very good job managing by yourself:

Your job is to prove to him that you can, and will, do much better. We've talked elsewhere about ways to demonstrate improved performance to your boss. See especially Problems 13-4, 13-5, 13-8, 14-1, 14-2, and 14-4 for ideas.

This is going to take some time. You can't just promise to do better and expect that you'll suddenly have full delegation. You'll need to demonstrate by continuing good performance that you can handle the job. You've already done something to raise questions in Carl's mind about your abilities. You need now to re-earn his confidence.

Something to Think About

One of the real classics of management literature discusses this problem of delegation at great length. It addresses both ways you can use delegation to increase your leverage as a manager and techniques you can use to obtain greater freedom and delegation from your supervisor. *Managing Management Time* by William Oncken is a "must" for any supervisor who wants to increase her effectiveness without increasing her toil. So is Clay's book, *The New Manager's Survival Manual,* which contains very practical suggestions for delegating effectively.

And If This Doesn't Quite Fit Your Situation . . .

Look at problems throughout Chapters 13 and 14 for discussions of situations where your boss inserts himself into your unit's management—and makes things harder for you.

Use Checklists 1 and 5 to develop a cure of your own.

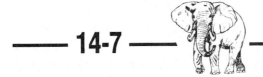

—— **14-7** ——

The Problem: He refuses to support your decisions when they're unpopular.

The Scene

"Now, Madeline, I know you mean well. I'd like to see your people produce more, too. But it's just not wise to fight over an extra 10 or 15 minutes at lunch. You can encourage them to get back on time, that's certainly okay with me. Writing them up for it, though, or docking their pay—that's just going too far. I want you to go back and tell Scott you've reconsidered and you're going to pull the warning out of his personnel file. I think everybody'll be happier that way."

It happened again! This is the third time *this month* that he's made you back down from an action because it was unpopular. How in the world does he expect you to maintain discipline and productivity if he undercuts you like this?

Possible Causes

He believes that you rely too heavily on negative supervision. He wants to see you develop more positive ways of motivating your employees.

He doesn't like to make employees angry. For whatever reason, he believes that this isn't an effective way to handle them.

He simply doesn't want your unit to cause him any problems. From his point of view, he has enough to worry about without you adding to it.

Hint: One of the facts of organizational life is that your boss's managerial style puts limits on what you can do. If you push these limits too forcefully, he may lose confidence in you (as in Problem 14-1). The limits may be frustrating, but you can't avoid them if you want to keep his confidence. The challenge is to modify your style so that he's comfortable with it and still deal effectively with your unit.

Cures

If he believes that you rely too heavily on negative supervision:

Look carefully at this alternative. If you think it may be the case, talk with him about it. You may have been leaning too heavily on "showing them who's boss" or "shaping them up." Ask him to suggest alternatives; then think them through carefully. Try them out and see what happens.

At the very worst, you'll learn some new ways to supervise. They may not work in the current situation—but they might be just the ticket another time. At the best, you'll find they really do make your job easier.

We all prefer to handle situations in familiar ways. Unfortunately, the preference can all too quickly become a rut. Regardless of your boss's style, it's an excellent idea to try new ways of handling situations ever so often. It keeps you flexible and growing.

If he doesn't like to make employees angry:

There might be any of several reasons for this. He may believe that you lose more from the anger than its worth. He may need for employees to like him. He may see himself as a kind person who doesn't make people angry.

It doesn't matter why he reacts this way. If he doesn't want employees angry, you need to find ways to supervise effectively without making them angry enough to complain to him.

We don't have the space to talk about positive ways of supervising at length. Here are a few brief ideas.

- Make sure that employees get rewarded for doing good work, and not otherwise. Use praise lavishly for a job well done; spend a minimum amount of time criticizing poor work.

- Give clear assignments with clear standards for successful completion. That will be enough for most employees to do a good job. When one doesn't, provide objective criticism based on the standards.

- Be a leader. We know—that sounds hackneyed. It's not. A leader sets goals and gets employee commitment to work toward the goals. A really effective leader does this *with* his people; they become everyone's goals, not just his.

- Above all else—and this is hackneyed, too—set the right example. Everything else you do is more effective if your employees see that you believe it enough to live it yourself.

If he simply doesn't want your unit to cause him any problems:

Some managers believe that they shouldn't have to handle problems from subordinate units. If a problem reaches them, the supervisor of that unit fouled up somewhere. If no problems come to them, their subordinate managers must be supervising effectively.

If that's what your boss believes, that what you do your best to give him. It's difficult. At the same time, it gives you the opportunity for real freedom in managing your unit. If you can keep problems out of his office, you can manage pretty much as you want. How often do you get a better deal than that?

The suggestions in the "cure" before this one are applicable here. You also need to let your employees know discreetly that they'll be in big trouble if they complain to your boss before they've talked to you. That gives you the chance to take care of the problem (which, of course, you'll do).

Something to Think About

You can't build effective supervision around the idea that you'll never make employees angry. On the other hand, if you *consistently* make them angry you'll never have a really effective unit. What's the answer? Your management style ought not make employees angry often; when it does, the issue should be an important one. The goal, though, isn't to keep them from being angry. The goal is to manage so that they do their jobs without the kind of intervention from you that makes them angry. That's good management.

And If This Doesn't Quite Fit Your Situation . . .

Look at Problem 14-10 if he won't support your unpopular decisions concerning a particular person because of friendship with that person.

Use Checklist 5 to develop a cure of your own.

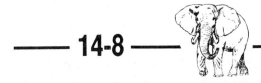

—— 14-8 ——

The Problem: She's new.

The Scene

"Hey, what have you heard about our new boss, Jeff?" you ask one of your fellow managers.

"Well, I've heard different things from different people," replies Jeff. "Paulette over in Accounting says she's really into controlling things, but Chris in Purchasing says she has a reputation for giving her people a lot of autonomy. Semia thinks she's going to impose a lot of reports and paperwork, but Luis heard from one of her old staff people that she likes face-to-face meetings—and confrontations. It's really hard to tell what she'll be like. I guess we'll just have to wait and see."

Possible Causes

It really doesn't matter *why* you're getting a new boss. It *may* matter why this specific person was chosen—especially if she was selected to address particular needs in the organization or if you were bypassed for the promotion. But those are things that you need to work out over a period of time. What we're concerned about here is how to get off to a good start with your new boss.

Hint: You have several, very important, advantages when your boss is new to the organization. While you have to work out the relationship between the two of you, there are a number of things you *don't* have to worry about: You already know the work—not only your general technical area, but the specifics of how to do business in this company and how to get things accomplished. You've also already established relationships with your peers and superiors throughout the organization. So you can afford to invest some time in figuring out your new boss—what she likes and doesn't like, what her management style is, and (most important) how to please her. It's an investment worth making. Any change in key managers causes a certain amount of trauma to an organization. It can't be "business as usual."

Cures

First impressions *do* count—a lot! While you can destroy a good first impression later on by poor performance, it's very hard to do the reverse and overcome a poor first impression. In your first few meetings with your new boss, you need to convince her of these things:

> That you're a loyal subordinate
> That you're not a threat to her
> That she can count on you for consistently good and timely products.

How do you do that? Well, *not* by making a sales pitch for yourself! What you need to do is *demonstrate* those things by what you say and do in the course of normal business.

These are some specific things you can do to make the transition as easy as possible for both you and your new boss:

Find out as much as you can about your new boss before she starts on her job. Talk to other people in the organization and any contacts you have in the organizations where she's worked before. If you have a good relationship with *her* new boss (your second-level supervisor), you might also ask him what to expect. Consider all of this as background information. Don't rely exclusively on other people's opinions in forming your own. But use what you learn to try to make the best first impression you can.

Soon after your new boss reports for work (in the first couple of days, if possible), make an appointment with her to talk about your unit and what you do in the company. Be prepared to talk in detail, but don't offer those details unless you're asked. This should be a kind of summary meeting—just to let your boss know what work you're involved in, what things are likely to come up in the near future, and what issues you're working now.

In this first meeting, ask specific questions about how your boss likes things done. Does she prefer information in written form; does she like to converse about the work; or does she like a combination of the two? Does she intend to hold regular staff meetings where you'll report on status, or would she prefer to meet with you individually? Does she want you to report on a scheduled basis, or just whenever you think something's going on she should know about? Is she interested in details, or "the big picture"? These questions about your boss' style preferences are legitimate questions to ask, and your boss herself is the best source of information. It's better to ask now than to spend the next few months giving her things she doesn't want (or not giving her what she does)!

This first meeting is *not* the best time to ask questions about how to handle specific work problems. If there are pressing issues, try to keep them on "hold" for a week or two. If you can't, let your boss know what the issues are and what you plan to do about them. Then let her know at what stages in the future, if any, she'll have the opportunity to reverse anything she's uncomfortable with. If she gives you specific direction, that's fine. But if you press her before she's ready, she'll probably be uncomfortable because of her lack of knowledge—and you'll have made a tactical error right at the start!

Use the information you've gathered beforehand to identify any areas where your management style is likely to conflict with your boss's. Try to work in some opportunities during your discussion to probe those areas to see how she reacts. If it's as you feared (for example, she likes to control things closely, but you give your people a lot of autonomy as long as they produce), stop there. Don't press the issue. Wait until you can come up with a strategy for working out those areas with your boss that will be likely to get you what you want without causing conflict. Look through the rest of this book to identify possible strategies.

We've talked about a lot of things that should happen in this initial meeting. In fact, you may want to do them over a series of shorter visits. The important thing is to know ahead of time what you need to accomplish, and plan to do it.

In the first few weeks after your boss has begun her new job, you will need also to introduce her to your staff. If you can arrange it conveniently for her, let her meet everyone individually—either all at once or in a series of meetings. Find out if she would like to address the assembled staff early in her tenure. And, of course, clean up the workplace so things look as professional as possible when she comes to visit.

Also in the first few weeks, talk to your boss about the reporting mechanisms already in place. Let her see how your work has been measured in the past, and give her copies of the latest reports. Find out which ones she wants to continue, which ones she wants to change, and which ones she's not interested in at all. (Let her know, of course, which ones higher management wants to continue—especially if those are among the ones she wants to kill.)

As you bring work issues to her attention, be sure to provide her summaries of the work to date in those areas. Remember that she probably has no knowledge of how things have been done in the past. She'll make her decisions based on *her* previous experience—not yours—unless you let her know what your previous history is.

Above all, in the first few weeks, it's important to go along with her wishes as far as you possibly can. Remember, you have the "home court advantage," and if you're to prove your loyalty and competence it's going to be on her terms. You'll have plenty of time later to work out the differences between you. For now, your first job is to build her trust and confidence in you.

Something to Think About

We've talked a lot in this book about how important it is that you have the confidence of your boss. This is a rare, and golden, opportunity to establish that confidence from ground zero. Sure, things will never be the same as when "Good Old What's His Name" used to run things here. They may be even better!

And If This Doesn't Quite Fit Your Situation . . .

Look at other problems in this chapter and Chapter 13 if the relationship seems to be getting off to a rocky start.

Use Checklist 5 to develop a cure of your own.

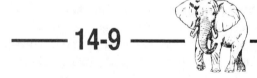

14-9

The Problem: She doesn't like you.

The Scene

"Mario, you really don't know why you have such a hard time with Ms. Estridge?"

"No. I do everything the way I think she wants, and it's never right. Nothing ever satisfies her. I'd love for you to tell me why."

"It's simple. She just doesn't like you."

"Why? What have I ever done to make her dislike me?"

"That I don't know—but I know she doesn't like you. I heard her in the cafeteria last Tuesday, telling Mr. Harris how much you irritate her."

"That's a hell of a note! What am I supposed to do about that?"

Possible Causes

The problem is caused by a cultural difference. Mrs. Estridge expects people to behave in a certain way, but you were brought up to behave differently. Just by acting normally, you're irritating her.

She finds your personal style offensive. This isn't a matter of ethnic differences, but of your own personality traits. She dislikes you simply because of the way you act as an individual.

What she really meant was that she doesn't like the way you manage. This is a very different matter.

Hint: We're going to suggest some ways to approach the situation, but there may not be anything you can do about it. Living with it or leaving may end up being your only two alternatives.

Cures

No matter what the situation is:

Talk with Mrs. Estridge. Carefully plan out what you're going to say.

If you think the direct approach will work, tell her that you think she doesn't like you. Ask if she can tell you why. Then listen; don't try to make points. You want the clearest picture you can get of why she feels as she does. You can try to deal with any wrong ideas of hers at a later meeting.

If you don't have confidence in the direct approach, you'll have to try to find out the same information indirectly. Perhaps you could work through her secretary or another manager who gets along well with her. If that won't work, try this: the next time she criticizes some of your work, ask her in detail how she'd have preferred you to do it. Don't argue; just listen closely to what she says. It may give you clues to some of the reasons for her uneasiness with you.

If the problem is caused by a cultural difference:

Whether you can solve it will depend on how willing each of you is to learn what the other expects. For instance, you may be used to expressing yourself forcefully (perhaps even loudly), while she believes that it's unprofessional to raise her voice. You may be very deferential and quiet, while she expects you to be friendly and talkative.

If you're both able to talk about the differences, you may start to reach an understanding. Don't expect it to be quick or easy. If you both want genuinely to build a good working relationship and are willing to really listen, you can make genuine progress. You'll know you're succeeding if you can each joke about the other's culture without offense.

If you can't discuss it openly, not too many choices remain. You can try to adapt to her expectations, and you may do it successfully. If you can't, you'll just have to accept that it's an unpleasant state of affairs. The remaining alternative is to move to another job.

If she finds your personal style offensive:

This feels much like the first situation, though the cause is somewhat different. She simply doesn't like people who act the way you do.

Again, if the two of you can talk it out you may reach an understanding. Even if you never become fond of each other, you may be able to work successfully together.

There's an "up" side to this. We've stressed in other problems the important of finding a variety of ways to deal with people and problems. Most of the time, the way you act and manage may be fine with people. Other people, though, may be put off or irritated by it. Why not use this as an excuse to learn some new ways of dealing? You don't have to change, or "give in" to anyone. You simply develop a broader range of ways to relate to people. Then you use the one that's most appropriate for the person you're dealing with.

If what she really doesn't like is the way you manage:

This is probably the easiest problem to resolve. ("Easiest" doesn't necessarily mean "easy," though.) There's really no "best" way to manage, and you may learn some valuable skills if you can change to a style she's more comfortable with.

Once again, if the two of you can talk honestly with each other about what she wants it will be much easier. Problem 1 in this chapter has some specific suggestions for dealing with this type of situation.

Things to Think About

It's disappointing, and often irritating, when someone dislikes you. If the reason is your management style, that's bad enough; if it's your personality or your culture, it's worse.

Our basic advice is simple and straightforward: don't take it personally. There's no rule which says you have to like everyone else, or that they have to like you. It may be inconvenient—even hard on your career—when they don't. It's not an attack on you, or a judgment on your worth as a person. Simply accept the fact that the person doesn't like you. Try to find out why. Then, if you can and are willing to, change the behavior that offends her. If you can't, put up with the situation or move out of it. Just don't let it "get to you."

And If This Doesn't Quite Fit Your Situation . . .

See Problem 14-1 if she may be trying to get you out of your job so she can put someone else into it. Or see Problem 14-5 if she may believe that you want to get her job.

Use Checklists 1 and 5 to develop a cure of your own.

—— 14-10 —— 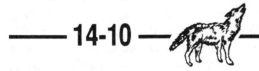 ——

The Problem: She's a good friend of one of your hard-to-manage employees.

The Scene

You enter Ms. Grimsley's office apprehensively and take a seat, wondering what kettle of hot water you've fallen into this time.

"Jon," she begins, "I've been hearing complaints that you're picking on Harold Schweibeck. Is there something wrong with the way he's doing his work?"

You *knew* this was coming. Ms. Grimsley and Harold Schweibeck have been friends since long before you came to this company. But Harold's been a problem for as long as you've been in the company too. And his continual bragging that "you can't touch me" makes it hard to demand anything of anybody else in the unit. But this is the first time Ms. Grimsley has actually confronted you about your attempts to tame Harold, and you're not sure *who's* side she's on.

Possible Causes

The question here isn't *why* Ms. Grimsley and Harold are such good friends (although knowing the answer *may* help you to view Harold in a somewhat different light). The real question is how you can get Ms. Grimsley to back your attempts to manage Harold without damaging her own relationship with him.

Hint: A little empathy on your part will make it easier to understand this situation. Ms. Grimsley is in a very difficult bind. She's caught between the demands of the workplace and the expectations of the personal relationship she has with Harold. Unless things are orchestrated *very* carefully, she's going to lose on one side or the other. Either the work of your unit will suffer, or her relationship with Harold will suffer. Since the latter causes her more personal pain, it's not hard to see which way she's likely to go, is it?

Cures

Regardless of the reason for the friendship between Ms. Grimsley and Harold, you still have a job to do. These suggestions may help you make things more palatable to Ms. Grimsley:

Make sure Ms. Grimsley knows exactly what problems you're having with Harold and how they impact on your unit's ability to do the work. She may know Harold *primarily* from a social perspective. And if no one's complained to her before (with hard facts to back them up), she may really not know what the problems are. Her attempts to protect Harold may spring from her lack of knowledge rather than a conscious decision to sacrifice your unit's productivity for the sake of her friendship with Harold.

In explaining the problems you have with Harold, focus on the impact they have on productivity and morale in your unit. Make it clear that these are not just differences of style or personality conflicts; they're problems that affect the unit's bottom line.

Suggest ways of dealing with Harold that won't require Ms. Grimsley's direct involvement. If you agree to take the heat from Harold, and arrange for Ms. Grimsley to be a sympathetic listener, she may be more willing to let you deal with the problem. Many managers have a stated policy of requiring their subordinates to deal with issues at their level—without intervention. If Ms. Grimsley makes it clear to Harold that her involvement would violate a policy that she (or her superiors) have already established, he may not blame her personally for all the "nasty" things you're doing to him.

If you can't gracefully arrange for Ms. Grimsley to remain uninvolved, you might suggest that Harold be reassigned to another unit that's not under her supervision. That would allow his new supervisor to deal with his problems without intervention and would take Ms. Grimsley entirely out of the line of command. The company could work out the problems with Harold, but Ms. Grimsley's friendship with him would remain intact.

What if Ms. Grimsley doesn't *want* to be uninvolved? What if protecting Harold, even at the expense of the company, is *exactly* what she's trying to do?

In that case, there's not much you can do about the situation except grin and bear it. If Harold's behavior or performance are truly intolerable, you *might* consider going over Ms. Grimsley's head. But you should weigh the consequences first. Ms. Grimsley will certainly be dismayed at your lack of personal loyalty to her, and may remember that during later key events—like appraisal time, or when the next promotion comes up, or when unpleasant assignments have to be handed out. If she's angry enough, she may even try to get rid of you.

If it's Harold's performance that's at issue, there are probably some things that you can do to minimize the damage he causes that won't upset him or Ms. Grimsley. Remove him from critical assignments; give him special projects to work on that will have high visibility with Ms. Grimsley—but few other people. He may not do you much good in those assignments, but he won't do you much harm either.

If it's Harold's conduct that's the problem, you need to evaluate just how bad his behavior is. Has he alienated key customers or suppliers? Is there potential harm to the safety or well being of himself or others? In those cases, the problem is important enough to elevate. Keeping on Ms. Grimsley's good side is *not* more important than the safety of your workers.

You may still be able to take some action without specifically involving Ms. Grimsley or openly ignoring her directions to you. Can you arrange for one of the other managers in the company, preferably at Ms. Grimsley's level or above, to observe Harold in action and put pressure on you, through her, to resolve the problem? If Ms. Grimsley sees that others are unhappy with Harold, particularly others who have influence over her, she may see the political necessity of dealing with the problem—regardless of her social relationship.

If Harold's behavior is not intolerable, just annoying, do what you can to minimize its ill effects and put up with him as best you can. Your job isn't *only* to produce for the company, it's also to keep your boss happy whenever you can. So look on this as just part of the day's work.

Something to Think About

One of the advantages of a small company is the solidarity and "family" feeling that are easily fostered among managers and employees. One of the disadvantages is that those feelings frequently lead to friendships that extend beyond the office and can complicate management. In a larger organization, such friendships still develop, but, when they do, there are more options. You can move people around to avoid potential conflicts of interest—without damaging either person's career or opportunities for advancement. If personal relationships get in the way of company management more often than you'd like, maybe you're in the wrong environment. But if you like the feeling of being "part of the family," you should recognize that these conflicts are a price you may occasionally have to pay.

And If This Doesn't Quite Fit Your Situation . . .

Look at Problems 14-1 if you think your boss is protecting one of your workers to replace you. Problem 14-3 has other suggestions for dealing with poor performers whom you're not allowed to fire.

And Problem 8-5 discusses the corollary of this situation—the worker who runs to your boss for protection.

Use Checklists 1 and 5 to develop a cure of your own.

14-11

The Problem: He bypasses you to your workgroup.

The Scene

"Eleanor, why aren't you out in the bindery? You know that we have to get the pageant brochures out today."

"Oh, no—first we have to get the 1000 Club certificates printed."

"What ever gave you that idea?"

"Mr. Schultz. He came by about an hour ago and told me to switch over to the certificates."

"Okay. Go ahead." You turn away, swearing under your breath. Once again, Schultz has gone straight to your people instead of telling you what he wants done. It's a wonder that any of them pay any attention to you any more!

Possible Causes

Mr. Schultz doesn't believe you relay his instructions accurately. He's concluded that the only way your people are going to get the right directions is for him to give the directions to them personally.

You're often not around, so he's given up trying to find you to tell you. It's easier just to find the employee and tell her what to do.

He doesn't realize how disruptive what he's doing is.

He's not used to being a second-level manager. He still thinks in terms of managing employees directly.

Hint: This circumstance may reflect a broader lack of confidence in you. Keep that in the back of your mind while you're dealing with the specific problem. If he does lack confidence in you, that's by far the more serious problem.

Cures

No matter what the cause is:

Instruct your people that if Mr. Schultz or anyone else in higher management gives them instructions they're to tell you as soon as possible. They're to do what they're told—but they're to see that you know about it quickly. That way, you can at least keep up with what's going on. You won't be surprised when they're doing something different from what you told them to do.

Try to talk with Mr. Schultz about the situation. See if you can find out why he bypasses you and how he looks at it. Remember that your primary objective is to listen; you can defend your position in a later conversation.

If he doesn't believe you relay his instructions accurately:

This one may take some work, but the solution is easy. It's probably best not to approach it head on. Try to intercept Mr. Schultz, so that it's awkward for him not to give you the instructions. Then listen carefully, repeat the instructions back to him, and make sure you understand them exactly. Then pass them on exactly. If you do it right, he'll begin to get the message and start dealing with your people through you.

You should also look at the reasons why you weren't getting the instructions right before. Did you get defensive if he seemed to be critical of you? Did you listen haphazardly, so that you got things confused? Just why did it happen? Is it happening in other situations, with other people?

Not listening carefully and fully is one of the worst habits which a manager—or anyone—can have. If it's a habit you have, take advantage of this situation to rid yourself of it completely.

If you're often not around, so he's given up trying to find you to tell you:

He may have started off wanting to give instructions through you. Because you're so often not there, he's gotten in the habit of going directly to your employees. It saves him time and frustration.

The simplest solution, if it's practical in your situation, is to have an employee who generally takes over when you're gone. Ask your boss to deal directly with him if you're not around. He can pass any instructions on, then see that you know about them when you return.

If this isn't acceptable, having your employees tell you what instructions they received is the next best solution. You might also be able to time your absences from the work area so that you're less apt to be gone at the times Mr. Schultz usually visits the area.

If he doesn't realize how disruptive what he's doing is:

He may have gotten into the habit of bypassing you and other supervisors because no one ever complained to him. He thinks it's okay with you. Or he may understand that you don't like it but not believe it really interferes with anything.

This is where a good relationship with your boss is important. If the two of you can be honest with each other, you can just bring the situation up with him. Hopefully, he'll see how disruptive it is and agree to change.

This is another one of the many situations in which your ability to listen carefully and ask effective questions is important. Of course, this automatically means that you've learned not to be defensive.

If he's not used to being a second-level manager:

This is almost the same problem as the last one, but with a small twist. Probably no one has told him that bypassing you is disruptive because he's been doing it so short a time. That makes it even likelier that he'll listen if you bring it up to him.

There is one caution, though. If he's new, he may be very sensitive to any criticism of his supervisory style. You need to make it clear that you know he's just being conscientious. All you're asking is the chance to show him that he can come to you and get what he wants done.

Something to Think About

You have one solid argument for having him deal with your employees through you—no matter why he doesn't do so at the moment. If he passes his instructions through you, you can see that they're carried out. If he doesn't, you may not know exactly what he wants—and it may not get done. In other words, it will be easier for him to do his job if he works through you instead of bypassing you.

And If This Doesn't Quite Fit Your Situation . . .

Look at Problem 8-3 if the problem is that an employee goes over your head to your boss.

Use Checklists 1 and 5 to develop a cure of your own.

—— 14-12 ——

The Problem: He takes credit for what you do.

The Scene

"Look here at the company newsletter," Craig offered at lunch this afternoon. "Mr. Newton's been interviewed about that new order processing system you put in a couple of months ago. And see what he says: 'I thought we needed . . .' and 'It seemed to me . . .' and 'I try to encourage all my people to be innovative, but I believe that as their leader I need to model creative behavior.' Reading this, no one would ever know you had anything to do with the project at all—and it was your idea to begin with!"

Possible Causes

There are two significant possibilities for why your boss is claiming credit for your work. Neither of them, unfortunately, is anything you can do much about:

He may believe that when he speaks of himself his listeners understand that he's referring to his staff also. He may not realize how important it is to the people who did the work to get specific credit for it.

He may be trying to enhance his own image by claiming credit for others' work. This behavior is guaranteed to make him plenty of enemies.

Hint: This is a tricky situation. Part of the job of any subordinate is to make his or her boss look good—but preferably not at the expense of other employees. Your goal here is to make sure your boss gets lots of credit for what you and your unit do—but for his excellent leadership of the effort, not for the idea or the work itself.

Cures

If your boss believes his listeners understand that his staff shares in the credit for the work:

Make sure that when you report progress or accomplishments to your boss you include the names of the major contributors. Give him the information he needs to pass credit along when he has occasion to talk about the project to other people.

Make gently encouraging statements to him about the positive effects of recognizing employees' contributions. Let him know how your employees react (such as with greater enthusiasm or productivity) when they know that someone above them is aware of their efforts. Your occasional hints may be all it takes to raise your boss's consciousness.

If gentle reminders don't work, and if your relationship with your boss is generally good, you might try a more direct approach. Tell him how discouraging it is—to you and to your workers—when it appears that he's taking credit for others' hard work. If he's a sensitive manager, he'll get the message. But, of course, you *won't* want to be this direct if you suspect that he really *does* want to claim credit for other people's efforts. See the "cure" below if that's the case.

If he's trying to enhance his own image by claiming credit for others' work:

Hints and reminders won't work here. Your boss is fully aware of what he's doing, and your pointing it out to him will only make him resentful of you. Your approach must be much less direct. But it's critical that you protect yourself someway. In the "cause" and "cure" above, your boss will presumably admit your contributions to the success he's claiming. In this case, he probably won't—and your record will look dismally bare if all *your* accomplishments appear to be *his*.

Try to work out an informal arrangement with your boss that you won't complain when he takes the credit for things you do—as long as he does what he can to boost *your* career. This doesn't even have to be a spoken agreement, as long as you both know what the rules are and live up to them. Drop a few hints here and there about what you want, and see if he picks them up.

If subtlety doesn't work, and if you can't even come to a spoken agreement about what he'll do for you, then you may have to start documenting your ideas and accomplishments. When you have something new to suggest, do it in writing rather than in informal conversation. Make formal written proposals rather than oral requests. Prepare regular progress reports that identify, specifically and in detail, what's been done and who did the work. Keep records, and, whenever possible, make sure your documentation becomes part of the unit's official files.

As much as you can without appearing to brag, let others know what you've accomplished. You can always tell friends and co-workers what you're contemplating and what you've completed. As opportunities arise in conversations with casual acquaintances, mention work you've done that's especially noteworthy. This is delicate. You don't want to look like a braggart or a "know-it-all," and you don't want to upstage your boss or contradict what he's been saying. But it's important to engage in a little defensive publicity from time to time.

Keep your sense of humor. If you're a talented and dedicated manager, especially if you have a proven track record in the company, people will know who's *really* doing the work. They'll soon recognize your boss for the scene-stealer he is and begin to discount his tales of great feats.

Something to Think About

While you're concerned about the credit your boss is taking for your accomplishments, are your employees concerned about your taking credit for *their* work? You can't expect workers to do their best if all their efforts go to your greater glory. You want your boss to be generous with his praise and credit; don't your workers deserve the same?

And If This Doesn't Quite Fit Your Situation . . .

Look at Problem 14-5 if you think your boss is grabbing the credit because he's afraid you're trying to take over his job.

Use Checklists 1 and 5 to develop a cure of your own.

Problem-Solving Checklists

Whenever you have a problem that doesn't exactly fit one of the situations we've described in the previous chapters, look here for hints on how to solve it yourself. These checklists will walk you through the problem and show you the steps to take to solve it.

We've included seven different checklists which cover the spectrum of "people problems" you're likely to encounter as a manager:

Checklist 1: Performance Problems (either individual or group)

Checklist 2: Conduct/Behavior Problems (either individual or group)

Checklist 3: Acceptance Problems (when one or several of your employees isn't accepted by the group)

Checklist 4: Problems with Your Peers

Checklist 5: Problems with Your Boss

Checklist 6: Your Personal Problems

Checklist 7: Substance Abuse Problems

THE GENERAL CHECKLIST

Whenever you have a management problem, these are the general steps you should follow to solve it successfully:

☐ *State the problem specifically in terms of*

  • *its source (who's responsible for causing the problem, not who's responsible for fixing it)*

  • *the kind of problem it is (such as performance, behavior, etc.)*

☐ *Ask questions and gather all the facts you need to make a decision.*

☐ *Identify the options available to you for solving the problem, now that you know exactly what the problem is.*

☐ *Choose an option that you'll follow (or a series of steps if that's the best way).*

☐ *Consider writing down why you chose the option you did, particularly if you think you'll be called on to defend your actions later.*

☐ *Act. Implement your decision.*

☐ *Evaluate how well your decision worked. If the solution is one that's implemented over a period of time, evaluate its success at specific points along the way. If it doesn't seem to be working out as you expected, go through the steps again to see if you can find a better approach.*

The patterns that follow take you through the first three steps of this general problem-solving procedure. It's up to you as the manager to make the final decision, implement it, and evaluate its success. GOOD LUCK!

CHECKLIST 1: PERFORMANCE PROBLEMS

Answer each of these questions:

☐ *Exactly what is the nature of the performance problem?*

☐ *Does the employee have basic self-management skills such as skill in organizing and prioritizing work and in sticking to deadlines?*

If not, look for formal training courses that will teach those skills. Coach the employee. Set short, progressive deadlines to help the employee manage his work as he assumes greater responsibility for managing it himself.

☐ *Does the employee have the technical work skills needed to complete his assignments?*

If not, teach the skills through training (either formal or on-the-job) supplemented with practice and feedback. Assign a mentor to review the employee's work and provide continuing coaching. If the procedures are hard to remember or seldom used, consider devising a job aid to list the directions in narrative or a diagram. (Standard Operating Procedures [SOPs] are a kind of job aid too.)

☐ *If training, practice, and feedback don't yield significant improvements, decide if the employee has the ability to learn the work. (Your Personnel Department or Training Department may be able to help in this assessment.)*

If he doesn't, transfer the employee to a job you believe he *can* do or terminate him.

□ *Does the employee have the interpersonal skills re-*
quired to establish and maintain effective work rela-
tionships?

If not, use formal training to teach the skills or coach the employee. Provide regular feedback on his progress. If coaching and regular
feedback and counselling don't result in improved performance, terminate the employee.

□ *Does the employee/organization have the tools neces-*
sary to do the work (such as supplies, materials, equip-
ment, sufficient time)?

If not, remove the obstacles or devise ways to work around
them.

□ *Does the employee/organization have a positive incentive*
for doing the work correctly and on schedule?

If positive incentives don't exist, design them into the system
to the extent you can. At the very least, remove any disincentives
and make sure employees understand how their work contributes to
the overall goals of the organization. (If you're not sure what disincentives might exist, ask your employees, "What gets in the way of
your doing the best job you possibly can?" They'll tell you—maybe
more than you want to know!)

NOTE: Look also at Checklist #7, Substance Abuse Problems,
to see if that could be the source of an individual employee's performance problem.

CHECKLIST 2: CONDUCT/BEHAVIOR PROBLEMS

Answer each of these questions:

☐ *Exactly what unacceptable behavior is the employee/organization exhibiting?*

☐ *Is the behavior serious or merely irritating?*

If it's merely irritating, caution the employee (or group) that the behavior isn't appropriate and that you may have to take stronger measures if the situation doesn't improve. Be prepared to live with most irritations, though, unless the behavior worsens or it begins to have a noticeable effect on the productivity of the unit.

☐ *Is the employee/organization aware of the rules in this area?*

If not, let him/them know what the rules are and warn of the consequences for not following those rules. Make a written record of the warning.

☐ *Is the behavior critical to the organization or to the safety/well-being of other people?*

If so, your first action should be to stop the behavior. That may mean calling in your company's Security Office or the police. After the immediate situation is taken care of, decide on the penalty for the misbehavior. In a situation this serious, termination is the most appropriate remedy unless there are unusual or strong mitigating factors.

☐ *Does the behavior undermine your authority or the basic supervisor/subordinate relationship?*

If so, consider terminating the employee or moving him out of your unit unless there are strong mitigating factors.

☐ *Is the behavior deliberate?*

If so, and if it's serious (even though it's not critical to the organization or to employees' safety and doesn't undermine your effectiveness), you still need to take action strong enough to stop the employee and others from repeating the behavior. Appropriate measures include suspensions without pay, writing up the employee in his official records, or moving him into a lesser position.

NOTE: Look also at Checklist 7, Substance Abuse Problems, to see if that could be the source of your employee's conduct or behavior problems.

CHECKLIST 3: ACCEPTANCE PROBLEMS

Answer each of these questions:

☐ *Exactly what problem is occurring?*

Are others failing to accept a worker because she is a woman or a member of a minority group?

If so, first make sure your workers know your policy, and the company's policy, on discrimination. Explain how you expect your employees to behave toward all their co-workers (for instance, including them in meetings and discussions that are relevant to their assignments). Model the behavior you expect of your workers, so that it's clear you practice what you preach.

Then work on changing the underlying attitudes that caused this problem. Examine off-the-shelf training materials. Discuss individual differences and individual contributions at staff meetings and other appropriate occasions. Arrange positive experiences for people of diverse cultures and backgrounds to work together.

☐ *Are others failing to accept a worker, not for discriminatory reasons, but because he irritates them?*

Encourage your employees to work together harmoniously. Make the establishment and maintenance of positive relationships a part of each employees performance discussions, and see that all your employees understand the negative effects on performance (and their appraisals) of failure to nurture those relationships. Then follow through.

☐ *Has one of your workers been accused of discriminatory behavior (including sexual harassment)?*

If so, first get the facts. Talk to the employee who made the allegation, any witnesses he names, and the worker who's been accused. Take notes of your discussions. If you believe the employee is innocent, talk to the worker who made the accusation to explain why you believe he misunderstood the situation and advise him of the right to file a discrimination complaint. If you believe the accused worker *did* discriminate, take appropriate action—even if it means firing her.

CHECKLIST 4: PROBLEMS WITH YOUR PEERS

Answer these questions:

☐ *Exactly what problem is the other manager causing you and/or your unit?*

☐ *Is what this manager doing (or failing to do) important to your effectiveness or the effectiveness of your unit?*

If it's not, you have your solution. Just live with what he's doing. You have other, more important problems to worry about.

☐ *If what he's doing (not doing) is important, are good relations with him important to your personal effectiveness or the effectiveness of your unit?*

If they are, forget trying to force him to change what he's doing. Instead, pick one of the alternatives below which doesn't require you to confront him or try to compel him to change. If none of those alternatives will work, just live with the situation.

☐ *No matter how important good relations are, do you have good relations with him?*

If so, your best alternative is to work out a resolution with him.

☐ *If you don't have good relations, or can't work out a resolution, do you have something to offer him in exchange for his cooperation?*

If so, see if you can't strike a bargain with him. Even if your relationship with him isn't that good, you can probably make a deal.

☐ *If you don't have anything to offer, is there another*
   way beside confrontation to get what you want or need
   or to minimize the effect of what he's doing?

If so, try to get around the problem he's causing without forcing
the issue.

☐ *If you have no good alternatives short of forcing him*
   to change, can you rely on your superiors and peers
   to support you if you try to force him to change?

If so, it's worth trying to pressure him into changing.
If not, your only good alternative is to live with the situation.

CHECKLIST 5: PROBLEMS WITH YOUR BOSS

Answer each of these questions:

☐ *Exactly what problem is your boss causing you or your unit?*

☐ *Is it a problem because it will harm the company, harm you, or require you to do something immoral or illegal?*

If it's not one of these, why is it a problem? It sounds like a disagreement—which means that you may try to persuade your boss to do otherwise, but if you can't you do what he wants.

☐ *Is the problem that he wants to take (or wants you to take) an action which will harm the company?*

If so, and if you trust your boss, discuss your misgivings with him. If he still wants to take the action after you've said your piece, do what he says.

If you don't trust him, decide whether it's important enough to force the issue. If not, do what he wants. If it is, follow the suggestions below.

☐ *Is the problem that what he wants to do will harm you (hurt your career, make you look bad, etc.)?*

If so, and you trust him, discuss it with him.

If you're not satisfied with the results of the discussion, or if you don't trust him, see the suggestions on forcing his hand below.

☐ *Is what he wants to do (or wants you to do) immoral or illegal?*

If so, and if you have effective connections with your boss's superiors, go to them with the situation.

If so, but you don't have effective connections, is what he wants to do serious enough to risk loss of your job? If not, do what he wants—and then start looking for a job somewhere else, because his next request may be more serious.

If so, and the matter is serious enough for you to risk your job, you have no choice but to refuse to do what he wants and threaten to make the issue public. Needless to say, you also need to start looking for another job—quickly.

(NOTE: There is a significant difference between an action that is immoral because it violates widely held moral standards and one which is immoral because it violates your personal standards. If it violates community standards, it may be easy for you to get support from others. If it violates your personal standards which most others don't share, they probably won't help you.)

CHECKLIST 6: YOUR PERSONAL PROBLEMS

Answer each of these questions:

☐ *Exactly what is the problem?*

☐ *Is your boss dissatisfied with your performance or generally unhappy with you?*

If so, talk to him about what he wants to see changed. Then, if it's something you can fix, fix it. If it's something you believe you can't fix, or are unwilling to change, you should know by now that your boss will come out the winner. It's time to look around for another job or prepare to live with your boss's continuing dissatisfaction.

☐ *Are personal problems interfering with your work?*

If so, talk to your boss to let her know that there are outside influences that may affect your performance for a while. Let her know how long you expect the situation to last, and try to work out some temporary accommodation that's acceptable to both of you.

Don't try to tough it out on your own. Your boss will notice the difference in your work, and she may assume you've just lost interest.

☐ *Are you burned out on the job?*

If so, try to find an interest, either on the job or in your personal life, that will revitalize you. Take some time off (no one's indispensable) to relax and reassess where you want to be and what you want to be doing. If you already have outside interests and the combined demands are overloading you—ease off. Give yourself some time to unwind and contemplate. If your dissatisfaction doesn't diminish in time, then consider whether this is really the right job for you. Get some professional help in identifying a career that will be more personally rewarding.

CHECKLIST 7: SUBSTANCE ABUSE PROBLEMS

A growing concern in the workplace is the impact of alcohol and drug abuse on employee productivity. Tremendous costs (many of them hidden) result from poor quality work, absenteeism, interpersonal conflicts, and other by-products of substance abuse.

There are several keys to identifying a substance abuse problem, but the primary indicator is *change*—

- change in an employee's behavior

- change in his patterns of work and absence

- change in the way he relates to others

- change in the quality of his work

- change in the amount he produces

Most of the time, you *won't* be able to identify impaired employees by physical symptoms—

- the odor of alcohol

- dilated pupils

- slurred or incoherent speech

- disorientation

- lack of muscular coordination (staggering, dropping things, shaking)

The clues will be much more subtle. And you won't recognize them if you don't already know what the employee's *normal* patterns are. Here's the checklist to follow:

☐ *Get to know your employees' characteristics and patterns—the way they typically act or react.*

☐ *If you notice a decline in work behavior or performance, talk to the employee about it right away. Evasion and denial are classic responses of employees with substance abuse problems.*

☐ *Look for changes in other areas. If an employee has been calling in sick frequently, has his performance also deteriorated? Or is he more irritable in dealing with co-workers or customers?*

☐ *Identify the specific performance or behavior problem(s) affecting the employee, then confront him. Make sure he knows exactly what will happen if his performance and/or conduct don't improve. Having related the problem(s) to work requirements, you should then offer the employee assistance or referral if he believes he needs it. Don't accuse! Your concern is getting the work out. If the employee recognizes that he has a problem, he'll need your understanding and support. If he doesn't recognize it, none of your accusations will help.*

☐ *If your company has an Employee Assistance Program Office, consult the coordinator for help in confronting the employee. If you have no Employee Assistance Program in-house, talk to your Personnel Department for help.*

☐ *Then follow through. Whether the employee gets help or not, make it clear that you expect him to improve his performance and/or behavior. If he does, congratulate him and offer your continued support. If he doesn't, take whatever measures are appropriate—including discipline or termination.*

Index

(NOTE: Numbers in brackets refer to topics)